ADVANCE PRAISE FOR *WHY ARE FAGGOTS SO AFRAID OF FAGGOTS?*

These essays—alternately moving and sprightly, contemplative and outraged—display the power of presenting an alternative to the mainstream: a world of greater tolerance, acceptance, support, and creativity.
  —*Publishers Weekly*

You may have thought you understood human nature before you read this book; after reading it you will be humbled by all you failed to grasp until now. America invented identity politics but here those identities have been multiplied and articulated as never before.
  —Edmund White, author of *A Boy's Own Story*

Mattilda Bernstein Sycamore's coruscating eye and clear head is what queers need if we are to survive as anything other than a tamed branch of consumer society, based on assimilation, repression, and despair. These essays come like a plunge into a forest pool of revitalizing joy, honesty, and common sense. Read them. Now. No—not tomorrow. Now!
  —Samuel R. Delany, author of *Times Square Red, Times Square Blue*

Why Are Faggots So Afraid of Faggots is a collection of essays that not only examine the intricacies of the current socio-political climate within the realm of the gay/queer/trans world, but also show how important it is for us to interface and aggressively seek to inform the world view of the culture at large… Thanks, Mattilda, for the insights, intellectual rigor and the glittering ammunition with which to destroy and rebuild.
  —Mx Justin Vivian Bond, singer, songwriter, and author of *Tango: My Childhood, Backwards and in High Heels*

This book plumbs the most important question facing queers in the 21st century: how the hell did we go from forming a crucial part of the '60s "lib" rainbow, and from mastering, refining, and successfully deploying nonviolent resistance with ACT UP, only to end up creating for ourselves a world of martial and marital law every bit as sterile, constricting, and amoral as the world we once fled like the plague?

    —Andy Bichlbaum of the Yes Men

These essays excavate masculinity, unearthing the complex and pervasive structures that police and construct it and exposing the beautiful resilience of its self-avowed refusers and failures. These pieces telescope between analysis of the structures of gendered racialization that produce body norms and the daily physical and emotional traumas and toils of surviving and resisting, providing complex and badly needed ways to imagine and reimagine faggotry.

    —Dean Spade, author of *Normal Life: Administrative Violence,*
       Critical Trans Politics and the Limits of Law

WHY ARE FAGGOTS SO AFRAID OF FAGGOTS?

Flaming challenges to masculinity, objectification, and the desire to conform

WHY ARE FAGGOTS SO AFRAID OF FAGGOTS?

Flaming challenges to masculinity,
objectification, and the desire to conform

AK PRESS | 2012
OAKLAND, EDINBURGH, BALTIMORE

Why Are Faggots So Afraid of Faggots?
Edited by Mattilda Bernstein Sycamore

© 2012 Matt Bernstein Sycamore

This edition © 2012 AK Press (Edinburgh, Oakland, Baltimore)

ISBN: 978-1-84935-088-4 (print)
e-ISBN: 978-1-84935-089-1 (electronic)
Library of Congress Control Number: 2011936325

AK Press   AK Press UK
674-A 23rd Street   33 Tower St.
Oakland, CA 94612   Edinburgh EH6 7BN
USA   Scotland
www.akpress.org   www.akuk.com
akpress@akpress.org   ak@akdin.demon.co.uk

The above addresses would be delighted to provide you with the latest AK Press
distribution catalog, which features several thousand books, pamphlets, zines,
audio and video recordings, and gear, all published or distributed by AK Press.
Alternately, visit our websites to browse the catalog and find out
the latest news from the world of anarchist publishing:
www.akpress.org | www.akuk.com
revolutionbythebook.akpress.org

Printed in the United States on recycled paper

Cover design by John Yates | www.stealworks.com
Interior by Kate Khatib | www.manifestor.org/design
Cover photograph by Charlie Stephens

TABLE OF CONTENTS

To the queens, the bitches, the he-shes, the not-mes, the runway reading divas, tumbling backroom baristas, swishy sissy sisters… and, of course… to all those faggots… who are afraid… of me.

For JoAnne (1974–1995)

For Chrissie Contagious (1974–2010)

For David Wojnarowicz (1955–1992)

Why Are Faggots So Afraid of Faggots?
AN INTRODUCTION

Mattilda Bernstein Sycamore

We've grown to appreciate the way our eyes give everything away, our hips sway, our voices flow up and down and then up again: hold me. We've embraced our hunger for bushes and beaches, back alleys and bathrooms and anywhere else we can find those bodies we once shunned: our own. We've come to terms with our deviance, our defiance, our love for fucking and flowers. We've pushed inward and outward at once; we've learned to hold one another even if it's only that moment, that taste, that tongue to tongue or the imprint of sweaty fingertips.

And still, we are losing hope. We wonder how our desires have led to an endless quest for Absolut vodka, Diesel jeans, rainbow Hummers, pec implants, Pottery Barn, and the perfect abs and asshole. As backrooms get shut down to make way for wedding vows, and gay sexual culture morphs into "straight-acting dudes hangin' out," we wonder if we can still envision possibilities for a flaming faggotry that challenges the assimilationist norms of a corporate-cozy lifestyle.

We wonder what happened to our dreams of a world of sexual splendor only bounded by the limits of imagination. Instead, we find ourselves in a culture where "party and play" means close the blinds, lock the door, and hope that no one will glimpse our degradation. Masculine ideals have long reigned supreme in male sexual spaces, from the locker room to the tea room, the bars to the boardrooms. Yet now a sanitized, straight-friendly version of gay identity exists side by side with the brutal, calculated hyper-objectification of internet cruising: scorn becomes "just a preference," lack of respect is assumed, and lying is a given. We scan the options: *HIV-neg, STD-free, UB2. Masc only, no femmes or fatties. Straight acting, straight appearing. No blacks or Asians. Must be discreet.* Is this what has become of the intimacies we crave?

Why Are Faggots So Afraid of Faggots is an emergency intervention. It's also a deeply personal project for me. As a genderqueer faggot and a queen with a certain amount of notoriety, I find myself incredibly inspired by the politics and potentials of trans, genderqueer, and gender-defiant subcultures. Simultaneously I find myself less and less hopeful in the male sexual spaces I also inhabit. I wonder: if the desire I hold dear has only led to a product-driven sexual marketplace, what are the possibilities for transformation?

This book comes hot on the heels of my previous two anthologies, *That's Revolting! Queer Strategies for Resisting Assimilation* and *Nobody Passes: Rejecting the Rules of Gender and Conformity. That's Revolting!* exposed the ways in which a gay elite has hijacked queer struggle in order to position their desires as universal needs, reimagining the dominant signs of straight conformity as the ultimate markers of gay success. *Nobody Passes* interrogated the act of passing as a means through which assimilation and cultural erasure often take place, and remain invisible. *Why Are Faggots So Afraid of Faggots* brings all of this analysis to bear on the question of what has given rise to the personal nightmares now intrinsic to gay sexual/social culture.

We are losing hope, but still we are hopeful. ML Sugie and Michael Faris skewer race stereotyping in online cruising, and argue for indiscriminate promiscuity as an antidote. D. Travers Scott reimagines the web beyond either/or limitations, and envisions an information "superfeyway." Chris Bartlett reinvokes the "gravity and levity" in pre-AIDS gay cultures. Eric A. Stanley explores the perils and possibilities of a relationship between faggots who came of age at the height of AIDS hysteria. George and Ayala and Patrick "Pato" Hebert discuss cultural production as a means of community building. CAConrad exposes the connections between body fascism, class striving, and a pro-military gay identity, and embraces a self-assured fat-positive sexuality.

We are holding our contradictions up to the disco ball, watching them refract. James Villanueva roams the West Texas bars (straight and gay), where he find himself fetishized as either faggot or Latino. Shepperton Jones wonders whether he deliberately approaches highly-educated Asian men for bareback sex because he considers them lower risk for masculinity obsession and HIV. Ezra RedEagle Whitman struggles to find a space for himself as a gay Native American man who doesn't want to be bounded by "Two-Spirit" expectations of spiritual purity. Matthew Blanchard flees gay-on-gay harassment at a Virginia college campus for the "crystal-lined, tina-torn, AIDS-quilted gay mecca" of San Francisco. Harris Kornstein describes a relationship between three theater queens, from kindergarten to adulthood, and the ways in which these childhood friends both resist and fall into homophobic ways of targeting one another. Francisco Ibáñez Carrasco challenges the sexual apartheid that divides the "healthy" from the "infected," while investigating the slippery slopes of self-medication through sex and drugs.

We are challenging hierarchies wherever we find them. Jason Lydon and Mishael Burrows expose homophobic prison norms—one as prisoner, and the other as prison guard. Booh Edouardo writes about a short-lived friendship with a rich, older gay volunteer coordinator who uses New Age spirituality to essentialize, sexualize, and harass Edouardo. Gina de Vries exposes a website that glorifies frottage as the manly alternative to anal sex. Willow Aerin Fagan shares his efforts to outgrow the homophobia of a Christian fundamentalist upbringing, as well as to unearth the roots of his father's violence. Larry Goldsmith questions the hypocrisy of the national gay organizations that enforce a promilitary agenda while refusing to support alleged WikiLeaks whistleblower Bradley Manning, a gay soldier imprisoned by the US government. Debanuj DasGupta flees a Master/slave relationship where he plays the docile Asian to his white Superman captor, in favor of a search for the routes that immigrant faggots take to find one another. Kristen Stoeckeler encounters gender policing in gay bars and bathrooms, as well as hierarchies of masculinity in drag king cultures and the possibilities of female-bodied faggotry. Ali Abbas confronts gay mythologies of homophobic Arabs, and the hypocritical agenda of gay do-gooders seeking to "civilize" the world.

We are in love, and we are in lust. And yes, we are cruising. Lewis Wallace writes about the tangle of desire and failure between two trans guys. Jaime Cortez illuminates a late-night streetscape where sex-for-pay and sex-for-play, sexual identity, and sexual desire collide. Khary Polk fights his fears that he and all other black fags are doomed, in order to find sexual satisfaction and develop personal standards of responsibility. Nick Clarkson romances a guy twice his age, but it turns out his catch is unable to conceptualize the pairing. Philip Patston describes the tricky conversations necessary in order to negotiate attraction between disabled and non-disabled fags. Thomas Glave watches gay men embracing on the street, and interrogates the childhood fears that become adulthood longing. Tommi Avicolli Mecca shows us the scene for queens and their critics/admirers on the streets in 1970s Philadelphia. Horehound Stillpoint plays by the rules he's learned over 30 years in San Francisco backroom bars, and still feels like he's failing.

We are all failing: the intoxicating visions of gay liberation have given way to an obsession with beauty myth consumer norms, mandatory masculinity, objectification without appreciation, and a relentless drive to police the borders. And yet, what might we conjure, create, and cultivate with our dreams that remain? *Why Are Faggots So Afraid of Faggots* reinvokes the anger, flamboyance, and subversion once thriving in gay subcultures, in order to imagine something dangerous and lovely: an exploration of the perils of assimilation; a call for accountability; a vision for change. We are ready.

FIERCE.NET:
IMAGINING A FAGGOTTY WEB

D. Travers Scott

STARING DOWN THE DROP-DOWN

When registering for the cruise site DadLad.com, a new user must choose how to identify herself from two choices in a dropdown menu: *Dad* or *Lad*. She can only choose one. There are no intermediate options, no descriptors of greater flexibility, as in the variety of choices for describing safer-sex preferences: *sometimes, most of the time, never, rather not say, let's discuss,* or *when appropriate.* There is Dad/Lad workaround, however. Later in the profile-creation form, a user can choose what type of partner she's searching for; there, she is allowed to make multiple selections. The form enables her to check both Dad *and* Lad. So, although her identity is fixed and singular, her appetites are allowed greater scope. She can be a Dad looking for Lads *and* other Dads, or a Lad looking for Dads *and* other Lads.

I'm not merely grousing over inadequate representation here, complaining of my mirror-mirror-on-the-web's less-than-exact reflection. The profile system has material effects in the hookup economy. If I choose to label myself a Dad, even though I note I am also hot for other Dads, I may not show up on those Dads' radars if they set their search parameters to look only for self-identified Lads.

It's tricky with Dad/Lad. The terms are pretty loose and not strictly linked to age or physical body type. There are lots of ripped, young Dads and greying Lads out there. The appellations refer more, but not exclusively, to one's predilection for sexual dynamics and roles. In contrast, the Bear community has a wider vocabulary describing roles with more shades of grey (if still rather fixed). *Bear* is generally for hairy, stocky guys with working-class affinities, *cub* for hairy and portly but typically younger and/or more submissive, *otter* for hirsute but slender, *musclebear* for gym-damaged but furry, and *trapper* for those neither hairy nor husky but feeling those who are. Typically uniting all of these is an appreciation for the rollicking, blue-collar-inspired Bear attitude (or lack thereof).

The dropdown menu on DadLad.com, however, omits many sexual shades of grey. Say he's a switch. To make matters worse, he doesn't physically map clearly onto either role, neither twink nor silver fox. The menu requires him to make an inexact, ineffective, and counterproductive choice.

I open with this admittedly-somewhat-petty anecdote as a concrete example of a larger concern. A dropdown menu is but one element of a user interface, but it is also one that is typically, traditionally masculine: it organizes and categorizes, and through this asserts identity, knowledge, and understanding. Like a Victorian scientist (or, hell, Kinsey) pinning his precisely-labeled insect specimens, it puts you into a box. What you see (in the label, in the search results, on the profile, in the museum display case) is what you get. The dropdown menu doesn't do nuance.

Worse yet, it suggests there's something wrong with anyone or anything that doesn't fit into those clear-cut, self-explanatory, "natural" options. Sure, you can express in your profile's personal statements the scope of your sexual tastes and practices as fully and with as much imagination as the text field's character limit will accommodate. But when you first encounter that dropdown, when you first look at the choices available and note that there are none with which you cleanly correspond, there is a moment of creeping doubt, of uncertainty, a nagging sense that there is something *wrong* with you. You *should* be one or the other.

In my best thrift-store drag of French philosopher-historian Michel Foucault, I'm suggesting that, if the online user runs up against enough of those moments of doubt, if she bumps up against them hard enough, maybe she starts trying to avoid them. Maybe she tries to simplify her complex identities and desires, tries to channels her tastes in a more specific direction, throws out the vest with the faux-leopard trim or the maroon herringbone slacks, but keeps the coveralls and cigars, instead of using both in her ensemble.

Imagine all that is lost at DadLad.com. Think of that exhilarating moment in cruising of staring down the unknown: Is he interested in me? Is his ass hairy? Does he kiss? Does he cry while getting fucked? Will he look me in the eye or zone out to some faraway place? In the online cruising experience, so many of these questions are already answered by profiles—correctly or incorrectly. And, whether accurate or not, they deflate the mystery of the unknown, the sweaty nervous risky stuttering heartthumping thrill of discovery and encounter. Uncovering a partner is exciting: the dodge and parry, the test and dance of sexual exploration and exposure. That moment he drops the façade, and all of the tension and building and uncertainty leading up to it—delicious. Online, it is often absent, defused by the endless registration and profile screens, the exhibitionistic runway of nakeddudesguysnudemenhuntersgearboishotfetishqueerromeoblahblahblah. Remember when you didn't know what someone looked like with their clothes off? Remember wondering what kind of cock he had? Remember shivering in an-tici-*pa*-tion? "The suspense is terrible. I hope it lasts."

Consider that short guy with the choppy, tousled, jet-black hair, the furrowed, uncertain, anxious brow resting uneasily above the clear blue eyes, a young lad who seems to have his heart bursting out in need of love and affection from his strong, comfortable dad. Maybe it starts out that way with the older, more muscular, confidently swaggering guy with whom he hooks up. Maybe Dad's salt 'n' pepper crewcut, confident grin, and dark brown eyes lead to strong embraces, deep hugs, and chest nuzzling—until the younger guy's switch kicks in, and he starts calling Dad "boy" and doing things to him that make him whimper. Moreover, what if he's a wiseass who wants to slip into some stockings while he disciplines his new boy? What if he laughs with a horrible, wicked, high-pitched fey cackle, like a wicked witch, while he's got his hand in Dad/boy, doing awful things to him? What if he later cradles the crying older man in his arms? Then draws them both a hot bath with fresh lavender? Where do these faggots fit into the dropdown menu?

The example of this humble and by now much-maligned dropdown menu is an illustration of how the web is not neutral. The technologies that constitute the online experience did not appear out of thin air or descend from Olympus as gifts from the gods. They are not separate from culture, somehow innocent and pure, but as deeply intertwined with culture as an episode of *The Hills*. The design and functioning of online technologies is far from immune to racism, sexism, homophobia, and other social ills.

IMAGINED COMMUNITIES, PHANTASIZED INTERFACES

I could continue to point out aspects of online experiences that are traditionally masculine, and therefore avoid, resist, or otherwise erase the complex, mercurial, and multifaceted: the feminine, the fey, the femme, the faggot. But rather than just reading the web's aspects of sexism, racism, or sissyphobia, I want to use a different technique. I want to imagine the opposite. I want to imagine what's lost, what's elided through the process of thinking of all the ways the web *could* be, but isn't. I want to point out how the web is such boring butch trade—one of those stupid-as-hair (and bad hair at that) regular "dudes" who just wants to drink beer on the couch and jerk off, bro—by imagining instead a queerer, more fabulous web. A faggotty web. An information superfeyway. A journey into cyberfemme. A world-wide sissy. What would this be like?

Well, for one thing, I wouldn't be sitting upright at a freakin' desk. Anyone knows sitting at a desk is a position of work and, in this fantasy, I am not working, although I definitely work it. The fundamental body position, muscle use, physical memory, and pose I strike should not be that of a desk jockey, office clone, or organization man, ass 'n crotch tucked way down below desk level, back upright, straight and tight, hands poised mid-air, my whole posture all formal right angles.

Oh, honey, no.

Here I must lounge, here I must be voluptuously loose and louche, here I must curve beguilingly. As Tennessee Williams famously wrote in *A Streetcar Named Desire*, "A line can be straight, or a street, but the human heart, oh, no, it's curved like a road through mountains." Well, so am I, dammit. So no desk for me, darling, I want to be supine on a sofa, to lounge on a chaise longue, to swoon on a fainting couch, to dally on a daybed, to stretch recumbent on a recliner. My cyberworld is not one fundamentally rooted in work but in leisure and in pleasure. I must recline if I'm to be able to nap, stretch in the sun, cricket my legs together seductively, flash a little ass, let my scarves and skirts trail flowingly down the side of the divan.

At least until I don't want to anymore. It's a queen's prerogative and a queer's obligation to change her fucking mind. So when I need to move, move I must. When some retro acid house compilation torrent finishes downloading and starts playing, I need to dance, baby, and I can't do that tethered to a desk. When I'm reading someone, not some book, I need to storm around the room, tickling with gesticulations, pivoting on my points and counterpoints—my rhetoric entails runway. And while a lazy snap tossed over the back of an overstuffed couch has its moment, other times I need full-body torque to make a point to which no impotent emoticon comes close.

So what kind of web does this entail? Something on bigger screens that I can see from more than a foot away. How about some widescreen wallpaper? How about a projector that plays my screen across an entire wall, or upon the billowing silks of my window treatments? (I know LCDs are expensive, sweets, but what about those groovy tricolor-eye psychedelic projectors the sports bars all ditched? I always liked them; they had a *War of the Worlds* meets Grace Slick vibe, and you could do all sorts of super shadow work in front of them, not to mention that nasty trick of spraying your porn across the wall, or your neighbor's wall). Hell, I can work with a super-8 projector if the situation warrants. I'm not expensive or high-maintenance, baby. I can adapt to the exigency. Pack my Hewlett Packard with transparency sheets and slide that inkjet output tray up into an old opaque projector—mmm, huff the dusty high-school goodness, get your-self a hard-on from poppers and purple mimeographs! Or go futuristic with sheets of cellophane flexible screens, or images floating midair like in that Tom Cruise movie *Minority Report*, how faggotty is that wrist action?

I want to bathe in my screens, I want them to be immersive and visible from around the room, whether I'm lounging, snapping, or catwalking. And mobile viewing would be facilitated by content that is big and visual rather than tiny and textual. Admittedly my glasses do have a certain geek-chic, I know, but eyestrain is far from fabulous.

I want big pictures, large text. Don't cram everything in so I can see it all at once, honey; I like to scroll—it's like a sashay! Zooming is a snap. I don't need some all-at-once Archimedian vantage point. I want a web I can explore, not survey, a cyberspace of cubbyholes, eddies, and dark private booths. I want to zoom, rotate, slide around, and manipulate the screen image with pinchy-strokey-snappy finger-motions on a touchscreen or touchpad. Why hasn't that long been our *primary* user experience, in all applications? Why can't large text and graphics, with twisty zippy pinchy navigation, be projected on giant wallscreens? Think about it, imagine it, imagine all you could do, all you could do differently, how much more such a faggot campy web could work it.

Audio and video chatting could become more integral. Everyone doesn't need a super-fast T1 connection to do it, even dialup can do audio and hell, notch my visual down to a low-res infrequent refresh. I love Flash as much as I love sparkles, sequins, and glitter. Why not? Just free my hands from this fucking keyboard! I want you to see my arched eyebrow and roll-ing eyes, to hear the shade dripping from my words. Feel the sonic boom of my snap. Twist inside my shrieks and giggles. Give your eyes a rest and my hands one, too—because there are much better things they could be do-ing. Much better, baby. Think of how much more meaning we could have, the intensified nuance, subtlety, inflection, irony, sarcasm, and flirtation we could communicate, how we could signify, how we could read, if freed from this hex of t-x-t! I can't type in nails and baubles. Give me more and better voice-operated operation, audio controls with consistent commands across applications and platforms, so I can input while testing out a new *pair* of platforms.

Finally, to return where I began: forms are fucked. Screw registration, age, verification, and marketing-tracking info-gathering. I can have as many identities as I want. My profile is a mood ring. All descriptors open-ended, with nothing required—I can put in any response to any criteria I want. If I want to cruise a chatroom and show you nothing but a picture of me biting a gummi eyeball, so be it. I can lurk in the shadows and show or hide as suits my caprice. Hooking up should not be rational calculation; seduction should not be schematic. And if you don't understand that, you don't know what you're missing.

Randomize is the next best thing to accessorize. I don't search for specifics, I browse, wander, cruise, poke, and pick through record bins and used clothes by the pound, bump into friends rather than targeting them. Accidents happen, and I love them. Bring on synchronicity, coincidence, and conspiracy. Such is the stuff of spirit, awe, and wonder. I have laughter and amazement, not search results. I have unexpected longings, not hierarchical ratings.

I prance among my large-scale, graphics-rich, immersive projected web, tossing off voice commands and burning through chat cubbies and bear caves, flying over Paris and sighing over a new crush. I savor depth, hues, sounds, and smells. This isn't just virtual reality: Too many issues of *Mondo 2000* wore out that wet dream. I am not trapped inside some other world. No, I have decorated, meshed, embellished, and beautified *this* world with my online friends, loves, and thrift shops. *First* life baby, no sloppy Second Lives.

COMING-DOWN CODA: DREAM LOVER

Perhaps I seem a bit bipolar, blowing up from a cruise site's lowly drop-down menu to my reimagined fantasy web, but, as some big modernist once said, God is in the details. The key to getting out of a bad relationship is being able to imagine something more fulfilling. We don't need to settle for the infohighway as planned by rational bureaucrats—imagine, look for, support, and help create something better.

And I said to myself, is that all there is to the Internet?

GOING FROM ZERO TO SEXY ON HIGH-CALORIC QUEER OVERDRIVE

CAConrad

After one particular reading in New York, a few young guys came up to me with knit brows while their alpha-boy addressed me: "Don't you think it's a bit much to be reading poems about having sex with your boyfriend in his taxi cab after AIDS?" To which I replied, "Have you never heard of SAFE SEX!?" They looked disgusted, and I thought, *How have we come to this!?* Is this really the result of the revolution started by Marsha P. Johnson and other Stonewall Riot drag queens and freaks? I'm speechless some days, and Marsha's in the afterworld with her picket sign: STONEWALL WAS A RIOT NOT A TRADEMARK!

When I was recently invited by a queer student group to give a reading at their college, it was faggots who got angry at me after I read from my book *Deviant Propulsion*. One young man angrily confronted me, "The things you write are not making room for discussion or acceptance! My parents love and accept me, but they would NEVER accept the things you write in your book!" Hmm. How weird to be in this position, I thought, but decided to say what I felt was best. "First of all, your parents SHOULD love and accept you, so stop giving them brownie points for something they SHOULD do! Second, this is your world too, stop walking on egg-shells and take up some space! And not only that, but do you realize you're asking me to write different books for the love of your parents? You need to get off that shit right away and get crazy and open to the possibilities of your life!"

When I was twenty, everybody hated us, and in many ways I can look back on that now and realize how great it was for me. Never once have I written a poem or anything else with the love and acceptance from others in mind—my writing is mine, and has always been mine! Society's hatred has kept me true to my creative punch. But how do I get young faggots to realize that this time of assimilation means that we need to become even angrier and more rebellious and creative so we can change the grim, apathetic direction in which we're all headed?

So much attention and so many resources now go towards creating a pro-gay military, and this has brought us a horrifying sense that we need to serve, we need to sacrifice, in order to be loved and accepted. FUCK ALL THAT! Being queer in this brutally homophobic world is more than enough sacrifice! And with the pro-gay military also comes the ever streamlined pro-military gay body, worked on obsessively, a machine for the common good of the state. It's never been more unacceptable to be fat, and no one knows this more than fat faggots like me. Being fat these days is not just unacceptable because it's unappealing and gross to mainstream society, but it's also now seen as contrary to the very movement for acceptance. The mainstream war machine regiments our appearances, actions, and lives. *Fat bodies do not fit into military-issue battle fatigues!*

An old friend asked me once, "Doesn't it disturb you that men only want to be with you because you're fat?"

"NO! I LOVE IT! How about your boyfriend? Would he like it if you got fat?"

"NO! He would LEAVE ME!"

"Ah, I see! Doesn't it disturb you that he only wants to be with you because you're skinny?"

My friend laughed, "OK, you got me!" His mouth watered as I drank my delicious chocolate milk shake. He loved chocolate milk shakes, but would only drink them vicariously through me. While others live in fear at the gym, I'm eating a cream-filled cannoli with a smiling man's hard cock hiding inside. Our love truly is free because it's unsanctioned! *The Joy of Gay Sex* has no chapter for us, and I'm glad! Fuck the experts and their claustrophobic parameters!

You don't know true freedom until you don't want what they want you to want. Coming from white trash has advantages people with money don't seem to understand. For years I've watched friends whose parents are doctors and bankers live in fear (even while rebelling) that they're not good enough, not achieving enough, not clean enough, and especially not thin enough. The quest for socially-acceptable body fat ratio has never been discussed in my family, too consumed with bill collectors and police reports and how the judge will react.

When I escaped rural poverty for life in Philadelphia I was still a kid, skinny and conventionally cute, and I made friends with guys my age who were turning tricks for quick cash. My first boyfriend in the city was a coke dealer who kept me out of the skin trade, kept me in parties, kept me high and frantic. When he went to prison, I was lucky enough to fall into friendship with a group of vegans and macrobiotic spiritualists. For ten years my life revolved around eating well, animal rights, paganism; it was a beautiful ten years.

When I started working at Giovanni's Room, the queer bookstore in Philadelphia, my diet became more vegetarian than vegan, and I started to gain weight. There was plenty of talk about this from customers, and especially my faggot friends who warned, "You better be careful, you're getting FAT!" One regular customer who had a crush on me came into the store drunk one evening to stroke my cheek and tell me, "If you lost forty pounds you'd be my ideal!" And I said, "Oh really? How much do you weigh?" He beat his chest, "I'M A HUNDRED SIXTY POUNDS OF PURE MUSCLE!" I nodded and said, "Well, if YOU lost a hundred sixty pounds you'd be MY ideal!" He didn't get it, standing there drunk and confused in his self-centered fantasy, as though I should have been grateful that he told me the secret to winning the trophy of his big hard cock.

They didn't seem to understand that I didn't care, and never had cared about my looks. And what they also didn't seem to register was that there are a lot of faggots who love fat men. And there are precious few of us fat faggots to go around. While my friends were warning me to be careful, lest I lose love, they were missing the simple fact that love is for everyone! At the bookstore, the guys buying the fat porn like *Bulk Male* and all the other blubber-zines were starting to give me the glad eye. Hmm, it was something new, and I felt adventurous and titillated.

Suddenly, and I mean suddenly, my dance card was very full—being a self-assured fat gay man made me an overnight rock star! Now men bake me endless chocolate cupcakes, make me peanut butter cream sushi, and prepare my favorite deep fried vegan ham and noodles dishes. They indulge me, I indulge them—full, fully loved. Food and sex over long blissful nights have plucked my fat flower from the massive bouquet of cultural shame and released me in ways I never knew when I was thinner and with men who were obsessed with thinness.

There are faggots I know who are only attracted to the fat Elvis, and you feel the soft purr as they talk about His chubby neck and breasts. Some people get angry when debating how long Elvis was fat, furiously whittling it down to six months as though the dead are anything but thin. Let me assure you that a photograph of the fat Elvis will not evaporate from your wall in six months. Yes, you can jerk off to it for the rest of your life, I give you my word!

Existing simultaneously outside queer and straight norms is liberating, and constantly exciting in ways I had never anticipated. The tedious, predictable world behind us, we have it our way—and I mean that sexually as well as politically! Outside the respectable domain, the vantage of an unjust world is always clearest.

TRANS/NATIONALLY FEMME: NOTES ON NEOLIBERAL ECONOMIC REGIMES, SECURITY STATES, AND MY LIFE AS A BROWN IMMIGRANT FAG

Debanuj DasGupta

On May 15, 2008 in a 4-3 decision, the California Supreme Court ruled that everyone has a fundamental "right to marry" the person of their choice and that gender restrictions violate the state Constitution's equal protection guarantee. Less publicized news from the same day reported that Immigration and Customs Enforcement (ICE) agents raided a well-known French bakery in San Diego, and arrested 18 undocumented migrant workers, some of whom had worked for more than 16 years at this bakery. ICE agents also raided the homes of workers who were not on the job that day, including an illegal raid on University of California at San Diego graduate student housing.

These two pieces of news from the same state and the same day neatly summarize the inequalities that mark my life. Even after the overturn of the California Supreme Court decision in a ballot measure six months later, the dominant LGBT movement imagery remains pictures of happy couples and their wedding cakes, cakes made with the sweat and toil of hard-working, underpaid laborers. Laborers who could be LGBT and/or undocumented. As the movement for sexual and gender revolution is hijacked by a narrow call to conform to a capitalist hetero-patriarchal core, the lives and aspirations of millions of human beings deemed "illegal" or simply unwanted are torn apart by imperialist regimes across the globe. While racially and economically privileged LGBT US citizens are finally assimilating into a US citizens' rights framework, and their humanity is being recognized, a whole new class of non-humans has been created.

As a brown, genderqueer, femme, leather boi, English-educated immigrant fag, I am forced to constantly negotiate my presence in this country, which is guided by complex gender, race, class, and border control regimes. My mobility across state and gender boundaries is restricted and contested—the cost of the contestation evident in my failing mental, physical, and financial health. I have worked as a nude house cleaner for rich gay men, inhaling ammonium and bleach for long hours. Many of these men would not hesitate to pinch my butt, or laugh at my hairy, brown body. I have also worked as a busboy at upscale bistros where I was slapped around by the gay male clientele, and yet I made sure to keep smiling at my customers, even when they would cross acceptable physical boundaries, in hopes of a fat tip. I have spent long therapy sessions crying over getting taken for granted as a femme-bottom in my relationships, and have spent thousands of dollars to figure out ways to exist "legally" in this land of opportunities. And I am not the only one.

LET'S START AT THE VERY BEGINNING

Our stories (as genderqueer, transgender, faggots) don't begin here in the US. We have histories sometimes rich, sometimes of terror and persecution in our countries of origin. Many of us were abandoned by our communities of origin since we were "Na-Mard" ("not a man" in Hindi and Urdu). We come from countries ravaged by wars, growing inequalities in income, and disinvestment in public services and schools—globalization has brought structural adjustments and a privatization of essential services. This has hit the poorest among us especially hard.

My friend Babu, from Bangladesh, has survived life-long torture from both his family and society at large due to his feminine presentation and Christian heritage. He lost his job at a government-sponsored development program and was unable to find another, since most folks would not hire someone effeminate like him. He then traveled around Bangladesh with a troupe of Kothis (femme men who have sex with other men). They would sing and dance at wedding ceremonies, living off a meager income of $50/ month.

After getting beaten and raped by local hoodlums, he escaped to the US and started working at Dunkin' Donuts, making $4.99 per hour, way more than he would have earned in Bangladesh. He continues to live in a makeshift room in a basement in Queens, and prays that he does not fall sick. He sends about half of his income back to his sister in Dhaka, hoping one day he can return to build a house there.

My journey across the globe begins with the immigration reforms in the 1970s and '80s, which brought medical and engineering professionals from recently decolonized nations of Asia to the US. Several of my maternal aunts were married off to professionals migrating to the US in search of a better future. Most of my childhood winter vacations in India were spent playing with my cousins from the US—as we explained to them the stories of over three million Hindu gods and goddesses, they shared their Lego toys and Disneyland View-Master with us. The dream of crossing the seven seas and living in the land of Mickey Mouse was firmly planted in my heart very early in life.

Growing up in an upwardly mobile English-educated family in Kolkata meant that I had access to the United States Information Services and British Council libraries, where I would spend countless hours devouring the *Atlantic Quarterly* or *Signs*, learning about the emerging LGBT and new wave feminist movements. The splashy images from the twentieth anniversary celebrations of Stonewall in 1989 inspired some of us to start the first gay and lesbian support group in Kolkata.

We would spend hours in cruising parks and women's studies gatherings doing outreach for support group meetings. Soon we connected with support groups in local cities and recently formed LGBT South Asian groups in major cities of the US and UK. We organized the first International South Asian conference on "Histories of Alternate Sexualities" in New Delhi in 1993 and in the following year the first International South Asian conference of gay men and men-who-have-sex-with-men (MSM). Tensions existed along class and gender lines, and any conversations with *Hijras* (often referred to as third-sex-third-gender in South Asian countries) were barely happening. Our publications had to be trilingual to reflect the complex linguistic contexts of India, but at support group meetings, Bengali and Hindi-speaking men and women would often remain silenced.

At the core of these tensions was our own internalized classism and homophobia. The key organizers of these fledgling LGBT support groups were all upper-middle class English-educated men and women. We were well-trained, respectable Indian citizens. The feminine voices and flamboyant mannerisms of the non-English speaking Kothis were too disruptive for us. I would act polite and smile as I met Kothis in cruising parks and I would hand them flyers for the support group, yet secretly I hoped they would never show up at meetings. In the parks, they would walk in small groups, wear facial makeup, and speak in street Bengali. Their loud mannerisms and shabby clothing felt alien compared to my English-speaking, denim-sporting, globetrotting "gay" world.

Yet when I was harassed by cops at the parks, it was Kothis who came to my defense. One such incident happened on a dark winter evening. I was caught carrying condoms in my bag by the local police, who would haunt the cruising joints hoping to extract money from "cocksucking Kothis." The two cops threatened to arrest me for distributing "profane materials." I was nervous, and yet kept talking to them in English and broken Bengali, telling them that I worked for family planning programs. The cops laughed loudly at all my pleas. Three of the Kothis came running, yelling and clapping loudly, cursing the hell out of the cops. A small crowd gathered, and ultimately the cops left. As I began to mingle more with the Kothis, I began to face my own inner prejudices and fears. I learned that loud mannerisms, claps, and street-smartness were their way of surviving the harsh realities of working class femme men in Kolkata. I went on to build friendships with several Kothis. We would sit on a park bench and giggle over how we would love to be the "wives" of hot butch men.

With increased visibility came increased backlash. Several LGBT organizers were beaten up, blackmailed, and harassed. I was attacked several times while doing HIV outreach at public parks and toilets. As some of us became publicly visible, our English-educated friends started to avoid us. Fear of bringing shame on their families if they were associated with such "disgraceful figures" lay at the core of these avoidances. In the wake of constant verbal and physical assault, the dream of Mickey and Minnie became more of a practical exit to the land of the Stonewall riots.

QUEER AND BROWN IN THE MIDWEST

In summer of 1996 I arrived at the Cleveland Hopkins airport with two suitcases packed with my favorite clothing. My well-built, basketball-playing cousin came to help with my luggage, as my aunt waited outside in her Jaguar. I recently went back to the picture my aunt snapped on my first evening in her house: my hair is long and curly and I'm wearing a tie-dye shirt, obviously femme next to my buff male cousins. We look awkward next to each other. The awkwardness in that picture continued to frame my next few years in the perfect white suburbs of Akron. I felt like an uprooted tree, cut off from my friends in India, not knowing how to drive, taking long bus rides to get to school.

Very quickly I found the cruising spots on campus. Back then cruising went on pretty heavily at a few of the men's toilets. You would make foot gestures from underneath the flimsy walls to pick up the guy next to you. I was surprised at the number of men who kept rejecting me, once they came around the doors and saw me up close. I guess being brown and having a medium sized penis did not take you that far in the white, blonde-dominated meat markets of the Midwest.

In summer of 1997, I met Kurt at one of the toilets. He was big-dicked, tall, and broad-shouldered, with sandy blonde hair and green eyes. He was the Superman I was told I could meet in the US. "I would love to tie you up and fuck you," he said. "I am not sure about that," I replied. I don't know why I said that. I had always fantasized about getting tied up, had always enjoyed reading the daddy-boy sex scenes in porn magazines. But I repressed those fantasies, thinking them to be "sick and perverted." But here was an open invitation from a gorgeous man to enact those scenes. I experimented once, twice, and decided to stick with him. We enacted countless scenes over the next three years.

I was the brown slave boy. I would stand in his dungeon, tied to a cross—unable to move, every part of my body restrained—as he would softly fondle me. Those were such intense scenes, all my thoughts focused on him, every single touch giving me goose bumps. His dark green sparkling eyes looked directly into my eyes, making me feel as though he was reading everything that was tucked away in the corner of my heart. He would play with my hair, saying how much he loved my dark black shiny hair. I distinctly remember feeling his warm fingers stroking back and forth. The intensity was overpowering.

Our entire Master/slave relationship revolved around race-based role-plays. He would pick me up from the school library, and we would fuck for hours. Some days he would be the white master raping my brown hole, and other days the white leather daddy punishing me for being a dirty brown fag. Most of our roleplays were supposedly negotiated, but as a lonely fag newly arrived in the Midwest I went along with whatever he proposed. Kurt was the hot white Superman that I had dreamt about; I would do anything to keep having sex with him. Our relationship never evolved beyond sexual buddies, and this began to disturb me. I would spend long sleepless nights wondering if I was merely his Asian sex slave. I ran into him at a local bar, and he refused even to acknowledge me. Back then, I was scared to confront him with this incident. Scared to lose my Superman. Years later, when I did confront him, he awkwardly replied, "I don't know why I did it! I am sorry!" Deep in my heart, however, I knew that while he enjoyed sex with me and several other Asian men, he wanted to fit in with his white upper class gay neighbors by dating another rich white boy.

FOR THOSE OF US WHOSE STORIES WILL NEVER BE TOLD

I left the unbearable whiteness of Akron, Ohio in January 2000 for the Big Apple, in search of a South Asian/people of color progressive queer community and a career in nonprofit management. Little had I anticipated that, a year and seven months later, one of the definitive events of American society was about to hit me and my home. "Debanuj, wake up, the Twin Towers have been bombed!" David's voice yelled on the answering machine. I turned on the TV and the first thing that went through my mind was, "My green card application is fucked!" I desperately tried to call work (an environmental canvassing agency) and went over how much I would receive in my next two paychecks, because there was no way that, as a brown genderqueer fag, I would be knocking on doors in Long Island right after 9/11.

In the days that followed we became a one-income household. David worked for his father's construction company during the day, and as a go-go dancer at night. I sat at home, cleaning and cooking, frantically begging friends to give me consulting gigs under the table. We were running out of food. Babu, my friend from Bangladesh, got us a ten-pound bag of rice from his church. I helped him with his asylum application. He was starting to feel unsafe working at Dunkin' Donuts.

Back in those days, there were a lot of community dinners at friends' houses. We would huddle in people's cramped Manhattan apartments, and silently eat. Yet soon these parties became rowdy with music and robust with our zeal to survive and thrive amidst growing violence and xenophobia. Since David, a Mexican immigrant, was very active in the Latina/o LGBT community, and I was involved with the South Asian Lesbian and Gay Association, our house soon became a venue to build cross-racial bridges. On David's birthday that October, my South Asian friends brought flyers for a teach-in on Afghanistan, and folks shared stories of how we were all oppressed by this system.

Our efforts to build cross-ethnic alliances were fraught with challenges. Most of David's friends were working income Spanish-speaking Mexican queer men and a few women, while most of my friends were English-speaking middle class South Asians. Let's just say there was a communication gap between us that had to be filled with rounds of tequila shots and food fights. Some of my closest friends would privately ask me: "How can you hang out with those illiterate Mexicans?" Very soon I would fall off the good books of the socialite South Asian queers, owing to my "wayward ways."

CULTURES OF FEAR

Post-9/11 was marked by an overwhelming culture of fear. I was attacked by a group of young men (they were a mixed racial group), and beaten up in an empty subway station. I was lucky that a few people came running down the stairs and I got away with a couple of punches and a twisted ankle. My attackers yelled at me, "Terrorist fag go back to your country!" In the first week of that October after 9/11, at least eight queer-transgender South Asians were physically attacked across Manhattan, Brooklyn, and Queens. South Asian drag queens saw a marked drop in attendance at clubs across New York City. One renowned South Asian female-identified DJ summed it up aptly, "People are afraid to be around brown people."

Policing in its multiple forms is so common in the lives of queer and transgender people of color that we normalize it. I learned how to walk fast in my neighborhood in Brooklyn, since there were always cop cars roaming. I also changed my style of dress—instead of wearing skirts with denims, I started to wear traditional male clothing, hoping to avoid ruthless comments from the streets. I knew I could not rely on the police for any safety, or to address any violence done to me; in fact, they might cause me more harm.

One of my friends who lived with his partner in Kew Gardens, Queens called me after receiving a notice from immigration authorities in the name of his lover (a gay undocumented man from Pakistan), saying that his lover would be deported to Pakistan due to a visa overstay. He could hardly do anything to prevent the impending deportation, since he also had just applied for political asylum. We found a pro-bono attorney and were able to get "withholding of removal," which allowed my friend to live and work in the US; today he is still unable to leave US borders. Several of my Pakistani and Bangladeshi friends were required to comply with new legislation that required them to register with Immigration and Customs Enforcement (ICE). Men who had grown to live their lives as women felt compelled to dress and behave "manly" when they went to register.

Needless to say, all of this put a heavy toll on our physical and mental health. I fell into depression. We got used to eating one heavy meal a day. Often we would pull in cash between three or four households and hold joint dinners. Soon tensions emerged in the community, and most of us just stuck to work and home. We were even scared to talk about immigration or 9/11 over the phone. The culture of fear and terror seeped into our efforts at community-building. Many of the Hindu middle class members of the South Asian Lesbian and Gay Association would warn me not to hang out with my Muslim friends. The nationalist divisions between Hindu Indians and Muslim Pakistanis became inflamed. Many of my Hindu Indian upper class friends would avoid their Pakistani friends, and often in all-Indian settings you would hear someone alluding to Muslims as gun-toting, backward folks. I would be warned by my fellow Hindu Indians, "You know they are all being watched! Don't go to their homes; you will be on the FBI list!" As I look back to the dim days after 9/11, all I can think of was how paranoid and fearful we were of everyone, including our best friends. All kinds of spying scenarios would go through my mind. I would wake up in the middle of the night thinking that the FBI had busted open my doors.

This is not to suggest that our problems started after 9/11. Prior to 9/11, fears and tensions about immigrants and queers existed in the communities we lived in. Detention was still high in working income communities, and trans folks were facing harassment, often rape, in detention centers. The NYPD had a heavy presence in neighborhoods like Bedford-Stuyvesant, Harlem, and Jackson Heights. The strategy was to nab immigrants on all kinds of misdemeanors and get them into the database. 9/11 gave the police and immigration authorities a reason to do everything overtly in the name of fighting "terrorism."

CONNECTING THE DOTS: WHAT DO NEOLIBERALISM AND SECURITY STATES HAVE TO DO WITH FAGGOTS?

Sometimes I am read as "respectable, upper-class, English educated," sometimes as the "brown other" and sometimes as "underemployed household help." In slowly waking up to these multiple mappings I have had to travel to my inner phobias of other gay/queer/genderqueer/faggotty and transgender people. The pain of loving a hot white stud in the Midwest who used me sexually while rejecting me emotionally served as a jolting reminder of my place in the race-class hierarchies of gay/queer men's communities in the US. In a twisted tale of global migration, I went from being on the top of the hierarchy in India to somewhere near the bottom in the US. I began to debunk my own internalized hierarchies by constantly challenging myself to love Babu and David during those dark days post 9/11. Honestly, a large part of it was prompted by my own survival needs. Yet, in attempting to survive, I was reminded that survival is never a singular journey.

Under neoliberal social ethics, human relationships, like the economic market, are left to laws of competition and individual gain. For those of us who find ourselves in the lower rungs of the racial-sexual-economic ladder, such notions are dangerous. As is evident from my stories both in India and

New York, my survival and ability to thrive is predicated upon my community's survival. Every time I have attempted to make it on my own, I have found myself isolated, hopeless, and often at the mercy of underpaid and overworked social workers.

Our journeys across national borders, in search of sexual and economic opportunities, are not singular journeys. We follow a global chain of movement—a set of hierarchies reduces us to nude housecleaners, go-go-dancers, and food servers. We are overwhelmed by financial stress and physical pain. Immigration regimes mark us as either "documented" or "undocumented," "highly skilled" or "unskilled." These markings manipulate our abilities to negotiate the price of our labor, often resulting in competition among friends.

Are we weak and silent victims, who choose to live in shade? Or are we strong resilient communities? To answer this question I invite everyone to imagine these two paradigms not in contrast with one another, but on parallel paths. We spend countless hours calculating the complex equations of immigration attorneys, international phone calls, and rising food prices. Sometimes the losses far outweigh the gains, and then there are times when our tired brown bodies wrapped around shining red and gold colors march down Fifth Avenue or Market Street celebrating all things queerly brown, and the very fact that we continue to survive, thrive, and cook cheap curried meals for each other. And in our survival, we win small victories against all-encompassing systems that would rather see us decompose and die.

LEVITY AND GRAVITY

Chris Bartlett

"I can never go back to New Orleans. I lost too many friends there, and I can't bring myself to go back to a world that is no longer there for me."
—*Sylvie, Nashville, TN*

This is a story about the lightness of a gay culture in the 1970s and 1980s that masked so much pre-AIDS heaviness related to being queer, or a queer of color, or a working class queer. I want to examine how, virtually overnight, the heaviness of death and trauma became inscribed in our communities by mass deaths due to AIDS, and the subsequent lightness with which we have treated these deaths. This essay is a map of my own simultaneous levity and gravity—my desire to resurrect and recreate the playfulness of 1970s and 1980s gay culture, while acknowledging that this same culture was dark and heavy for many people.

In discussions about long-term trauma and where it fits into queer history, people are sometimes a bit confounded as to why I would involve myself in a project of remembering. "Isn't it haunting?" asked one. Another said, "I've had to put those stories behind me in order to cope." And I do feel haunted at times, and sometimes I wish I could put the history behind me. But I feel so pulled by these powerful queer stories of the past, and I imagine that they might inspire or move someone—and maybe even make a difference in a life or a community. So here I offer up some rememberings—with the hopes that they will show you a bit of those light/heavy worlds. These are the memories and myths and the accretions of stories I have created to understand things that are incomprehensible.

THE HEAVINESS OF NUMBERS

"Things just happened. Friends sick on Friday, dead by Sunday."
—James, Liberty, TN

When I imagine the impact of the AIDS epidemic and the related trauma after so many deaths, I think in terms of the heaviness of numbers. In my own city of Philadelphia, approximately 4,500 gay and bisexual men died of AIDS between 1981 and 2009.

In a city that has an estimated 25,000 gay and bisexual men alive and well today, that's about one-sixth of the current adult population killed off. This wasn't just a decimation of Philadelphia's gay community (the Roman military term for killing one tenth of a population)—but, far worse—the killing of one-sixth, or 17 percent. Losing one in six meant fewer leaders, fewer dancers, fewer of everything in the surviving culture.

I think too, though, of what those people who survived did and do, and of what those who were dying taught us about living.

Numbers in the thousands or tens of thousands tell the toll from other cities—New York, San Francisco, Chicago, Los Angeles, Houston. Smaller cities had death tolls that were equally large in the context of their gay communities. How does this feel to you? Do you know how many gay men died in your city? Do you know where they came from?

Many of us have not stopped to do an inventory of these deaths or to consider the impact on the fabric of our queer communities. I believe we need to do both in order to understand our origins, and to imagine where we might go from here.

THE LIGHTNESS OF RISK-TAKING

"We grew up in a risky gay world, where we learned how to take risks to survive, and then public health told us to reduce our risk and that risk in fact was to be avoided."
—Peter, San Francisco, CA

Just stop for a moment to think about what could have been created by these men who died. Many of them were risk-takers—in community, in the arts, in drug use, in business, in sex, and in relationships. Can we even imagine what was lost—would one person have created an operatic masterpiece? Would another have gone on to transform a community, or develop a vaccine, or act as an elder to someone who really needed one?

I'm not saying that everyone who died was a risk-taker or an artist. I am saying that as a result of a virus our communities and cultures became suspicious of risk—*fearful* of risk—and sought safety, either perceived or real. And most of us thought that safety couldn't be a bad thing—but perhaps we forgot about the benefits and advantages that risk-taking had brought us.

We were taught, by public health institutions, community organizations, and each other, to fear certain sexual behaviors, but in fact many of us couldn't separate the behaviors from the people, so we ended up viewing other gay men as vectors of disease, regardless of sexual practice or HIV status. The "risk reduction" we practiced often meant avoiding intimacy with the very people we needed in order to overcome generations of internalized shame. We ended up limiting the types of connections that had historically led to personal health and community well-being.

Generations of pre-Stonewall gay men knew what it was to live their lives amidst risk—the risk of the paddy wagon, the risk of media exposé, the risk of family ostracism. But despite this, resilient urban gay cultures developed, cultures that celebrated the role of the outsider. My own experience of risky gay men leads me to celebrate the role of risk and risk-taking in gay culture, and to grieve that risk has been pathologized and demonized as the result of a virus.

My inventory of dead risk-takers includes many powerful and insightful leaders whom I met through ACT UP Philadelphia. I'll take a moment to name some of them here as a ritual, shared with you, of remembering:

Dominic Bash (died 1993, age 46), was the South Philly hairdresser and diva who walked right up to Philadelphia's Cardinal Bevilacqua and gave him a piece of his mind about condom distribution and sex-ed in the schools. One story of Dominic sticks in my head: as a boy, he had confronted a bully by sticking a broom into the wheels of his bike so that the bully went head-over-heels onto the ground. I remember thinking that Dominic preferred to attack the machine (the bike) rather than the person directly (the bully).

Harry Reid (died 1992, age 45) was a city sanitation worker who showed up at ACT UP demonstrations with shakers of martinis and a much needed sense of humor. I always thought it was notable that working class gay men whose lives were so much at risk during the epidemic showed up to fight. Harry was a bit impatient with some of the intellectual debate in ACT UP, and he was one of the voices propelling us forward when we got bogged down in too much process or unproductive argument.

Arnold Jackson (died 1998, age 40) was a poet and advocate who constantly made a stand for treatments (including alternative therapies) for black gay men. He forcefully advocated for alternative therapies for people with HIV, even when the doctors were dismissive. He was also a writer and artist, and I saw the ways his creative life nurtured and intersected with his activist life; he wrote poems and stories that described and celebrated black gay culture, even amidst a tsunami of death. He was a clear intellectual descendent of another black gay Philadelphian who died of AIDS: Joe Beam, the editor of *In the Life*.

The unstoppable Kiyoshi Kuromiya (died 2000, age 57) was a major figure in many of the liberation movements of the '60s and '70s, and taught me to see the intersections in activist movements. Kiyoshi had an endless energy to show up at every action, demonstration, and meeting to bring the power of his broad vision and perspective derived from decades of civil rights activism. He was a mentor to dozens of men and women who now lead HIV/AIDS and gay movements and organizations. His house on Lombard Street was accessible 24/7 to those who needed support, drugs, or company. At the end of his life, I worked with a team of twelve ACT UP Philly veterans to provide him with 24-hour companionship and care.

Ted Kirk (died 1998, age 31) was, like me, a Radical Faerie, and we traveled together to the Short Mountain Sanctuary in Tennessee. He went to the faerie gatherings even toward the end of his life, and we had to take a few unexpected trips to Nashville-area hospitals when pneumonia developed. I remember how scared I was, driving on the mountain roads to get him to the hospital. I'm sure I didn't discuss this with anyone. Since Ted didn't let illness keep him from living as fully as he desired, even to the end, I felt that processing my own experience of his sickness would be a luxury. He included his faerie friends in the process of his death, and we accepted that.

The death of Dominic Piccirelli (died 2006, age 39) was particularly poignant for me, because we were the same age. I loved Dominic. He was adorable and flirty, and helped me and artist Jackie Cassels in an early project to create small paintings to memorialize ACT UP Philly members who had died. He was also a poet who continued to write throughout his life. He worked the coat-check at Woody's, the largest and most well-known gay bar in Philly, and I remember seeing him grow thinner and knowing that soon I would need to grieve him. Dominic is one of 24 Woody's staff members who have died thus far. Our meccas of dance and pleasure were flipped, spun, and reconfigured by the large numbers of deaths.

Jonathan Lax (died 1996, age 46) was a treatment activist and an inventor. He invented the surge protector as well as that little piece of metal used to keep you from tripping over cords on the floor. They always said

Jonathan was equally comfortable in a board room or at a demonstration. Early on, he took me under his wing and invited me into his projects, including the Lax Scholarship for Gay Men, whose selection committee I serve on to this day.

John Kelly (died 1992, age 33), also known as Camille, helped organize the AIDS Library of Philadelphia and combined camp with seriousness. He was levity and gravity personified. He involved his dad and family in his dying process, and by the time of his passing, he had connected his diverse worlds to one another. By doing this, John ensured that the communities he had built survived his death.

These are but a few of a much larger list of beautiful gay men who inspired me, mentored me, danced and partied with me, and taught me each of their own unique takes on what it means to be gay. In many cases, they died so young; at 43 I've already lived longer than many of them. It's almost dizzying to see the trick that time plays on our minds: when I was younger, 32 seemed so old. Now it seems so young. But it always seemed a young age to die.

Today's young gays (and their allies) are unlikely to even know who these men (or others like them) were, and how much their work created what is possible today. Solidarity with an older generation whose experience is either unknown or alien might seem unnecessary or perhaps impossible, but I am asking for solidarity. If we don't tell the stories of men like these, their stories will no doubt die out in a few decades. Without clarity about what happened to our people and culture in all of its diversity, how could you even imagine the fabric of a community that survives the ripping and rending of so many deaths? Perhaps you couldn't.

For those of you who have similar lists of friends lost, I urge you to write down their stories before they are forgotten. And for those of you who have as yet lost no one, I ask you to learn a few of the stories and remember them. I think that any hope for intergenerational solidarity relies upon doing this work.

THE HEAVINESS OF SHAME

What stops us from taking a complete and descriptive inventory of the deaths, from telling these stories, from expressing solidarity? Likely shame. Shame that those were our "adolescent" years when we hadn't fully grown up and assimilated. Shame that those guys died and we didn't. Shame that we haven't done anything yet, so why should we now? Shame that we just aren't up to it, and isn't it awful that we lack the courage? Shame over funerals or memorials shrouded in secrecies. Shame that we abandoned some of the powerful ideals of gay liberation, and sold out for rights. Shame that when protease inhibitors became available and white gay men could (largely) afford to survive, we abandoned the fight. Shame that we can't even remember the names of all our friends who died, and we are occasionally reminded of someone we loved and forgot, and we are appalled.

How can we even inventory an unquantifiable and unqualifiable loss? And who would take on the remembering and inventory? Do we need a community occasion to acknowledge that history, or is the process best left informal? Could younger queers, who haven't lived through this trauma so directly, share in the collection and documenting of these thousands? The inventory must be done—we need to capture all of these stories to explain our advances and the missteps.

I have my own stories about the '70s and early '80s that started with lurid tales captured from *Philadelphia Magazine*, *Time Magazine*, and other mainstream periodicals. Then I discovered books and articles written by gay men themselves. As a teenager, I secretly devoured these, including Andrew Holleran's *Dancer from the Dance*, John Rechy's *Numbers*, and the fabulously sexy *Gay Guide to New England*. Having discovered what was possible through these books and articles, as a gay teen in the early '80s I rode the subway into Philadelphia and wandered the streets—many times spending hours walking up and down Spruce Street with the hope that I would find another gay man. I was 18 years old, and I did find those men— they invited me back to their apartments and initiated me into the sexual world I'd fantasized about. I hadn't yet been taught to fear older men, and so I embraced them. My years in ACT UP acquainted me with more thinkers who challenged our communities, from the celebratory writing of Eric Rofes to the shaming tone of Larry Kramer. I read and noticed quite a bit. And I remember.

MAKING LIGHT OF THE HEAVINESS

I remember the paradox of a light-hearted gay culture that faced the serious threats of gay bashing, job discrimination, family ostracism, and racism from both within and without. I remember a light-hearted gay culture that danced and laughed, while doormen at bars excluded black men and women of all races. I remember a light-hearted gay culture that honored its gay leaders each year, and they were almost all bartenders. I remember a light-hearted gay culture, serious about sex and sex culture, serious about the need for liberation from a world that feared sex. I know gay men who have described this lightness through stories of sitting in the bathhouse on each other's beds and talking about their lives and politics. It's the lightness of old-school camp, all kinds of intermingling encouraged by random encounters, and the lightness of Sylvester's songs, gay rallies (not just parades) with a sassy political edge, and cruising through it all.

I remember a light-hearted gay culture where cruising was the norm. Does anyone cruise the streets anymore? Younger gay men often seem fascinated (and/or appalled) when I talk about my ability to meet random and unknown men on the street, to have a conversation, to engage. This behavior seems like ancient history—a time when you didn't first pre-determine all your similar interests through Manhunt checkboxes and online surveys. Friends remind me of a time when sex was much lighter and more playful. There was not always the spectre of HIV, the spectre of fear in every interaction, or the spectre of denial of both these realities. It was just lighter, because it *could* be lighter. But like all light, it came in many forms: the lightness of possibility on the dance floor; the strength that came from chanting with thousands at a rally; the lightheadedness that came from fear.

When I have shared drafts of this essay with gay men who came up and out during the '70s, some have cautioned me not to be too nostalgic for a decade that was painful, dark, and difficult for many. They remind me of the horizontal hostility between gay men, the cattiness, the elitism. And I get that and acknowledge it, while I celebrate the assets that were no doubt there.

In my life, I have seen this hostility directed mostly at those viewed as gender traitors—especially sissies and ultra-butch women, or anyone viewed as having transitioned outside of their "given role." I have also seen the hostility directed towards elders, or to the idea of growing old—so that we create an invisible older generation whose wisdom and learnings aren't accessible. And, most pertinent to levity and gravity, I have seen an unspoken hostility toward the memory of those who have died and toward those who are currently living with HIV—risk reduction has pulled us apart.

My gay elders remind me not to let my own sadness and pain and anger consume my sense of purpose, my faith in what we can do next. They also remind me to remember the tremendous achievements we made individually and collectively, in the face of the multiple challenges we confronted.

THE HEAVINESS OF ANGER, THE LIGHTNESS OF THE FUTURE

"I loved the incredible generosity—we really needed a community for life and death reasons."
—Peter, Philadelphia, PA

I do wonder whether many gay men of my generation and older are walk-ing around just waiting to explode in anger, and how much of that is about aging and unfulfilled promise and how much is about what we lost, about what has been marginalized and forgotten. The gay men of the '70s and '80s who died of AIDS, or really from any cause, must be so pissed off that their lives and traditions haven't been better remembered. Why do we think we can just brush their lives and stories under the red carpet? Don't we indeed think that? I want to better understand the anger I see in older generations of gay men—especially when that anger is channeled against younger gay men in ways that further the divisions in our communities.

I want to confront the shaming hostility put forth by the likes of Larry Kramer and other finger-wagging fogies who chastise queer youth for not being serious enough, or for being too sexy or sexual, or too hedonistic. Though I was raised on Kramer's writing and was frequently inspired by him in my youth, I have found that embittered gays like Kramer can't even take a moment to step out of the impact of their trauma to see the inspiring new generation of queers who are recreating and regenerating, making new the old traditions of lightness and camp. These new generations seem to in-stinctively know the heaviness and seriousness of what is at stake. And out of the gay traditions of the past, they are able to tell the difference between that heavy knowledge and living forward with a lightness of touch.

DEATH BY MASCULINITY

Ali Abbas

In 2007, I was expected to attend an LGBT leadership conference in order to maintain a scholarship that helped to pay for my undergraduate degree. I was anxious to meet other scholars and activists who had been selected based on their concern for social justice. While sitting down with a fellow attendee, I became engaged in a conversation about current projects we were pursuing. The conversation started out light but soon turned serious when the focus shifted to the Middle East. As a self-identified Arab, I quickly found myself the target of interrogation and criticism. At one point, I was asked how I could still be proud of my heritage and simultaneously "identify with the politics of the LGBTQ community." According to the other scholar, "the Muslim world just isn't ready for it." I was not just offended at his obviously loaded and prejudiced comments, but I felt pressured to fit either the stereotype or the demand: I could be an Arab or an advocate of the LGBTQ community, but never both.

> *"You really are playing into your culture. Think of the possibilities of reform!"*

Because this individual asked me where I got off still "playing into" my culture, he assumed that somehow his upbringing as a white middle-class US American (as opposed to those Americans who are immigrants, non-US citizens, or otherwise choose not to identify with the US) was the norm. This gung-ho attitude resonates with the masculinist attitudes ubiquitous in gay spaces, where men who are "nelly" are routinely denigrated, and paranoid fantasies about feminine men trying to "take over the community" are commonplace. Of course, this is a community that drag performers, butch dykes, and men who patronized dark, damp bars in basements fought for after they were ostracized by employers, friends, family, and society—a battle that was later appropriated by upstanding white men who came out years after they made their money. The argument voiced by the man at the conference had a no-less-hateful intention than the all-too-common hatred directed at queeny men. Just as traditional gay masculine men must protect their (stolen) personal property—bars, gyms, gayborhoods, etc.—from repulsive feminine invaders, a new generation of *liberal* gay masculine men must defend their cultural property, the LGBTQ (most often just G and sometimes L) community.

Those on the top will claim that identity is dead only insofar as this releases them from any responsibility for their words or actions. All over the internet, gay personals websites valorize "straight acting" as a universal value that is both desirable and positive, linking it to a set of norms that eerily imitate moral code in religious law (thou shalt be butch). In bar scenes, men stand in lock-step formation, patrolling the behavior of those who stray outside the borders of masculine performance, imposing fear of social deportation. Likewise, the largest LGB organizations prioritize the privileges and choices long upheld by patriarchal US American society, like the right to receive benefits through marriage or the right to kill under order of government.

"Straight-acting" does not only prioritize a certain gender presentation, but also inherently assumes whiteness and ableness of body (people of color or anyone using a wheelchair need not apply). Personal profiles use the words "masculine" and "feminine" as a way to marginalize, though the authors claim that they are simply helping out the browsers to narrow search results. By claiming that "Hey, it's just what I prefer, dude," the writers fail to realize that, in a community formed by and built upon identification with the body and its practices, the simplest marginalization becomes a vehicle for exclusion and opens new channels for bashing. Not only should a gay man prefer someone masculine (one who avoids "playing into" other value systems), but also someone clearly US American. Supposedly, by laying claim to the pride of stars and stripes, one can overlook years of US segregation, oppression, and imperialism of the body, in favor of something more fitting—like a shiny new BMW in which to cruise ethnically-cleansed parks.

"Not that I think they're backwards or anything, I just wish the gays of the Middle East could learn from the gays of America."

Why? So publications purporting to be LG (again, sometimes B, less often T, almost never Q) can advertise expensive watches and handbags while discussing privileged politics in articles positioned next to images of young fit white men? The "Dude, I just don't do femme" hypocrisy of gay men (last time I checked the lexicon, sex with men was society's ultimate act of femininity) is echoed in these claims of intercultural "dialogue." It is as though the "I just" or "but" placed in compound sentences somehow relieves the speaker of any accountability for racism, misogyny, femme-phobia, or hate.

Somehow, the existence of gay bars in urban and usually expensive geographies becomes proof of social equality. Yet how secure can a space be if it will inevitably be out-gentrified by rich straight white couples? Only then does migration to new underprivileged areas become trendy, and the cycle begins again. I am terrified at the thought that social justice can be measured by the size of a bar or the make of a car. Even with the protection of "historical landmark" status for gay bars and dives, there is no guarantee that individuals in the LGBTQ community will ever find their own sanctuary in a relationship between body and society. Why are gay bars so crucial to LGBTQ politics in other countries? Why is the amount of repetitive dance music produced and distributed in bars dominated by men the marker of queer activism?

On the basis of my upbringing in the Middle East and from what I've observed during recent trips back, I can assure those afraid of not having a welcome vacation spot that bars with a multitude of same-sex interactions are alive and kicking. Yet I unapologetically declare that they are not a mirror of the bars in major US cities. If a community strives for autonomy and individuality, then why is it so important that every space emerge as identical? Why is it so hard to believe that queerness can exist outside the model we have come to know in the United States? Perhaps it could be that liberal gay masculine men, as often as they pretend to be strong in singularity, depend upon the masses. No one would buy into the hype of mass gay consumerism if they were sure that alternative modes for living and creating culture existed and were easily accessible without shelling out the cash.

"I just feel bad for them, you know? They live in these conditions where they cannot even speak out without fear of death. If their relatives believe so strongly in suicide bombings and honor killings, they can't help but fuck things up for the gays."

It is inevitable that with the performance of masculinity comes a strict belief in nationalism. How can one imitate the white, US American, able-bodied, middle-class, masculine lifestyle without including extreme and often violent patriotism? With the rise of anti-Arab/anti-Muslim (anti-brown) sentiment outside the gay community, it was only a matter of time before gay men and their allies aligned themselves with the politics and hateful policies of the normative public. Rather than fight to uphold human rights and dignity, LGBTQ politics remain narrowly focused on civil rights and privileges linked to citizenship (e.g. gay marriage). Liberal masculine gay men assume that gay marriage is a sign of equality because it allows for (limited) mobility in a system that distributes health and tax benefits based on the state-recognized relationship between two people. Everyone, both citizen and "alien," contributes labor into this system, yet there is no room within it for the undocumented, or anyone who poses a threat to "national security."

Liberal masculine gay men wholly support the US American marriage complex and the "right to serve" in the military, a right that currently leads to the murder of millions of people of color and the illegal detainment of many more. Political gay bloggers valorize their "out" lives in rich urban neighborhoods, while speaking of the threat of radical gay-bashing Islamo-Fascists. They claim that anyone who has been following the headlines should realize that men and women of color who happen to hold citizen-ship in developing nations are out to blow themselves up in order to target Americans, and in this attack they might take out rich gay urban men! These men are obsessed with the word "terrorism" (politically far-removed from poverty, war, occupation, and sickness—leading causes of death, but not connected to marriage and the right to serve) and safeguarding of American traditions. Ironically, I see that masculine gay men have very much in com-mon with the bodies they name as threats to their freedom. Perhaps the racist, essentialist, and Orientalist remarks about "Middle Eastern" culture aren't personal fabrications but a projection of the current climate in the US American LGBTQ community.

"You're just being an apologist [for Arabs]. You really need to be honest with yourself."

The word "apologist" surfaces quite often in these heated conversations. In the classroom, it is used against those who challenge misguided statistics with real-world narratives. In the social scene, it is used to silence those who might speak out. It is a an accusation that forces one to "be grateful that you just live here, many people would die to have the opportunities you have." How ironic that an LGBTQ movement should focus its liberation on equality and freedom by comparison. As long as there is someone out there living in much less desirable conditions, then somehow our oppression is more tolerable; I personally see no correlation between the two. Yet the white gays and lesbians who reside at the top of the privilege food chain identify their current surroundings and experiences as universal goals that everyone else just fails to realize.

The growing trend of "tolerance" demands that leaders direct funds into the legalization of gay marriage, which could otherwise be used to fight hunger and homelessness; the benefits of gay marriage, like tax breaks and healthcare, only benefit a particular minority of LG people who hold a majority of power. Why fight for the ability to receive health benefits through a state recognized partnership when we should be pressuring the state to pay for everyone's healthcare? Who benefits most from partnership tax cuts and will that bring an end to financial inequality? These are the questions that are never raised when the subject of gay marriage is discussed. It makes me wonder: who exactly is the apologist?

"Some cultures just have a problem with the way they treat their women."

Perhaps the women of "some cultures" should be liberated so that they may become excellent producers and consumers like their US American sisters. Why should women have the freedom to choose a *hijab* or language preference in school when proper French and English educations would dictate otherwise? It seems that liberal masculine gay men, who ordinarily take no interest in the well-being of women, have no problem using women (as inherently feminine victims of circumstance) to demonize others. This dichotomy of us/them and right/wrong somehow always positions the liberal and masculine as the civil, the hero, and the master, while everyone else is tolerable at best.

The same gay men support overcharging women at gay bars (if they let them in at all), and the removal of locks on women's bathroom doors. These men not only target feminine gay men, but any female body, in their war to gender-cleanse the bars. Women are able to access these bars, but only as specifically indicated guests who will accessorize the male body. The very same gay men will justify their actions by claiming that women, both straight and queer, should patronize their own bars or that the traditional resentment towards women in gay bars is a reaction to the homophobia of straight bars. Both excuses are simply ways of justifying a subculture that continues to mistreat women. By pretending that "some cultures" ultimately have a problem with the way they treat women, rather than all cultures (including gay culture), gay men, riding high on the homo-nationalist bandwagon, can sleep soundly.

"Why don't they just come out of the closet?"

This question arose after my biography and interests were carefully examined by a group of fellow scholars. It is the essence of the problem. How can gay white men who wear designer suits to work and drink designer cocktails at night sleep knowing that my consciousness may not be completely focused on granting them approval? How can anyone be a legitimate LGBTQ activist while defending cultures that the media portrays as anti-queer? Masculinity (often resulting in hyper-patriotism) requires our undivided attention. Because liberal masculine gay men claim to be the crusaders of the LGBTQ community, they can decide who is and who isn't acceptable—not only in body, but in action.

It is inconceivable to US American gays that there are men and women in the world who engage in same-sex sexual practices yet don't identify as L, G, B, T, or Q. Yet there are infinite ways that relationships exist everywhere. All these relationships come fully assembled with as much joy, sadness, anger, love, and violence as traditional US monogamous relationships (gay or otherwise).

I have to wonder what our masculine liberators intend to do with the people of the Middle East de-rooted from their "savage ways." Will they be free to assimilate into US American LGBTQ culture and take a backseat in bars like their counterparts of color? Will they be free to serve the masculine power structure that claims to "know what's best"? I sense that as long as they wear the nicest clothing, patronize the trendiest bars, and keep their mouths shut about the injustices their newly paid taxes commit, they are more than welcome to join the LGBTQ community in the United States.

WITHOUT A FACE

Thomas Glave

This is the truth: that someone whom I do not in fact know and whom I have never seen face to face (so far as I know), but for whom I feel a great amount of affection and respect, unexpectedly asked me, completely without warning, to write something—to write a "short piece," I think the words were in the inviting email months ago, or something along those lines, similar words—to write something about "fear"; about a particular sort of fear. About the fear that one might have (that I might have) of certain men, *those* men—a fear of them long held, though I am, know myself to be, one of them myself. I was asked to write something about this fear, and immediately thought, with much anxiety, Me? Write something about this fear that is very personal, very secret, and perhaps even (yes, of course) shameful? *The fear of a particular and omnipresent You*, I thought upon reading the email invitation: *You, who, as one of those men, as all of them, I have watched and longed for and run from and wanted so much, yes: wanted and yearned so much, sometimes, to be like*…to be like you, to be as lovely as you, to be as (apparently) admired as you and as popular, as confident, as calm, as free, as (apparently) utterly unencumbered as you: light in your laughter, easy in your stride, and (often, though not always) so muscled. Muscled. Beautiful, young, and (apparently) indifferent to fear. You who (whomever you were from time to time) were often a kind of hero, a sort of god…yes, absolutely, of course you were; someone and something to worship, as you might be even now; as you *are*, in fact, even after all the years…for in my very privatemost, most secret and most very hidden realm, this is still how I think of you. How I think of you and all of *them*.

But then why? Why the fear, this particular fear, and why so much of it? So much, enough to bring a cold sweat (felt often at the most unexpected times—yes, tell the truth, as it persists); enough, this fear, to bring a trembling in the hands, an unsteadiness in the knees, and that heat to the face: that most awful heat, the heat of remembered shame. Shame occasioned again by … was it someone else's disgust this time? Your disgust? Your scorn, contempt, even sheer loathing this time? What was it? And why write about all of it? Why write about it when it still hurts so much to think about it (yes, tell the truth: *hurts*); when it has hurt so much in the past to think about it and feel it and remember it? Remember it—

But please, I really don't *want to remember it. Don't want to remember or write about all of that anymore. About him: about—as a place to start—that young man; that very young man, in fact just a boy, really, a teenager; in truth really just a child, naïve as he remained for the longest time—but never mind, then, all right; let him think that he was something of a man, almost one. Almost a man at fourteen years of age, or fifteen, or something like that; that child, standing there on some street corner somewhere, or walking quickly somewhere with, as usual, his head cast downward, though he loved the sky, loved birds, loved green things and bright colors and of course snowflakes and even—in spite of everything—blinding white light. That child, brown boy, large-eyed, often clumsy (his legs and arms, rather long, often got in the way of his simply being); that creature at fourteen or fifteen or whatever age, always a bit scared…or no, in fact very scared. Very scared as, in those years, he began to seek out the places where they, those men who seemed to know so much and so much that was utterly unspeakable, and even, in his world quite different from most of theirs (he thought), unthinkable, congregated, passed time: big grown men who seemed at ease and not at ease with each other, and who sometimes embraced and kissed each other on the street—on the street!—in front of him, in front of others, not always caring…not caring, certainly, if they found themselves in places that they considered safe, on streets where they would not be killed. He had to travel far, so very far, from his own quite different world, in order to find them. In his each-and-each-day world of Jamaican accents and North Bronx kitchens, that known world of grandparents who spoke regularly with the dead and people who could never, it seemed, forget that island from which both they and their deepest memories had come, such men were not—at least so it had seemed at the time—very easy to find. As a child thinking himself almost a man (whatever that would ultimately mean; already he knew even as a child that it would be both a challenge and triumph to grow up to* become *a living breathing black man with body and mind intact), he found himself frightened to look at them, those men—perhaps because, in those days, looking at them in the city so far from the North Bronx kitchens and island accents, so many of them were white, seemed only to be white; was it possible to be like them only if one were white?—*

as he also thought: Am I going to grow up to become that—*to become them? But how do you do that? How do you do it, he wondered, I don't know how... how do you look in another person's face like that and let them know—let them know that you want—that you want to ---o—*

But then remember that this is partly a story of birds' wings. The birds' wings that he, that child, as he grew to be a man (an actual man and not the fanciful one of his youthful dreams), did not possess, and so fervently longed for whenever he found himself in the company of some of *them*: those men of whom, in his own very different way, he grew up to be a part, but not a part. (But a part.) The birds' wings he wished for to take him far and suddenly away from them—away from their eyes from which, in great shyness, in the fear of not being enough—*I'll never be enough for them, never truly wanted or really truly cared for by any of them,* he had so often thought. *They will always laugh out loud when they see me coming. I dared not look at so many of them,* he had so often thought. *Never into their actual eyes,* he'd thought, *because I so feared that I would find there the scorn and contempt that I had seen so many times before; seen when I was younger, when I was not younger. The scorn and contempt of Who is this little faggot, this little immigrant kid reject bitch looking at me.* (But in fact, according to the laws and the reality, his parents had been immigrants, not him. Did that mean that they had been rejects? Bitches?) *This little shithouse sissy faggot reject looking at* me. (Yes, because supreme masculinity, even with them, especially with them, had to be supreme.) *Who is this faggot looking at?*

Who?

But that was me. (*But it hurts. It really hurts, and why the hell did So-and-So ask me to write these words? And why, like a fool, did I say Yes? Yes, I will write something about this, like a fool? But still.*) But since "me" does hurt, and since it is frightening and much too revealing to have "me" at last so exposed, let "me" once again now become "him," although without birds' wings.

Without birds' wings to fly away whenever, in years to come, he was around them: at parties, at gatherings, in public places. He was around so many of them who, lovely as they were, tall as they often were, broad as they so often were, made it clear to him time and time again—didn't they?—that they had absolutely no use for his limper-than-limp wrist, for his embarrassing st-st-st-st-stutter, for his "girly" faggy laugh. ("*Damn, man, even when you laugh you sound like a faggot. What the fuck?*" *one of them had once said to him...in the teen years, in the very difficult years.*) *Be a man, be a fucking man, so many of them had said, but how do you do that, he had always wanted to know, can you show me, I just don't know. Nobody knows. He couldn't know then that they themselves were ashamed, and more ashamed, of all that they had learned to be ashamed of, beginning with their own wrists and the swing of their own hips, forcefully quieted by many of them in the pursuit of true,* true *manhood. But all that would be only the beginning of so many things for him. And the end? But there would be (though he could not know this at the time) no foreseeable ending.*

"I suppose I was afraid" (he wrote; found in a bottle tossed out to sea many years after his death; the bottle and its contents now situated in the Museum of Utter Truths, in the northernmost region of yet another global and ever-shifting region of dreams) "—afraid of them because I wanted so many of them, you see—so many—just to love me. Yes, just to love—that was all. Just to look at me, look *at me, and say, in words or with their eyes, 'Well ... well, yes. You. You will be just wonderful. Yes, of course.' To look at me and say, in words or in other ways, 'But this will be just fine. This one (large-ish eyes, and a little awkward, but never mind, all right) will be just enough.' I wanted to say those things too. To—to really* love, *feel loved by... by... by one of them. To hold out my arms and hold him—hold them. Perhaps I even wanted to sing then when I began to feel that way about one of them; and I suppose that in that way, so given to joys of the heart and joy in celebration as I have always been, I have always been a bit of a fool—what some call a dreamer, I know. But I speak what I know was* felt, *and felt again. I never wanted to talk with one of them and find, as had happened on more than one occasion, that his eyes traveled in so many different directions whenever another man came into the room, or walked by. I never wanted him, or any of them, to feel embarrassed about being near me because of my wrists, or my voice, or my 'mannerisms,' as one of them termed such things. I just... but, well. And some of them de-spised me, I know, for being what they thought was so not-masculine: what was so hateful. But then some of them, when it came to—"*

[The remaining contents of this note are indecipherable, having been blurred and smudged by the sea over time. The sea, perhaps mercifully, has erased the writer's memory and even identity. Thus some sadness, and perhaps even a small register of grief, have been wiped out, obliterated, and pulled,
pulled, down to the bottom of the sea.]

(Present Day; A Faceless Voice)
It's nice, really nice, when you can speak about scary things without a

face! In this way, you can say all the things that you might at some point have been afraid to say, without anyone knowing that it's you who is saying them. When you speak facelessly, you don't have to worry about the birds' wings you always wanted—*needed*—for your flight and safety, but never managed to secure. You can look at people without them really seeing you, and live, I mean really *live,* without them really seeing you—and if that isn't safety, what is?

These days, in the faceless time, I love watching them walk down the street, holding hands. Holding each other. Kissing each other. Saying things to each other that only they can understand. I'm invisible to them now, more than ever, maybe, so what I'm feeling when I see them doesn't matter, because whatever I'm feeling won't show on the face that I haven't got. Since I'm invisible, I don't have to be afraid anymore. It's like now I know that none of them, not even the handsomest or the most stylish one, will look at me with that *What-the-fuck-is*-he-*looking-at* expression. So now I really love watching them, wondering as I watch what it feels like to feel all the things they must feel together. All the things they probably feel as they hold each other and are just together. As they touch each other again and again, and say things like (listen to them, *listen!*)—things like ". . ."; things like that, for instance, that you can't really describe or write down because there's always so much, isn't there, in the not-said thing, and in the breath between; so much in the look, the *look*, that both precedes and follows the very chosen word. I think that you can read all about this in books, though; read about what all these things feel like and what people who enjoy all these things call all of it: the feelings, the being, the…I guess it's what you would call joy. You can listen to people sing their voices raw about all these things in so many songs, and go see plays and movies that are all about all of it. After a while, thinking about all these things, you begin to understand how important it is to people—to people who have faces and even to some who don't.

If I were to tell the truth, which I can do now because I don't have a face (but which I wouldn't even try, trust me, if I did have one), I'd say that I'd be really afraid of doing all these things, feeling all these things, with one of those men—with *a* man—because, one night—one day—I might dare to look right at him, right into his eyes, and see that he actually really did like me; that, in fact, he more than liked me, as I'd been hoping so much he would and had been so fearful he would; as I had felt all those things for him. (Is that what they call joy? I just don't know.) If I had a face, a real one, I would never dare say that I can still hear all those voices from those earlier years, and see the scornful eyes, the disgusted mouths, and especially see how their mouths curl just before they say something like "Faggot," or "*What* a little bitch," even though they, the ones saying it, are "faggots" themselves, or will soon be. With my own face on, I would never admit that. Because…well, sure: I can still hear and see and feel all that, the same way I know that it's all still deep-twisted up and twined in me, Jesus, barbed and so crooked…the same way I know that it still jabs sharply into me now and again, *sharp, you little faggot,* whenever I turn the wrong way, this way or that one, on the bed, on the big old there-it-is-and-always my bed. And so with my actual, proper face on, well!— With it on, I wouldn't dare talk about how I *want* to reach across to them; about how I want to put out my hand to them—in fact, to *him.* To him right there, standing right there the way he always does in the front-most part of my dreams. Can you see him? He's there, sure enough…maybe not waiting, not waiting for me, at least, but just…and if I could, maybe, just once, I would, looking at him in the dream the way I have always wanted to, I would be—I would just try to be—

What? Be *what?*

Oh, but I'm forgetting! Forgetting that I don't have to worry about any of this. That's the nice thing, one of the sweet things, my God, yes, about not having a face. You—I—can just disappear, or go way down into the bottom of the sea, or just move on. *Move on.* Leaving everything behind.

Walking.

Without a face.

Moving onward.

Nowhere.

FUCKING WITH FUCKING ONLINE: ADVOCATING FOR INDISCRIMINATE PROMISCUITY

Michael J. Faris & ML Sugie

The following is our attempt to interrogate personal profiles on websites such as gay.com and manhunt.net where men congregate to meet each other for friendship, relationships, or sex. We're focusing primarily on the sex. And why the hell not? Sex is fun. Sex is creative. Or it should be, which is more our point. Largely, we're interested in the ways conversations in hookup chat rooms reproduce and enforce dominant narratives with regards to race, gender, sexuality, and sex. We've chosen to write this essay as a dialogue between the two of us, in order to separate our voices and acknowledge our different experiences.

ML: I'm a queer brown drag queen faggot. *Queer* and *drag queen* are purposefully chosen—not because they were necessarily conscious choices I made, but because I actively participate in their discursive use. *Brown* and *faggot* are more political and pragmatic instead of being indicators of an active selection; I acknowledge my brown faggotry as a salient feature of my identity because that is how I am most often perceived in the world. I know this because I've spent years feeling pissed off at people for calling me a faggot, or mistaking my ethnicity. But while the term "faggot" is generally off-limits in polite conversation, my ambiguous ethnicity is always in the domain of the appropriate. This includes times when I'm waiting in line, sitting in class, riding in a car, or meeting someone for the first time (online or otherwise).

"What ethnicity are you?"
"Um, I was wondering where your family is from."
"So, what's your heritage?"
"Are you part Mexican?"
"You look a bit Asian."

Each time my ethnicity is questioned, I feel an assault on my dignity. I am no longer *me*. I am something to be discovered or explored. Or, perhaps worse: an unknown quantity.

In the beginning of my forays into online sex culture, I stated my ethnicity explicitly, as a way to avoid further discussion of a topic which is at best complex and confusing. Most of the responses were chilling:

"Ohhh, I LOVE half-Asians."
"I think hapas are really hot."
"I always get along great with Asian guys."
"I think mixed guys are the most beautiful."

As a bi-national with roots planted nowhere, I detest the idea that you could know anything about my life by looking at me. Or from reading my relatively banal responses to questions of race and ethnicity. You can't tell where I've lived, what language(s) I speak, how I like to fuck, what my genitals look like, or my sexual history. How could you tell anything about whether I like to bottom simply by looking at a picture of my face? Ask me what I want to do, tell me what you want to do, and let's talk about the boundaries of our interaction. Anything else seems irrelevant to the project at hand.

Michael: It does seem naïve to believe that we could just talk about fucking and not categorize ourselves in these chatrooms, but also, I believe, *hopeful*. And I think that as we interrogate racist (and many other) assumptions, we remain hopeful that we can get to a place where meeting people for sex is more about sex. I feel, as someone with white privilege, that I should admit to my own hangups here. I'd like to be able to enter one of these chatrooms, find someone I'd like to meet, and have the kind of sex I'm looking for at the moment. But my own internalized conceptions of race, gender, class, and even "scene" get in the way of that. Even for those of us who are aware of racist social constructions in our society, it's disingenuous to claim that we aren't still influenced by racism through our own internalization of these constructions.

I don't think that either you or I is trying to write from some "objective" or "enlightened" position. Instead, we're both influenced (and even formed) by structural racism, sexism, and homophobia, as well as a system of compulsory gender normativity. For instance, I've gone on chat rooms and talked to African American men and decided not to meet up with them. Did my decision have to do with anything about those men *as individuals*? No. I have to admit that it had to do with my own racist assumptions about black men and masculinity, informed and supported by societal stereotypes about black men.

These men, as individuals, could have a variety of gender expressions and feelings toward their own masculinity and femininity. But because of my aversion to stereotypical masculinity (the type wrapped up in domination) and my own racist assumptions about black men as sexual aggressors, I decided not to meet many of these men.

I admit to my own racist assumptions and how they've played out in online chat rooms because I think it's important that we all interrogate ourselves and our own desires, until we can get to the point where we fuck based on what we want to do, and not on the type of body we want to do it with. Our society has fucked up our sexual desires so that we're so fixated on other people's bodies that we forget about what we actually want to do in bed (or in a car, in a park, in a porn booth, and so forth). What if we just said in these chat rooms: "This is what I want to do with someone" rather than "This is who I want to do something with?" As you said, ask me what I want to do, not about my race.

ML: But having the ability to ignore race is great if people ignore your own. I have no such privilege. Case in point: I was exhausted from the blatant racism and fetishization I found perusing online profiles and chat rooms. So I removed the information on my ethnicity to see what would happen. With nothing but a picture as a guide, more questions came up. "Are you gay? Are you closeted? Are you Latino? What's your ethnicity? I am so curious!" The details of how we would hook up became secondary to the need to know where my sometimes-jaundicey permanent tan came from. What this information would reveal was a mystery to me. Was I expected to play the Taiko drum during sex? Should I wear my Japanese geta shoes while you suck my toes? Were we going to talk about Anime in the middle of coming? Yes I use chopsticks—is this some sort of kink I hadn't considered? Do you want to lay sushi on my body and use my ass to hold wasabi and ginger? (Check, please!)

With no luck and a limp dick, I decided to start throwing the question right back at people. If someone asked me what my ethnicity was, I said, "What do you think I am?" I became a global hopscotch and a game of 20 questions. Which continent? Was I close or far off? Were you born here? Do you have a bit of _____ in you? The more I answered the questions, the more angry I became at the ignorance of the people I met.

I finally decided to make the (brown) elephant in the room visible and explicit, and solicit responses to the inevitable question. I headlined my profile "Guess my ethnicity … and win a prize!" I used the same set of pictures over the course of six months and documented what happened. I realize now that asking the question turned the responses into a game, like there was some reward waiting for those who answered.

In no particular order, I was told that I "looked" like I could be from Albania, Lebanon, Greece, Saudi Arabia, Egypt, Algeria, Morocco, Spain, Turkey, Italy, South Africa, Libya, Brazil, Mexico, Argentina, Indonesia, Thailand, Korea, China, Vietnam, Cambodia, India, Pakistan. Or from ill-defined regions like Latin America, South America, Pacific Islands, Asian, South Asian, East Asian, South-East Asian, Middle Eastern, Mediterranean, North African. Races and ethnicities also came up: white, Latino, Asian, Native American.

What was more interesting to me was when people paired up countries, regions or races/ethnicities as proportions: "half Mexican," "part Native American and part white," "Maybe some Latino," or "some sort of Asian." Was there a formula I was missing? Was I cut from the same come-stained cloth and slutty pattern as these monolithic groups? What part of my picture easily identified quantiles of ethnicity?

Of course my questions indicate my rage. Rage at people who felt annoyed when I refused to answer the question, rage at the people who felt like they could guess my ethnicity, rage at the realization that my race and ethnicity online—like anywhere else—were constructed within and toward a specific white dominance and white hierarchy. The internet—the great liberator. The internet—the great equalizer. The internet—yet another tool to totalize my life. If you're white, great, you can be whoever you want to be. The rest of us brown faggots don't have such an option.

Michael: I agree that as a white man I have the privilege to ignore race. It's easier for me not to bring it up than it is for people of color who have others ask them idiotic questions. I have a lot more mobility than brown folk to define my own presence and my own sexual preferences on this "great equalizer" of the internet.

How then, I wonder, can we express our sexual preferences? I mean, an obvious answer could be that we can list activities: I like fucking and getting fucked, ball-stretching, receiving head, making out, biting, and so forth. How, then, can we describe the bodies we want to fuck, be fucked by, to see naked, to hold. Like you, I am disturbed by preferences for certain raced bodies. Additionally, I'm often disturbed by stated preferences for certain gender performances. Those men who write "into masculine men—no sissies" seem to be proclaiming, "Even if I want to fuck men, I'm still a man—and you should be too." This preference seems to express a fear of femininity and a belief that "real men" can't be feminine. What this does is create a hierarchy of masculinity: "manly" men are better than sissies (because, ultimately, according to this logic, sissies aren't men at all).

Perhaps what it comes down to is that we shouldn't state preferences for our sexual partners. It does make sense to have preferences for a romantic partner. For instance, I wouldn't want to date someone who is conservative or overly invested in masculinity. But these aren't bodily preferences: I'm making preferences based on someone's attitude toward life, politics, and gender—not based on bodies. I'm not going to play like I'm some kind of angel here; I certainly have my own biases I'm trying to get over, in regards to looks, body size, ability, and even race and gender. The point here isn't that you or I are trying to pass down judgment from some almighty place of perfection in regards to who we'll fuck, but rather to point out that this whole system is fucked up. I'm reminded of an essay I read from the 1974 joint issue of *Fag Rag* and *Gay Sunshine*, two zines from the 1970s Gay Liberation Front. In his essay "Indiscriminate Promiscuity as an Act of Revolution," Charley Shively wrote:

> We need to be *indiscriminate*. No one should be denied love because they are old, ugly, fat, crippled, bruised, of the wrong race, color, creed, sex or country of origin. We need to copulate with anyone who requests our company; set aside all the false contraptions of being hard to get, unavailable—that is, costly on the capitalist market. We need to leave behind the whole mentality of measurement; it is a massive tool of social control. We all measure ourselves against some standard, find ourselves wanting, and feeling inferior, guilty, wrong, weak—in need of authority, direction, correction, ruling and enslavement.

ML: So let's be indiscriminately promiscuous. Let's move our desire back to the acts we want done, and not think about who's doing them. Let's complicate things. If you want someone to come on your face, who cares what type of dick is involved? Why should it matter if I am able-bodied enough to hop on your chest and point my cock at your face? After we consider what we want to do together, we should experiment. We should discover new ways to get off (or not get off) with each other. We produce creative fucking when we stop talking in the language and inscribed bodies we are handed, and start imagining new ways to produce our sexual selves.

If what we want is intimacy, if we want to feel connected, if we want to *experience* sexuality then we have to *actively participate* in it. Let's just be honest about what we want—cuddling, making out, teasing the asshole, hours of fucking—and let's put it out there. Thinking that we can find the fulfillment of a particular sexual pleasure in a particular sexualized body is a myth. Big hands can be just as gentle as small hands. Our bodies are more flexible than we imagine.

Michael: Part of this takes a radical interrogation of one's own desire. What do we find attractive? Who do we want to fuck? Why do these physical attributes of bodies turn us on? It seems obvious to me, but perhaps it isn't to many, that these desires aren't solely our own: that they've been constructed, in part, by what our society deems beautiful or erotic. Advertisements, movies, television shows, music videos, magazines—even our families and education—in some ways construct our desire, portray what is normatively attractive, whether to straight folks or queer folks or both. We get an image and we ingrain it in our bodies: the sexually attractive is the thin, white, toned, tall, middle class, and able-bodied. We are "trained" to desire this normative body. When we don't, or when society portrays a desire that doesn't fit into this ideal, it's either not meant for the mainstream (e.g., "fat porn" that makes fatness into a fetish rather than a normal desire), or it's an eroticization that plays into racial stereotypes: the masculine black man, the over-sexualized black woman, the anal-retentive dominatrix Asian woman, the innocent school-girl Asian, the emasculated, boyish Asian man, and so forth.

Men who have sex with men, just like most people in our society, seem to be stuck thinking in binaries, in regards to race (white vs. color), gender (masculine vs. feminine), and even sex (top vs. bottom). I detest the questions that arise when I am cruising online and *simply looking for sex.* These questions reek of banality. "Are you gay?" I was once asked. My immediate response in my head was to ask, "Why the fuck does that matter?" Who gives a damn if you're "gay," "straight," "heteroflexible," or "queer," if you simply want to fuck!

ML: It's the totalization of another without their consent and without their input. "Oh, you act like a faggot in your daily life? You MUST be a bottom!" You don't know, will never know without asking, what my life is like and what it is I'm looking for or want to do. Do not look at me and assume you know my life well enough to be deemed sexually acceptable or unacceptable. I am not a pear at a fruit stand.

Michael: There's no complication in the question of top vs. bottom.

ML: Where is the power bottom, the lazy top?

Michael: Yeah! Furthermore, where are blowjobs, handjobs, and even sex that doesn't rely on the penis? Where is making out and grinding? Where is the sensuality and sexuality of our nipples, our ears, our lips, our eyes? We've reduced the gay body to anus and penis. If two men are going to fuck, the implication of this question is that they must fuck as a top (dominator) and a bottom (dominated). Although I don't think gay sex is exactly like heterosexual sex, the way we talk about it is in terms of straight sex. If straight sex is seen so simply as the penis penetrating the vagina, gay sex must be equivalent—the penis penetrating the anus. I want hookups that are messy and experimental. I don't want to be asked if I'm a top or bottom. What we do is what we discover about each other and ourselves. Predetermined sex is boring.

Straight sex is scripted. We're not straight. We're fucking queer.

ML: I no longer want to feel alienated from my sex life. I feel isolated in my own sex life, I feel uncreative and unconnected with the commonly reproduced discourse on fucking. Even if I know better, intellectually, I still feel estranged from my own agency while fucking. I have power, sure, but why bother? Maybe I could just play the part so I could get it over with. Sure, I'll be Latino today; why yes I'm Turkish, how did you know? You like people from Thailand? I make a killer peanut sauce! Fuck that bullshit. I want to be able to feel like I am an active participant in *making* my own sex life, not just following some script handed down to me using all the racist, sexist, heterosexist, ableist, capitalist modes of thought.

DIFFICULT CONVERSATIONS

Philip Patston

When I came out at age 19, I went to see a counselor. He told me to expect gay men to be harder on me about my impairment than heterosexuals. For a heady moment I thought he was trying to prepare me for the probability that guys, finding me extraordinarily attractive, would be ragingly turned on by my uniqueness. I had a fleeting fantasy of being inundated with both offers of—and requests for—love and sex from all and sundry. I would have my pick, my veritable fruity smorgasbord.

Alas, he didn't mean that at all.

He was suggesting that gay men would find my physical deviance from the norm a challenge they would avoid rather than rise to. I would remind them that the illusion of physical perfection, so voraciously projected by and to the gay community, was, at best, a fantasy and, at worst, temporary. Gay men would judge me for my difference, rather than celebrating it.

Young, scared and gullible, I remember swallowing hard and setting off to battle against intolerant non-disabled people, yet again. I thanked the counselor for his wise counsel but, on reflection, I should have thanked him for the self-fulfilling prophecy. What a stupid thing to say to a 19-year-old disabled guy, who had just watched a made-for-TV teen coming out movie and thought, "Yes! That's me!" Just when I needed some affirmation, positive self-image, and general morale boosting, my therapist decided to get real on me.

Looking back, this exchange reminds me of something a family friend said to me when I was about 12. She asked my twin brother if he liked a certain girl we knew. Sitting right next to him, I observed him blush as he murmured, "Maybe." I waited for her to do the twin thing and compare our responses.

I tired of waiting. "Er, what about me?" I asked.

"Oh, she wouldn't be interested in a disabled person."

I couldn't help feeling naïvely defensive. I shouted in my head, "Yeah, but I might be interested in her!" But I'm sure I internalized the message.

I wish she'd said, "Don't be stupid, you're a flaming poof!" Similarly my therapist could have said, "Gay men are a shallow, fickle lot. You're far too good for most of them."

But in many respects both my therapist and the family friend were right. There are a myriad of unspoken rules that guide non-disabled people's response to intimacy with disabled people. I began thinking about this stuff at 16 and I still haven't really sussed it out nearly 30 years later.

There's this thing that usually happens when I meet a guy. It goes like this—poetry, really:

I notice him.
He notices me.
>   I look at him.
>   He thinks he could find me attractive.
>   I fancy him.
>   He thinks of everything he's heard about attractive guys.
>   I still fancy him.
>   He thinks of everything he's heard about disabled guys.
>   I look away, bashfully.
>   Attractive. Disabled. He notices his oxymoron.
>   I look back and meet his eyes.
>   He realizes.
>   I realize he realizes.
>   He freaks.
>   I freak.
>   He looks away, shamefully—a degree of self-conscious panic.
>   I roll my eyes.
>   I pluck an expletive from my dog-eared repertoire.
>   Then there's a hiatus where one of two things will happen:
>   Nothing,
>   or
>   I'll go over and say, "Hi."
>   Usually it's nothing because I fantasize, assume, judge, eradicate
>   — nah, not worth it.
>   My fear of fear, masked by nonchalance.
>   Sometimes I wish I was a lesbian.

From the distance, I remember thinking that disabled lesbians seemed *en vogue*: they had organized groups to go to, all over the world, like the Brighton and Hove Disabled Dykes Club in the UK or the disabled lesbians group on DailyStrength.org. It felt like women wore double and triple minority labels proudly, like metaphorical medals emblazoning their ample, natural bosoms.

But whenever I was in a group of gay men, I felt like I was wearing the wrong uniform—and therefore accentuating my lack of uniformity. It didn't feel like gay culture was about exploration, but about fitting in, following the rules. I had to keep in step, and woe betide me should I fall out of line. Eventually I gave up.

The men I have truly loved, and who have dared to love me—and, to a lesser extent, a few brave enough to sleep with me just once ("Go on, I won't tell … and, let's face it, no one's likely to dare to ask.")—have been prepared to go one step further. On some level they've understood the dialectic complexity and simplicity of who I am in relation to who they are, which has demanded a varying degree of self-awareness and self-confidence on their part.

Usually, to be honest, they've stood a bit apart from conventional gay norms too. Indigenous, older, addicts, genderqueer, or connected to disability through family or profession. Something about their unique experience resonates with mine and, *voilà*, a common experience is born.

A recent sexual partner was a trannyboy. It was a wonderfully queer dynamic—we would often joke that the common ground between people who experience functional and gender diversity is the accessible toilet. I'm certain our inner lesbians saw each other across a crowded room and were bedazzled by our emblazoned, breast-less chests.

Our affair lasted 18 months—the closest to a fuck-buddy relationship that I've ever had, but, in many respects, more. We had a very "political" relationship—pillow-talk was about society, systems, and structures, about which we were both distinctly dubious. And now our relationship has morphed into one which is more collegial than anything, with our professional lives melding through similar interests and networks.

We were never publicly a couple and, though we've not openly discussed it, I'm fairly confident neither of us was hiding the other—we just started falling into bed with each other and it didn't feel necessary to declare it to the world. After a while I began telling close friends about him and received wholly positive—if not intrigued—reactions, in the main because they knew us both and who would've thought?! The majority of those I didn't tell would probably have felt as much—or more—offended by the illicit non-formalization of our liaison as by the deviance of his gender identity.

Right now I am seeing this guy I've known for about twenty years. (Let's call him "Guy.") We hooked up drunkenly three weeks ago at a work party I threw at my home office at the end of 2010. My entrenched single identity, born of 43 years with nothing near a "traditional" relationship, is challenged by Guy's comfort with coupledom (he recently ended a 20-year partnership, complete with kid and dog).

My personal hangups about commitment aside, the last three weeks have offered an interesting opportunity for reflection. In spite of knowing Guy for 20 years, there have been lots of things we've needed to talk about that other couples wouldn't. Some are somewhat mundane matters, like letting him know that I occasionally fall over around the house. ("I'm fine—no, don't call an ambulance."). And there are slightly more vital issues, like whether he should offer help or wait to be asked ("Erhm, either, but if you offer and I say no, it means no—even if I look like I'm struggling—and please just go and do something else rather than turning into a spectator.").

And there have been downright intimate things, like explaining that, because of my high muscle tone, it can take me quite a while to relax in certain situations ("I know it's been half an hour and you're still not in, but keep it up, dude, it'll be worth it!").

It leads me to believe that the fear, on both sides, is not so much of the disability factor, but rather of the need to communicate about the difference and allow this new shared experience to deepen the relationship. It takes trust, respect, strength and a whole lot of faith to engage in unusual and sometimes difficult conversations. These are the kinds of conversations that gay male culture, with its focus on sameness over difference, categorization over fluidity, often seems unwilling to allow.

PENIS IS IMPORTANT FOR THAT

Nick Clarkson

I walked into his salon at the end of the day, needing something new. I had been going for a surfer boy look, but I'd had two bad haircuts in a row and was starting to bald. It was time to give it up. He looked up from the head of chestnut curls he was clipping away at. "Can I help you?" he asked as I admired him. He had a shaved head and a neatly trimmed Tom-of-Finland mustache. He was stocky, with a bit of a belly, wearing 501s, a thick black leather belt, and black boots, with a black leather scissor pouch slung around his hips. He looked me over, sighed resignedly at the thought of staying late on a Saturday afternoon, and said he'd be with me in a minute.

I sat down with my book and tried to read a bit, but I was too busy stealing glances at him. When he finally called me over, I tossed my book up on the shelf near his tools. He asked me what I needed. A faux-hawk, I was thinking. As he looked at me in the mirror, his fingers in my ear-length hair, I could see exuberance flashing in his eyes. "A faux-hawk will help mask your thinning here on top," he said.

I'm usually more awkward than smooth, which means that my typical response is to sit silently in situations such as this. But the beautiful fall day was making me feel a little more saucy than usual, so I asked playfully, "An update on the comb-over, you mean?" I was quite impressed with myself for pulling off this bit of flirty repartée.

"A younger haircut that suits you better," he corrected. As he started cutting my hair, he asked about the book. It was John D'Emilio's *Sexual Politics, Sexual Communities*, which I was reading for a class called "Gay Histories, Queer Cultures." I was more interested in talking about his leather aesthetic than the book, so I mentioned the paper I was researching for the same class about discussions of safer sex among leather men. "What have you seen here in Indy?" I asked him, hoping for tales of dungeon debauchery. He launched into an Indianapolis leather history. He didn't offer the dirty details I'd hoped for, but his eyes betrayed mischief. I was enjoying his anecdotes, watching him in the mirror as he talked. He was watching himself too. He'd snip at my hair, I'd ask him a question. He'd stop snipping, and his glinting blue eyes would fix on themselves in the mirror as he smiled, reminiscing. Some might have taken this as a sign of self-absorption, but I was charmed. The impish gleam in his eyes enticed me, whether he was looking at me or at himself.

Aside from the Indianapolis leather history that day, I got one of the best haircuts I'd had in a long time. I saw Joshua regularly for haircuts over the next two years, more for the thrill of his fingers on my scalp, his hard stomach pressed against my arm, and the opportunity for shameless flirting than for the fantastic haircuts. These visits were interspersed with evenings of admiring him from a distance at the bar. My friends were introducing me to the Metro during their intermittent evenings of drinking in Indianapolis, and it quickly became my bar of choice for martinis and conversation. Among the three bars where I spent most of my time, the Metro was most brightly lit, with music videos and cocktail specials. Greg's and the 501, my favorite cruising spots, were more dimly lit, played stills of well-muscled men or video porn, and frequently featured bottles of Miller Lite on special. I only ever ran into Joshua at the Metro. But I had already guessed that he preferred cocktails and conversation to cruising.

After many months of glancing at Joshua across the bar, I ventured a "hey" as I walked past his bar stool. The next time I saw him there, I stuck around for an extra beer after my friend moved on to Saturday night dancing with the other twenty-something boys. Joshua was sitting at the opposite end of the bar. I made eye contact a few times, wanting something more, but too shy to make it happen. After a few more of my fleeting glances, he brought his pink drink over and sat down across from me. His lips deliberately formed his greeting as he explained, "I was trying to say hi to you." His blatant drunkenness should have been a turn-off, but it wasn't. He was so adorable, smiling underneath his neatly cropped mustache, leaning towards me as he spoke, arching one purposefully shaped eyebrow. My gleaming blue eyes mirrored his.

"You look innocent," he suggested, "but I'm not buying it."

I arched my not so carefully shaped eyebrows and asked, "Why's that?"

"Your eyes say something else." He was noticing the unabashed desire. He was probably thinking that a shy, young boy like me shouldn't so brazenly cruise a man of his stature. But I continued to stare at him.

He told me a number of stories that night, and surprised me by including his coming out story. There was a point in my life—around seventeen—when, not knowing what else to talk about with other people, I always asked about coming out experiences. At this point in my life, though, twenty-one and having been through three or four (who's counting?) coming out processes of my own, friends had stopped telling me coming out stories, and I'd stopped coming out. At the very least, I tried to avoid the tortured confessionality of the declaration. If I wanted to talk about being queer, I dropped it into conversation where relevant, encouraging people to keep up with the conversation. It also seemed ridiculous to come out as gay after transitioning; I often feel like my transness is an invisible secret lurking beneath my clothes—a secret that demands confession—but I assume that my gayness is apparent to anyone who has met me.

But Joshua was telling me his story during our first conversation outside his salon. It was clearly still relevant for him. He told me about growing up a farm boy in rural Indiana. "I can build a barn or sew a gown," he proudly declared. His four football-playing older brothers had tormented Joshua the gymnast, but he was nevertheless able to hold his own. He had come out at twelve, marching into the kitchen to tell his mom he was gay without giving any thought to the consequences.

Off he went to military academy. The pain of the memory flickered across his face, but he said nothing about it, quickly launching into a story about his roommate at the academy. "He slept in the top bunk, I slept in the bottom bunk. Every night, he'd do push-ups naked before he got into bed. Every night it took him longer to get up to his bunk until eventually he didn't make it up there at all. After that, we'd lay in bed in the dark, playing with each other's penises like they were stick shifts on cars." His eyes glittered impishly again, the pain of his initial coming out gone.

So much of my desire for this forty-two year old gay man—and for older gay men in general—centered on the self-knowledge he'd excavated growing up gay twenty years before me. Coming out as a dyke in high school had been relatively painless. As a result, I hadn't learned much about myself in the process. Coming out as trans had scared me much more and required more introspection: How do I know I need to be a boy rather than a butch dyke? Where do I find people like me? Can I fit feminism and testosterone in the same body? Though not the same as Joshua's experience, my trans coming out had offered me a grounding that mirrored Joshua's experience more than that of most male-born gay boys my age.

Though I had hoped our conversation might continue outside the bar that night, he said good night and went home without me. I kept thinking about him, though. And while I wasn't generally much of a bar-goer, I started going out more often, hoping Joshua would be there. I walked past him one night a few months later while he was too absorbed in conversation to notice me. I slid into a chair and nursed a pink drink or two myself, eventually making eye contact with him, interrupting his conversation with a wave. He walked up behind me and wrapped his arms around my shoulders, allowing me to savor his big biceps at my neck for a few short moments. I had just finished my drink, so I asked him, "Should I head out, or should I get another drink and stick around?"

Joshua said it was up to me, laughter glinting in his eyes. I had another drink by the time he got back from the bathroom. "How did I know that's what you'd decide?" He grabbed his drink and came back to sit with me. He told me a few of the same stories he'd told me the last time we'd talked, but he also had some new ones. He described his bedroom décor to me. "You should see it sometime," he said, and I agreed. He explained that his roommate Kevin, an interior designer, had played a major role in the design decisions. They'd been close friends for years.

"How did you meet?"

"It was here. I was in my twenties, wearing some short white shorts, doing E. Have you ever done it?" he asked. I shook my head. "It makes you feel really attractive. So I was here in my short white shorts and I jumped up on the bar. I walked up and down shouting, 'I'm stunning, fucking stunning, and everyone wishes they were me!' I kept walking up and down shouting, 'I'm stunning, fucking stunning, and everyone wishes they were me!' Then I slipped and landed in a puddle of alcohol. My white shorts got all wet. Kevin was walking by and stopped to say, 'Honey, you're a mess.' We talked, we went home together, we tried messing around a few times before we realized we were going to be really good friends. And we still are."

This story was followed by other stories of exhibitionism and drugs. There was the dance party where, dressed in a black body suit covered in mirrors, Joshua the human disco ball had pirouetted from end to end of a twelve-foot high scaffolding in the middle of the dance floor. His friends told him he would fall, but he just kept on pirouetting.

These glimpses into gay culture around the time I was born are also central to my love of older men. In addition to the wisdom and genuine confidence older men often exude, I appreciate the sense of lineage they offer by telling stories about being gay in the '70s and '80s. If Joshua had told me stories about participating in SM clubs in the '70s, I would have melted. I came of age in a time of LGBT politics focused on marriage, and have a nostalgic, romanticized attachment to the sexual forms of community of the '70s.

After a little more chatter, he got up to head to the bathroom again. I grabbed his elbow as he walked past me, massaging the curve of his bicep with my thumb. He paused, gazing at me inquisitively. Then he kissed me. It was a delicious contrast to the ravenous, penetrating nonsense most men call kissing.

As he settled into his chair again, he said, "Penny for your thoughts." I wasn't sure what he meant, but I figured he was just pointing out that I hadn't talked much. I babbled on about school.

"How old are you?" he asked.

"It doesn't matter," I assured him. I already knew he was forty-two. I had also already heard his "horror story" of being hit on by some twink (who probably didn't look all that much different from me) who had called him a "really hot daddy." I wanted Joshua because he was a "really hot daddy," but I knew better than to call him that. And though it's clear that I couldn't be older than mid-twenties, I was reluctant to let him know that I was younger than he was assuming. I was tired of the predictable reaction that always follows: these forty-something men, approaching me knowing that I'm significantly younger than them, theatrically exclaim at the age difference.

He wasn't letting me off the hook, though. "Well, if it doesn't matter then you can tell me."

"I'm twenty-one," I confessed.

"I'm old enough to be your parent!"

Tell me something I haven't heard. "But you're not," I responded wearily, annoyed at having to talk another guy through this age difference "problem."

"That's for sure! I've *never* been with a woman." More bad news. I guessed that the gold-star gays were more likely to be skittish about the I'm-a-fag-with-a-cunt conversation. I suspected Joshua—like so many other gay men I've tried to have these conversations with—would insist on the equation penis=man and vagina=woman. He'd think that sticking his dick in my cunt would basically mean he was having sex with a woman. He might tell his friends that he fucked a vagina. He might try to talk about having sex with a *boy* with a cunt—taking account of my identity and my whole body in relationship to my cunt—but these hypothetical conversations would quickly devolve into "Well, if you want to stick it in a vagina, you're not gay."

These gay men don't consider that my understanding of my body and identity might offer them insight. My mastectomy scars archive the history of breasts. I appreciate the experience represented by those scars, but my cunt and the little dick that has grown from my clit are not a reminder of where I've come from. I don't think of my cunt or my dick as remnants of my female history but as part of my present. In the context of my trans body, bordered by muscular and hair-covered thighs, belly, and ass, my cunt is an important part of the shape of my body, the shape of my trans identity. My cunt is not a female part, out of place in the context of an otherwise male body, because my cunt is at the center of my *trans* body.

Insisting on the femaleness of cunts is, I imagine, so much of what causes problems for men grappling with their identities in response to the apparent incongruity of my body. I do want them to understand my body as different from their own rather than collecting evidence of masculinity from my body to declare me seamlessly male. To do this, they need to see my whole body as neither male nor female. Thinking of my cunt as the void or the misfitting piece in the jigsaw of my body is not going to get them where I need them to go. I sometimes suggest that they think of my cunt as a self-lubricating bonus hole rather than as a vagina. Though I don't really like giving them a way out of dealing with the reality of my cunt—I don't want to let them off the hook for naming it and re-imagining its meaning in the context of the rest of my body—I hope that offering them a new lens will encourage them to see my whole body at once. I hope to ease the process enough that they will be encouraged to actually *do the work* rather than shut down.

But Joshua and I would deal with that process later. In the meantime, we were dealing with other hang-ups. "I don't like to mix business and pleasure."

"Oh, come on. It's not like you're one of my professors or something. You don't have any authority over me." He chuckled, unconvinced. "Well," I conceded, "if you have to stick with that, I'll understand."

"That was totally insincere, but nice try." He paused before challenging, "So what do you want?"

"What?"

"Oh, come on, don't play coy with me."

"Are you asking me what I want to happen between us?" He raised his eyebrows, not deigning to nod. I clearly should've already known. My face growing hot, I stumbled through another confession. "I thought you were fucking adorable the minute I met you. I really like talking with you. I like that I'm so attracted to you but still so confident around you. I don't know how to describe it, but there's something I really like about our interaction. Something about the space between us feels really good. I'd like us to be able to spend more time together and at least be friends. Hopefully more."

"You really are an academic. You talk in circles like one. I try to be very direct. I thought we were getting ready to go home together earlier, so I asked you what you thought. You never answered my question."

Penny for my thoughts? Now I knew that he'd offered a penny for my thoughts about "us," but I still didn't know what he'd actually been asking. Was that when I was supposed to confess my lust for him? Was it an invitation to invite myself back to his house? I was feeling vulnerable for having said as much as I had and was getting frustrated with *his* circumlocution. "Is it a deal breaker to know that I'm trans?" I asked. I'd avoided coming out as trans until then, waiting for a moment to casually drop it into conversation rather than being forced to confess. The moment hadn't come, though, and I wielded the confession now as my most reliable defense mechanism: I come out as trans and push people to respond to ever higher standards until they inevitably fail to live up to the standards. I then feel comfortable walking away.

"What? What do you mean?"

How would I put it this time? There are a few options for framing my explanation depending mostly on my intent (fucking, dating, or friendship?) and how many drinks I've had. I could simply state the facts: I was born female and transitioned to male three years ago. I could be more explicit about my body, playing up its advantages. I could point out to him that my dick is any size he wants it to be and is always hard, that I have three holes instead of two. The first option intentionally evades his unasked questions about my genitals and how sex would work. The second option gives him a much better idea of how sex might go but risks exoticization. I wanted him to appreciate my body as I do, but I didn't want him to cross the line to obsessing over my cunt, no longer seeing me as a whole person.

I decided to start gently, explaining, "I was born female."

He looked at me apprehensively and started to ask, "So do you…"

"I was born with a cunt and I still have it. I've been taking testosterone for two and a half years, and I had my breasts removed two years ago."

"I like to consider myself worldly, but this is a new one for me." He repeated this a few times as we continued trying to process together. "I have to say," he insisted, "I'm gay, and penis is important for that."

The drinks I'd had made it easier to retort, "Having a detachable penis has its advantages." He laughed, still unconvinced. He wasn't going to be convinced, and his friends were antsy at the bar a few yards away from us— "Seal the deal, Joshua!" one had shouted—so I got up to go. I stepped up between his knees to hug him as he said goodbye. I asked if I could kiss him again. "Of course." The end of the conversation had been frustrating but I assumed that ending it with a kiss was a good sign.

I gave him my phone number, but he didn't call. I spent a lot of time at the bar making myself available on the weekends, resisting the temptation to go in the middle of the week when he was there drinking with his friends. When I saw him a few weeks later, he let me know that he'd been thinking a lot about it and was still figuring out what being attracted to me meant for his identity. He liked to consider himself worldly, he repeated, but this was something new for him. I listened, concealing my impatience, before telling him to call me sometime so we could talk more about it. He nodded.

This was new for Joshua, but it was new for me too. Until then, my self-preservation strategy for the trans confession with boys had been to walk away from anyone who so much as flinched when I came out. I hadn't been sure enough of my body or identity, and I hadn't sorted out my relationship to gay men. Helping someone work through their issues about the supposed "inadequacy" of my body would have done too much damage to my fledgling identity. I walked away from everyone who didn't already know how to talk to me about my body and experience on my terms. Joshua's gay-boy-meets-trans-fag identity crisis was the first one I'd stuck around for. Noticing that I was secure enough in my body and identity to do this made me proud, but the vulnerability of waiting it out scared me.

He still didn't call. The next time I saw him at the bar, I stood awkwardly in line near his bar stool, waiting to order a drink. I was insecure since he hadn't called, so I wasn't feeling nearly as charming as last time. I complained about not being able to get a drink. He asked what I was having, explaining, "Honey, we don't wait in line." He called the bartender over and ordered my drink, then didn't accept the money I held out to him. This was the first drink he'd bought me, even though there had been a number of opportunities for him to do so when he was planning to take me home. I sat down next to him, fidgeting as I waited for him to say something.

"Look," he began, "I try to be very direct and honest. I have to tell you, this isn't going to go any further. I'm gay, and penis is important for that." Though he'd never called, I was still surprised to know he wouldn't be working through his identity crisis. I wondered what my face was supposed to look like to communicate gracious acceptance of rejection. Or if I wanted to be gracious about getting rejected because I don't have a penis. He kept talking. I sat there, mind spinning, trying to hold my face in whatever expression I'd settled on as he continued to explain himself in an apologetic sort of way.

I tried remembering what it felt like to have a sexual identity restricted to one—of two—sexes, trying to wrap my head around where he was coming from. I could almost sympathize, remembering in flickering glimpses the thoughts that followed my first sexual encounter with a biological boy two years earlier. I had started testosterone but hadn't yet had chest surgery.

Though I was well on my way to becoming a boy, I was still holding a certain amount of masculinity away from myself, thinking I needed a flat chest before I could relate to men as the boy I wanted to be. My fragile, androgynous identity was threatened momentarily by my enjoyment of vaginal sex with a boy-with-a-penis. How could I be a boy if I liked having things in my cunt? Fortunately, the masculinity and the trans boy body I was headed for didn't require a penis or denial of my cunt, and I'd enjoyed vaginal sex enough to quickly dismiss any threat to my boy-ness. But I ruminated a bit longer over the threat of penis-in-vagina sex to my queerness. I was disconcerted to enjoy the configuration of genitals typically thought to define heterosexuality.

Maybe Joshua was thinking some of these things. Maybe he wasn't delving deeply into the details. Either way, maybe if he'd talked to me about the things he was thinking I could have offered him some insight. He said something about the importance of penises a few more times. I told him emphatically, "Honey. I understand. You don't have to explain *that* to me." I understand worshipping penises. What I *don't* understand is speaking of vaginas with any less reverence.

"I really respect and admire you for what you've done, especially at such a young age," he offered. But that's not the respect I wanted. I didn't want him to admire me for that period of my life three years ago. I wanted him to respect me *now* by appreciating my trans body, recognizing the meanings I've imbued it with. I didn't want him to admire me for my dealings with therapists, surgeons and parents at the start of transition. I was sitting in front of him at that moment, carrying the experiences of transition in my movements, my understanding of the world, and my ability to listen to him defend his own carefully bounded identity. Respect me for what I'm doing *now*.

"I really like myself," he affirmed repeatedly. "Well," I wanted to say, "I like myself too, Joshua. Stop talking about my body as thought it's the problem when you're the one obsessed with penises." He kept emphasizing how much of a struggle it had been for him to assert his gay identity and to become who he had become. It seemed that who he had become, though, was someone who couldn't date a boy he was attracted to. Maybe my trans coming out and his gay coming out were less alike than I'd thought. I wanted to ask, "We do all of this work to assert ourselves as gay men just to conform to a new system of homo-regulation?"

That's not what I asked, though. Instead, I asked, trying for a bit of levity, "Is the problem that we're both bottoms?" Though there had been guys I'd cruised and gotten cruised by who'd been put off by my transness, none had commented on my lack of penis. I'd had plenty of fun with tops who seemed to enjoy my bodily configuration. I still didn't understand why it mattered to him that I didn't have a penis.

"What? No! I haven't bottomed in—oh God, eight years!" I needed to get away from the conversation, but he kept talking. At some point he bought me another drink. When he launched into a conversation with someone else, I slipped over to another table for a moment of consolation with a lovely boy I don't often get to see, knowing that my conversation with Joshua wasn't yet over.

Eventually I found enough of an opening in Joshua's other conversation to say good-bye. "Are we okay?" he asked.

"Yeah!" I responded a little too enthusiastically. Of course I'm okay with being rejected by someone I was really attracted to. Of course I'm okay with meeting an unwillingness—or inability?—to work through a narrowly-configured gay identity the first time I'd made myself vulnerable enough to let someone do that work. I tried to conjure up some righteous indignation about his characterizing my body as insufficient. I tried to convince myself that *my* desires didn't include anyone with such rigid and narrow identity boundaries. Somehow I couldn't convince myself that I wasn't still disappointed. "Yeah, Joshua, we're fine."

GLASS BLOWING

Khary Polk

We were leaving a place that no longer exists, reminiscing about a bar that had recently closed. I wondered why the measure of love was loss in this city.

"I don't follow you," Ricky said, beginning the game of touching my arm as we moved north on Seventh Avenue South, walking towards a late-night pizza joint.

"It's the first line of a novel by Jeannette Winterson. 'Why is the measure of love loss?' I didn't understand it at first, but I think it means you don't know what you got 'til it's gone."

"Oh. Like Joni Mitchell," he said.

"Exactly."

I brushed back, keeping my hand away from his. I wanted a bit of friction, too, but I wasn't ready to handhold. Though I had never met Ricky before tonight, I knew him from Wonderbar, the East Village dive whose closure we were both lamenting. It was the only bar in New York that ever felt like home to me. Its multi-culti caste of color-me-queers reminded me of my life growing up as an Air Force brat, where every kid I knew was mixed with something or another. Ricky partied there all the time. He was taller than your average fag; I remember watching him stick out in the bar's dank interior, even using him like a lighthouse to navigate the sea of bodies packing the spot. He caught me clocking him a few times, but neither of us took the extra step to exchange names. I always figured I'd meet him maxing among the Andres and Big Bois at Wonderbar, crunk under Bill Coleman's poly-genre groove. Instead, we met earlier that evening at Bar d'O during a book party for the first volume of *Think Again.* Conceived by two fly boys—one from Trinidad and another from Toledo—the essay collection was a dissident cog in the AIDS industrial complex, challenging those working in HIV prevention to examine how fear and loathing of black gay bodies girded their prevention efforts. I had a piece in the book and came out to support the fête. Meeting Ricky there made me think again about all we had lost with the closing of Wonderbar; and what we might do to recapture those memories in the meanwhile.

I guess he felt it, too. We drank and talked, talked and drank until it was clear we both wanted to spend the night together. Drunk and hungry, we bade Bar d'O adieu and headed out into the November air, giddy as schoolboys in love. By the time we sat down to eat, our game of grab-ass had petered into silly innuendos and knee rubs under the table. I wolfed my pizza down. Turned my slices to breadsticks in a matter of minutes.

We were almost ready to leave when Ricky's eyes changed. Something was up.

"Khary, I want you to know. I'm positive."

I stopped, and in that brief pause a host of memories flooded my mind. I had forgotten about Paul, a man I'd met my first summer at Oberlin College. Like many a Negro before me, I had run north to Oberlin, Ohio in search of certain freedoms. Paul was the live-in curator of a Frank Lloyd Wright "Usonian" house built on the outskirts of the college. One night we went drinking with his friend, Micah. Never before had I felt so alive in my own pursuit of happiness, so fresh and so free. We closed three bars in the city limits before heading back to the Wright estate, lounging within the modern wonder of wood and brick. Frank Wright designed Usonian houses as pre-Ikea American dream homes you could snap together yourself. He thought they might save our nation. With my knickers loose, I thought they might too. As the porn came on our clothes came off; soon the three of us were naked, our bodies interlocking like the fretwork of the redwood ceiling. In Usonia, our family fit together. We even moved our play outside for a time, and the boy who had led a life sheltered by the barbwire fences of his military childhood was suddenly fucking two men on a tree-lined lawn, protected only by the shadow of night.

The next day, I ran into Micah at the first bar we'd crawled the night before. He pulled me aside and quietly asked whether I had known that Paul was HIV-positive.

I had no idea.

"Well it should be ok, we used condoms," he said, and I went back to my dorm room and began to cry. I was sure I'd been infected. I wondered why my first taste of freedom should come at so high a price. I held fast to this anxiety for years, folding it into my very character, always afraid an HIV test would confirm the worst of my fears: that black boys were the expendable subjects of social engineering. The most modern of creatures, we were the sacraments of a New World Order—those sacrificed so that others might live.

The fear of being just another nigger made it easier for me to forgo tests and medical check-ups for the rest of my college career. I didn't want the drama or the responsibility. I did still want the dick, though. Sex became a game of goldfish memory: How fast could I swim to the other side of the bowl before forgetting what I had done with him, and to him, and what he had done to me, and what *had* he done to me, and what *was* his name?

Four years later I found out I was a bone marrow match with a sixteen year-old girl battling leukemia in Cleveland. Though I had no memory of ever registering—gay men are barred from giving blood, after all—the National Marrow Donor Program had tracked me down in New York City. They hoped I'd agree to become a marrow donor for the girl. Of course I would. Problem was, I knew the blood center would ask me whether I'd ever had sex with a man, or whether I'd ever had sex with a woman who had sex with a man. A "yes" to either question would mark my marrow ineligible for harvesting. They asked. I said "no" on both counts. I knew they'd test my blood.

The staff at the New York Blood Center kept telling me what a hero I was for donating bone marrow. They showed me photographs of firefighters who had given marrow transplants, pointing out the three who died on 9/11. You all are heroes, they said to me as they drew my blood for infectious disease screenings. You make us proud. Was this my version of life on the down low, submerging the most salient part of myself in the service of a greater good? How many people had done the same thing? I spent the next week on edge, thinking about the girl whose body had mumped its way to 250lbs during chemo. My ability to save her life depended upon the history of my sex, the fitness of my blood. She paced the waiting room of my thoughts, waiting for my news, stopping only to watch daytime TV, listening to Oprah tell America to hide her little girls because Bigger Thomas is back! Willie Horton is back! Nushawn Williams is back! Magic Johnson is back! Easy E is back! And *girlllllll*, don't be no fool now. Don't be no fool, baby girl; he will end your vagina monologue if you let him.

The results came by priority mail. I was too afraid to open the envelope. My breathing went shallow. I called up the center and asked them how my blood work went. A center rep told me the results looked pretty good.

"But what about the AIDS test?" I asked.

"You passed that, too."

The woman heard the relief in my voice. She asked me why I was worried.

Leaving the pizzeria, Ricky and I took a cab back to his apartment in Fort Greene. We made out in the back seat the whole ride, oblivious to the driver's eyes as we crossed the Manhattan Bridge into Brooklyn. When the cab pulled up to Ricky's building we were more than ready to head indoors. He paid the fare and led me up the steps to his brownstone walk-up. Inside, we began to undress, letting our layers pile upon the floor, shedding our skin on our way to the bed.

We kissed for a time, and my lips grew sensitive from the rasp of his beard. I made my way down his body and took his length into my mouth. It was a Cinderella fit. Ricky nudged the back of my throat with every thrust. There was no gagging, however; I'd grown gills. I pivoted, and soon his head was at my crotch, matching me stroke for stroke. The seesaw of our rhythm shook the bed.

Ricky rolled me upright. I wanted so badly to earn his trust. My legs were open; I could feel him loitering just outside my ass. His lips parted and pursed above me; a line of spittle fell from his mouth and landed into mine, hitting the back of my throat. I coughed. Ricky waited, and lowered another soft, clear jewel into my mouth, the saliva cool and congealed as blown glass—

I swallowed.

And I realized two things:

That to love anything was to risk its loss. And risk, itself, is the oddest barometer of love.

APPEARANCES AND ALL THAT

Tommi Avicolli Mecca

That hot summer night in 1974, I was standing on the corner of 13th and Locust streets in Center City Philadelphia. It was becoming a habit. The intersection was well-known for sales transactions. The world's oldest kind.

I wasn't interested in the local economy. I just wanted to hook up with someone. I was horny. The gay bars on the other side of town were out of the question. The boys who went to those establishments wanted "real" men. The owners served their clients and their bank accounts well by keeping my kind out. "Two pieces of ID, please." The boys barely needed one. No matter what a queen produced (birth certificate, driver's license, high school diploma etc.), it was never enough.

I was living in drag. I even went to work at a record store in South Philly in outrageous outfits. The owners were hippies. They thought I was trying to be David Bowie in his "Ziggy Stardust" incarnation. Glitter rock sold.

The store was located inside an old warehouse turned shopping mall. The owner tried to get me fired for inappropriate dress. Fortunately, the employees were all members of Retail Clerks and our shop steward, an amazing African American woman, wouldn't hear of it. I think she secretly loved queens. Maybe she was a dyke. Once, when a group of black and Puerto Rican queens came sashaying into the store as loud and proud as could be, the owner tried to throw them out. Our shop steward intervened and happily waited on them. She even let one of them try on a dress in the women's dressing room, while the owner looked on disapprovingly.

That night at 13th and Locust, I was wearing one of my favorite ensembles: hot pants, platform shoes, a shirt tied up at the waist to reveal just a bit of flesh. My hair was long, gnarled and unruly, as it always was in the extreme humidity. The temperature may have been dropping a bit that night, but not the humidity.

I was sporting face paint, but not too much: I wasn't going for Marilyn Monroe. The most I could hope for was Bette Midler or Barbra Streisand on a bad hair day. They were my role models anyway. I was too ethnic looking for those washed-out blonde Hollywood types. A Jewish friend with similar Mediterranean features had already undergone her first nose job. There would be many more to come. I thought about it, but altering my family's "snozzola," as Papa lovingly called it, was not on my list of priorities. Not only would Papa have killed me, but generations of ancestors with Roman noses would have cursed me with the *mala occhia* (evil eye) from beyond their graves. I didn't need that.

It wasn't the smartest thing to be standing out there so visibly. My uncle the cop worked in that police district. He might drive by in his patrol car, though I knew he usually did the day shift. He probably wouldn't recognize me anyway. He hadn't seen me for a while. He certainly had never seen me in radical drag. Of course, if my faggot ass got hauled off to jail, he'd find out for sure.

I didn't care. I hated my uncle. When I was younger and worked at Papa's gas station, pumping gas and washing cars, he'd come around and mouth off about the "damn hippies" who were ruining the country. He'd ask me when I was going to start "acting like a boy." As if that was something I really wanted to do.

I hated cops. The boys in blue bothered queens all the time. They hassled the gay boys, too: raiding the bars when the owners didn't make their payoffs, stopping all of us from hanging out together at night on the streets, and arresting us for selling our bodies or having sex in the parks and tearooms. There was actually a law at the time that made it illegal for several homos to be walking down the street together after 10PM. Cops routinely stopped us and told us to disperse or they'd take us in.

They also bothered us a lot in Rittenhouse Square, the beautiful park in the center of the gay ghetto. When I was a teenager, I used to bring my $15 folk guitar to the park on clear summer nights and jam with the hippies under the stars. I wanted to be with the queens, but they were off in their own little corner where I didn't yet feel comfortable. The cops would come through as soon as it got dark and start hassling the hippies and the queens. They also went after the gay guys who walked around in circles cruising each other. Sometimes two guys would duck into the bushes for a little grope session. In the dark they could usually get away with more.

Some of the activists at the local Gay Activists Alliance wanted to meet with the police to try and stop them from hassling gay guys on the street or in Rittenhouse Square. They also wanted the police department to start hiring gay men and lesbians. They weren't thinking of people like me. I wanted to disband the police department altogether.

It was sometimes difficult to work with the gay activist types. They really had a different agenda. Respectability. Fitting in. They were always saying that "gays are like everybody else." I didn't want to be like everyone else. Normalcy was overrated. And boring. As Oscar Wilde or Jean Genet might have said.

Some activists thought that queens like myself were giving them a bad name, that we hurt their cause. By being out there on the corner of a street known for hustlers, whores, and queens or making a lot of noise in Rittenhouse Square (instead of silently parading around looking for dick), I was setting back the cause of gay rights.

If the truth be told, I tried hard to set it back. I worked on it every day. Most times, I succeeded. Like that night on the corner of 13th and Locust.

"Hey, how's it goin'?" I heard his voice before I actually saw him. I turned. The guy was standard-issue South Philly macho. Jeans, t-shirt, sneakers. Not too tall. Talked like Rocky Balboa on testosterone.

I knew the type well from growing up in working-class Little Italy where the guys stood on the corners in tight jeans and tee-shirts. I spent many a summer afternoon staring out the window of my parents' room fantasizing about those *guaglioni* (homeboys), as we called them in my mother's southern Italian dialect.

He had nice thick eyebrows and a Roman nose. I liked the combination of olive skin and black hair. It was a turn-on even when I was a young fag staring at male classmates in Catholic school. A nun once called me out for it, telling me that if I looked at the other boys that way, people would get the wrong idea.

Except that was the right idea. From the moment I started playing with my sister's dolls and jumping rope with her friends to the day I tried on my first dress, I had nothing to hide.

"Whacha lookin' for?" I asked Mr. Macho.

"Company," he said.

"You're just a lonely boy, huh?" I asked, echoing the lyrics of an old '50s song I liked. I think it was by Paul Anka.

"Yeah, real lonely." I could tell. As Mae West would have said: Was that a gun in his pocket or was he just excited to see me?

It didn't take long to figure out we wanted the same thing. Lucky for both of us, he lived within walking distance. I made it a rule not to go far.

You didn't hear much about queens getting murdered in those days (which is not to say it didn't happen), but I still didn't take chances. I had even stopped hitchhiking. I did it in college before I came out. Sometimes I pretended I didn't notice that guys were coming on to me. Other times I let a guy grope me before I dashed out of the car.

When we got to his place, I was relieved to see that he lived alone. No roommate or partner to come barging in. He wasn't the best housekeeper. No surprise there. He offered me a beer. It was years before date rape drugs were the rage, but I still made it rule number two not to accept anything to eat or drink.

Formalities out of the way, he grabbed me and tried to kiss me. I pulled away. Affection wasn't part of the deal that night. "I don't do that." I paused.

"That's cool," he said defensively.

"Let me get somethin' straight. Just cause I dress like this doesn't mean I'm passive. I ain't here to suck dick or get fucked." That was rule number three.

He seemed scared at first. I liked that. A butch old fag like him. Of course, I didn't know for sure that he was queer. Could've been a straight guy who preferred getting sucked off by a queen. Maybe his girlfriend wouldn't do it. Maybe she was lousy at it. Maybe he was exploring his sexuality. Guys did that even back then.

We called them "trade." "DL" hadn't been invented yet. When they turned violent or hostile we called them "Neshinu." There were quite a few Neshinus in the City of Brotherly Love.

"I'm all yours," he whispered. He was getting with the program. More like he was so horny he was willing to do anything.

"On your knees."

He hesitated before dropping down.

"You know what I want," I said in a firm voice.

He got right to it. He pawed at my pants and undies until they dropped down my legs. Then he started sucking my dick and loving it. He kept looking up at me like a puppy desperate to please his master. I started to smile. What a sight that would have been for the gay boys on the other side of Broad Street in their dark, noisy Mafia-run bars. In their view, closeted straight guys sought drag queens because they secretly wanted other men but couldn't admit it. Gay men liked other men. Other men who dressed and looked like men. Only pure and unadulterated freaks liked queens because they were queens.

Queens knew better. We lived on the outskirts. We saw things that other people didn't see. We were like that fool on the hill the Beatles sang about. We watched the parade of gender-obsessed people in the world with amusement. We knew it was all more complicated than dreamed of in anyone's philosophy, even our own. The radical chic shrinks of the day only hinted at the world to come if the walls came down and people were free to invent their genders.

I got a taste of it that night. My trick was doing his job well. He was bringing me to the edge. I decided I wanted more.

They had a saying in those days: the butcher they are, the faster they roll over. Before I left that guy's apartment, I would discover the truth of that saying firsthand.

GIRLS
Gina de Vries

It's Jodi's fault that I find it. She, Rebecca, and I have just come from the excellent bánh mì place, bags full of sandwiches and Vietnamese candy. It reminds me of slumber parties, even though it's a Tuesday afternoon and not a Saturday night. Jodi has bunk beds in her apartment, so that helps with the 24/7 sleepover feeling. We're tearing into sandwiches the size of our heads, sprawled out on Jodi's carpet with pillows underneath us, listening to music and telling stories.

Jodi is talking about a fag friend from high school, a friend who told her he wasn't coming out to his parents because his mother had once said, voice full of venom, "Do you know what THEY do? THEY do THIS!!!" Then his mother stuck out both of her index fingers and slapped them together to illustrate gay sex, which, according to her, looked like a phallus battle. Jodi sticks her fingers out to approximate the penis duel as she tells the story. I almost choke on my sandwich from laughing so hard. Then she says, "Wait, Gina—have I shown you the website?"

"Uh… There's a penis-battling website?"

She grabs her laptop, and opens up a website called HeroicHomosex.com. The first shot on the opening page is a fair-skinned man's naked torso, his arm in the Pledge of Allegiance pose, next to a billowing US flag. I think it's a parody at first—until I see that there's a lot of text underneath the image, and whoever is writing is awfully earnest and humorless about masculinity.

> *This is a FREE site for guys into*
> *COCKRUBBIN*
> *FROT*
> *COCK TO COCK*

DICK2DICK
BONE ON BONE
and
WRESTLIN.
And who are
PROUD
of what they like to do.
HEROIC HOMOSEX
TO LOVE ANOTHER MAN
AS AN EQUAL AND A MAN
WITH TOTAL FIDELITY …
AS A MAN
not a top
not a bottom
not a butch
not a bitch
not a gay
not a bi
not a str8
A MAN
WITH TOTAL FIDELITY

It turns out the creator of the website is a guy named Bill Weintraub, and he has a singular and all-consuming fetish: frottage, or, in his words, "cock2cock, man2man." There's a lot of circular, repetitive, and entertaining-but-not-particularly-well-written information about how "frot" is the most superior, masculine, and "equal" way for two men to have sex. Weintraub calls men who exclusively practice frottage "cockrub warriors." There are little illustrations of scantily clad guys in Roman soldier meets heavy metal meets Dungeons and Dragons outfits—lace-up sandals and kilts, but big headresses with lots of spikes. They have vaguely Scandanavian-sounding names ("Blaadokz and Krundoun"), and they pop up as the site's mascots. Masculinity-affirming forms of address like "dude" and "bro" are sprinkled throughout the website to refer to the readers: "New to Frot, Dude? Click Here to Find Out What's Hot About Frot!"

Jodi starts reading aloud: *"Not into anal? Gay, bi, or str8 curious? You don't have to surrender your masculinity to be sexual with another man. Frot is the safe, hot, intimate, and masculine alternative to anal sex."* We click on links to more articles, all by Weintraub. There's a lot of talk about how anal sex is disgusting, dirty, and degrading;

that it makes men who should be masculine and heroic into sissies and queers; that penetration of any kind should be left to straight people. Rebecca starts reading out loud, too: *"What was the anus, after all, but a sorry substitute for the vagina?... It was just a convenient hole for one man to use while pretending, on some level, that he was fucking a girl. And I had no interest in that—either in penetrating women or being penetrated the way that they were."*

"Penetration is for girls! Cockrub Warriors aren't girls, they're MEN!" Jodi is trying to keep a straight face as she says this, but she collapses into giggles pretty quickly. Rebecca and I are grimacing at the misogyny, but we're laughing, too. It's difficult to take The Cockrub Empire very seriously. Rebecca keeps reading: *"Indeed, I had no patience with any of those parts of homosexual culture which sought to equate gay men to women: the derogatory use of the words "girl," "she," and "her," to refer to other gay men, and the adulation of drag. I wanted to sleep with men, that is, other gay men who were male-identified; I did not want to have struggled all those years to become a self-accepting male homosexual only to end up sleeping with people who thought of themselves (or me) as girls."*

When we read the parts about how fags aren't girls, I think about middle and high school again, about the stories Jodi, Rebecca, and I were telling before we got sidetracked. The fags I knew at the queer youth group I went to—almost all men of color, almost all working-class or poor—called each other "girl" and "honey" all the time. They called me "girl" and "honey," too, which made me feel dear, loved. All of us wore bright colors and glitter on our eyelids. We played dance music in the common space and told filthy jokes; laughed loud and long. There was a lot of voguing, drama, and cattiness, and underneath it all, a fierce and relentless sweetness. Those fags would do anything for me, and I would do anything for them. At 12, when I started going there, I was the baby of the group, and one of the only young women. The faggots protected me, and taught me how to protect myself—deliver scathing come-backs, walk down the street with my head held high.

I learned a lot of what I know about being femme from my first fag friends. My femmeness is about acting sweet and playful, glittery and queeny; it's not about being perfectly-coiffed and deliberately cool. My femmeness involves looking hot and fabulous, but not in a way that means wearing the most expensive clothes or fucking the most popular people. It's about how being a girl is a joyous, precious, absolutely great thing, and I first learned how to find joy in girlhood from faggots. Some of my first fag friends growing up in San Francisco were homeless, or right on the edge of homelessness. Some of them lived with their families in the Excelsior or the Mission (in the parts that weren't trendy or gentrified) or the Ingleside, Bayview/Hunter's Point or Sunnydale—all poor, working-class, and lower-middle-class neighborhoods, and all neighborhoods that were predominantly people of color. My once-working-class Italian-Catholic family had moved from Sunnyvale to San Francisco's Ingleside District when I was 8; my father got his first "good job," and we began to class up. But our house was still ramshackle, and we were still an hour's streetcar ride away from the queer youth group in the gay and monied Castro District.

Sometimes, the boys and I would ride back to our neighborhoods together. They'd always yell to me as I got off the streetcar three blocks from my house to be careful walking home, to not let any of the boys from my neighborhood throw me shade. After telling my friend Luis the story of a particularly awful fight with the homophobic school bullies, he said to me, "Okay, from now on, you are half-Samoan, and I am your Samoan cousin, who will beat the living shit out of them if they even look at you funny. I will come to school with you and look hella intimidating to those boys. They won't call you a dyke again." I know, logically, that there are rich and middle-class fags who are femme, who mama people. I know that money and privilege don't necessarily make you a jerk, that it's all about whether you own where you come from, acknowledge your advantages, and don't use the privileges you have to fuck people over. But my association with that kind of protective, tough-mama faggotry has always been with working-class fags. There was a camaraderie among us, this sense of not having anything left to lose. I wasn't a gay boy, but I was a queer femme girl from a similar background, and that made me part of the gang. Why cling to masculinity if it wasn't us? What did we have to be scared of? We were fabulous, goddammit.

Then I started high school, in a neighborhood that felt like it was a million miles away from my little family of queer boys. I met fags who could have been my friends if they weren't so scared of girls, or of being called girls. I went to a hippie prep school in the Haight-Ashbury on scholarship. It was the kind of place where we sat in circles and called our teachers by their first names, but the school still sent a lot of kids to the Ivy League. There were things I loved about it—the dedicated teachers, the pack of sweet and nerdy queer friends I eventually found—and there were also problems. I was the token baby dyke, the smartypants queer youth activist getting my picture in the paper, getting flown across the country to speak at conferences. The administration milked that for all it was worth, because they wanted to score diversity points with the good liberal rich parent crowd. It was admittedly nice at first, that even the Dean of Students noticed me, and seemed proud. Then a rich boy started sexually harassing me, and the administration did nothing about it, because I was a scholarship kid and his parents donated to the school. There were a couple of teachers who were truly sweet and supportive, but speaking out would put them on the line, too. My harrasser's fate was in the hands of people who wanted his parents' money, people who wouldn't dare punish him, because it meant a loss of income for an already extravagantly wealthy school. And I dressed punk and slutty, in short skirts and fishnets, and I brought my lunch in a bag instead of buying it on Haight Street, and I bussed in to school from an hour away. Somehow, this all meant that I asked for the creepy emails, the notes in my locker, his cold, predatory stare lingering over my breasts in the hallway. This boy who was harassing me, he'd raped a girl who went to my school, and that had gotten hushed up, too, because they'd dated, and if you date a boy you're supposed to have sex with him, especially if he's rich and you're not. One of the out faggots at my high school, a boy I thought could maybe be my friend, said to me, "But I heard he didn't rape that girl who said he raped her!" He didn't say that he didn't believe this guy was sexually harassing me, but he didn't need to. The message was clear: *Boys tell the truth. Girls lie.*

The few out fags at my school didn't really like me, either. I didn't connect it to class or girlness at the time, but the fact that they came from rich families and had the high school version of a butch, boys-only clubhouse makes me grimace now. I remember really wanting to be friends with this one faggot because he was punk and he seemed sweet. But we got into a fight in a Gay-Straight Alliance meeting, where I said we should do programming about trans issues, and he said "Well, I don't want to wear a dress!" "That's not what being trans is about, nobody's gonna make you wear a dress, and besides, wearing dresses isn't bad!" I said back. I was wearing a dress that day, so I was particularly pissed off. Didn't he know dresses were fun? What the hell kind of faggot was he?!

Then, there was Angel-Miguel, who, I swear to god, had an angelic face— those big, bright choir boy eyes. Angel-Miguel had gotten bashed a lot in middle school, and my sense is that when he came to high school, he wanted a fresh start, a place where no one would have ammunition to gang up on him. In high school, everyone wanted to talk with me about sex—the queer kids, and the straight kids, too, because queers teach straight people about sex. People would approach me with their sex questions in the hallway during lunch, during break between classes, at the cast parties after school plays. Angel-Miguel cornered me at one of these parties, so drunk he couldn't stand up straight. He told me that he wasn't gay, but he liked having sex with guys. But he wasn't gay, he wasn't bisexual, he wasn't queer; he just liked having sex with boys. What are you supposed to say to that? I think I said, "You know, it's okay if you are queer," but I don't know if it got through the alcohol haze. Angel-Miguel never came out in high school, but he did these insanely sexual dances at our talent shows, grinding and shaking his ass to whatever hip-hop song was most popular that year. The big finale would always occur when he tore off his pants (granted, he was wearing a second skin-tight pair underneath) and threw them into the audience. You can get away with a lot at hippie schools. Angel-Miguel and I never talked about it, but my sense was always that we came from similar neighborhoods and backgrounds. He was one of the few kids of color at my high school. Sometimes, he reminded me of the faggots who raised me in my queerness. Sometimes, he reminded me of the other boys at school, the ones who were not girls.

But back to the Homosex Heroes.

Weintraub's best lines, by far, are from the essay "Hyacinthine Love, or, Some Thoughts on Cock-rubbing and the Cultural Tyranny of Buttfucking." Weintraub very thoroughly criticizes the "The Buttfuck Dictatorship": *"Thirty years after Gay Lib first took on that smug, complacent group of social arbiters and moralists it called the Heterosexual Dictatorship, gay life is controlled by a Buttfuck Dictatorship."* Jodi, Rebecca, and I start talking about how we want to start a band called the The Buttfuck Dictatorship, or maybe just make a lot of t-shirts that say "Buttfuck Dictatorship." Weintraub writes a lot about experiences he's had with men trying to chide or pressure him into having anal sex when he doesn't want to. Even though I find Weintraub's sexism, misogyny, and homophobia gross, I have to agree that his partners pressuring him into doing sexual things he doesn't want to do is upsetting—at best it's boundary-pushing, at worst it's sexual assault. I understand how it feels to have your kinks degraded, or treated like they aren't cool enough; I once had a particularly insensitive lover tell me I had "too many sexual boundaries." The relationship didn't last much longer than that, but the words still stung. On that front, I can empathize with Weintraub a tiny bit. But only a tiny bit. Because when you turn your personal preferences and boundaries (like, no anal sex) into a blanket judgment of other peoples' sexual behavior (*"And what was the anus, after all, but a sorry substitute for the vagina? If the penis corresponded to the clitoris and the scrotal tissues to those of the vagina, the anus, it seemed to me, corresponded to nothing. It was not an organ of sexual pleasure"*), and then you back up your hatred of said sexual act by spewing some really twisted homophobic and misogynist rhetoric, I have a problem. If you don't like anal sex, you don't have to do it. You also don't have to condemn people who enjoy it.

The whole website is fascinating and repulsive—sure, we could spend our time and energy doing things besides reading Weintraub's ramblings, but we can't look away! We need to see what other fucked-up and entertaining things Weintraub will say! There's a lot of rhetoric about "equality" and "fidelity," about letting go of roles like top/bottom and butch/femme and being men together, "as equals" and "with total fidelity." All the language about equality, egalitarianism, and mutuality reminds me of lesbian-separatist sex-writing about equal and egalitarian love between empowered women—which is ironic, considering how masculinity-obsessed and girl-hating the site is.

Weintraub's position on AIDS is one of the scariest and most complicated parts of the website. He doesn't *exactly* say that queer men are bringing HIV upon themselves by engaging in anal sex, but he gets close. Even anal sex with barriers isn't 100% safe—the only truly safe (and masculine!) sex is frottage: *"Still, when we look at all the problems associated with anal—the feminization, the inequality, the drugs, the pain, and the disease—we say, you know dude, there's an easier way, it's pure male, and it's very hot."* Weintraub doesn't differentiate between barebacking and anal sex with condoms and lube. According to him, both are equally bad; both are worthy of scorn and ridicule. Weintraub says he lost the love of his life, a man who was his lover for over a dozen years, to AIDS. I wonder if the website—if the whole anti-anal-sex schtick—is a product of all-consuming grief, and I feel a twinge of compassion again. Can watching dozens, even hundreds, of your friends and lovers die unhinge you this deeply? I think about the older fags I know who survived what they refer to as the plague years. None of them are misogynistic and homophobic like this, but that could just be the result of my lack of tolerance for those behaviors. I'm remembering that more faggots than just Weintraub think similar things—not that they're "Cockrub Warriors," necessarily, but that they decide that certain types of sex are "good" and certain types are "bad." That certain types of sex make you a girl. Or just that a girl is the worst thing you can be. Weintraub's website is an extreme example, but my head starts to hurt when I think about it for more than a few minutes.

I remember that I ran into Angel-Miguel on the dance floor at a queer youth conference after high school. We were maybe 19 or 20. I was shocked to see him in an explicitly queer space, considering how deeply conflicted he'd seemed about his sexuality when I'd last seen him. He grabbed me, spun me around, laughed, and pointed out the boys on the dance floor who he was having sex with. He told me he was working as a stripper. Given the pants-throwing dances in high school, I can't say I was surprised. I told him I was doing porn modeling, and he laughed. We had a sweet conversation about sex work, about being femme. He seemed so relaxed and sexy. He wasn't drunk, he was just in his body, and happy to be there. He called me "girl" with a queeny joy, and kissed me on the cheek. He seemed so excited to finally say the word.

STRAIGHTENING THE SHAWL

Ezra RedEagle Whitman

Among Native Americans there is this notion that gay people contain both the spirit of a man and the spirit of a woman, and that a *Two-Spirit* person doesn't fully identify with either sex. Historically Two-Spirits have been looked upon as teachers, advisors, and all-around mystic beings. I know this may sound overly romantic and new-agey, and I won't deny that a sizeable portion of participants in Two-Spirit gatherings across the US are non-Native gay people. I remain skeptical until proven an asshole in most cases, but *Two-Spirit* is actually a legit concept. I learned this while attending my reservation high school, still very much in the closet, when one of the cherished basketball stars of my graduating class, the half-breed Christian that he was, said out of nowhere, "I hate gay people. They make me sick." I cringed when he said this because he and I usually got along well.

Back then, I couldn't admit to myself how much I desired cock, so instead I presented myself as a blossoming metro-hippy who wanted free love for all. Like a beacon of hope, however, one of my closest friends—a loud-mouthed, long-braided jock—shot back, "My grandpa said *those* people were special. He said they could feel different sides of an issue because they possessed male and female power as leaders." The debate was closed; there are very few ways to contradict a reservation kid convinced of what his grandma or grandpa says and come out alive. My friend's claim that a person could feel two different things—the spirit of a man and a spirit of woman—lingered with me until graduation day.

I considered this spiritual take on homosexuality as a way to ease the transition into living as a gay person; nothing can be wrong or unacceptable if it is done in the name of spirituality, right? I quickly learned, however, that this left one flagrant dilemma: nothing felt spiritual about my raunchy sexual desires. Accepting the mystic power of a Two-Spirit made me feel like I had to give up sexuality altogether and hover about humbly voicing the visions that came to me in my sleep.

This is where my hang-up lies. I'm so utterly in love with and loyal to my cultural heritage. Yet I feel as if I need to forfeit some part of me in order to accept the description of "Two-Spirit." There's too much obligation to *walk the red road, the good road*, as the traditionalists say. I can't help but think that a spiritual person, someone who provides guidance and wisdom to others, couldn't possibly want to slut about or get smacked on the ass and told sweetly distasteful things.

As Native Americans, our community is more than just neighborhoods, it's a collective sense of family and homeland, a shared past and honor—honor that is, at times, held hostage if a member wants to act decadent or pornographic. Sex is still pretty secretive on the reservation, and any openness to exploring or declaring the sexual self is both subject to ridicule and met with warnings ranging from the typical "What will your family think?" to larger—if abstract—pressures like "What does this do to the tribe's image?" or, "Is this what your ancestors died for?" I could be subject to these warnings for an act as small as walking hand-in-hand with my lover down Main Street, past the high school, the tribal government headquarters, or on the way to the local grocer; or as a writer describing my own sexual experiences or even writing graphically about sex in my fiction. I could never abandon my spiritual post if I knew people counted on me to provide counsel. Nor could I stand the thought of one person waging words against another in defense of my role. *He's special, he can help us. No he can't, I heard he swallows.*

As a result I've become such an awkward version of a gay Native American man that I wonder just where I fit in. I mimic the goofy antics of consumer-driven gay ideals: prioritizing gym memberships and physical fitness above all else; maintaining frequent wardrobe updates; dropping hints of frivolous travel in a bragging-not-quite-bragging manner; navigating silly club scene hierarchies—*I don't wait for drinks, I know the bartender...excuse me while I go say hi to the DJ*—stuff that I cling to in order to feel a part of the crowd. Likewise, for fear of being a sell-out, a faded red, it has taken me most of my life to declare that I don't agree with certain social aspects of modern Native America, especially the constant blame towards white America for the taking of land, of livelihood, or for "trans-generational trauma" in order to distract from inconsistent Native leadership and poor health choices. I'm fearful of accepting spiritual duties founded within my tribe due to the lockdown of the sexual self as the price I would have to pay.

Feeling anything less than enthralled to remain in the perpetual plight of reservation life shouldn't prove someone to be less of a Native American. In fact, it was that very desire to say "Fuck the reservation" (as a system, not the people, mind you!) that drove a faction of men, women, and children from my tribe in 1877 on what is known as the Nez Perce Trail—a now famous journey for freedom of over a thousand miles with the US government in close pursuit. I belittle the memory of that perseverance if I cannot confront and question what it means to be my own person, in order to be the homo I really want to be.

My tribal history allows me to see religious views not as separate, compartmentalized parts of life but as intrinsic components of everyday living. In essence this means that some part of my day is always spiritually significant. I can attest that some part of my day is also sexually significant. I know that mentioning gay sexuality and Native American spirituality together is almost sacrilege, and my main challenge is to understand why.

I'm a prancy nancy at heart. As a child, I remember dancing with my sisters in the middle of the street in broad daylight. Native Americans have these social gatherings called Pow-Wows, which typically consist of dance competitions showcasing different styles of traditional dance. It's a culture within a culture, laden with popular tunes, trends in dance and outfits, and famous drum groups. There are dances performed strictly by girls, though as a young boy I was quite good at these dances. My sisters and I would practice using household towels in place of the trademark shawls, and conduct our own mini Pow-Wows out in the street. I danced, twirled, skipped, mimicked a little bird picking through the grass. It was great fun. I knew I wasn't supposed to do these dances so any time a car passed I kept my "shawl" wrapped about my shoulders but turned my face away from the street, hoping the driver would see me from behind and think I was just a short-haired girl.

There was an old retired white couple who lived next door and they gave us popsicles in appreciation of our shows. I have never felt such acceptance as a girly little boy as the one time when the old lady once looked at me while handing me an orange Dreamsicle and said "Darling, your shawl is crooked," and reached out to unroll one side off my shoulder. I'm not sure if she actually knew I was a boy, but she gave me such a significant blossom of pride deep within my chest. She's gone now, but I think about her sometimes when I've got a cute little outfit on and I'm ready for the night's prowl. I check my collar, check the way the jeans ride the hip. *Darling, your ass looks flat in those...*

There is documentation of both the existence and the acceptance of gay and lesbian figures in Native American history. Most interesting to me was a case mentioned in the writings of Pacific Northwest explorer Captain Bonneville who came through Nez Perce country in the 1800s prior to establishment of the reservation. With the help of Sahaptian interpreters ("Sahaptian" is the general term given to the group of languages spoken in the region), this explorer was able to observe two men living as women, in that they dressed in women's clothing and performed female roles of gathering and crafts. It was relayed that these two men were told by their guardian spirits to live in such a way. Whether one or both were actually homosexual or not, this obligation to their guardian spirits was unanimously respected by fellow tribal members. Their masculinity was never brought into question because such a priority took a backseat to ideals of honor, duty, and spiritual strength.

If, in fact, Native Americans historically didn't bother with generalized notions of what defined masculinity, why are so many men from my tribe pressured to do so today? Much of this pressure comes from previous generations who rejected homosexuality as a result of accepting Christian homophobia installed when the reservation system was implemented. This is a component of contemporary reservation life that stems directly from non-Native ideals. With this in mind, who, then (and I stoop a bit), are the sell-outs?

Searching for a guardian spirit is a practice that has all but disappeared in modern times, but it doesn't mean the idea of acting straight needs to then become the new priority. If I cannot have a guardian spirit to help me decide what is acceptable and what isn't, why am I allowing a jumbled heap of strangers to define that for me?

As silly as it sounds, maybe my laptop has become the guardian spirit these days. I feel like I need to consult it before making any decisions and it provides all the answers I need in getting places or understanding certain issues. I get a little nervous if I am unable to access my machine for a few days, and more to the point it's a way to explore my sexual self. I'm a cyberslut and I love to peruse ads if for no other reason than to appreciate the general freakiness out there. I have my preferred sites that lend a helping hand on those more lonely mornings— a chat room, video communities, and on occasion the personal ads of hook-up sites. I also give not-so-tasteful tours of my apartment on my webcam. My online identity is a bitchy one, and at the core of my terse little online personality is a generalized fear that I'll be condescended to or rejected by someone who I would in other circumstances consider irrelevant. I'd like to think it's because they, like me, would rather be the ones to deliver the bad news than to receive it. Then again it could be I'm just a bland conversationalist.

I'd venture to guess, however, that I'm not any more bland than a large portion of the personal ads out there. *Hey bro, let's hang out, drink some beers and see what happens. Be STD free, in shape and under 25yo. No fems. Your pic gets mine.* Seriously? Is this my chance to prove just how much of a real dude I am? Is this why, for a few seconds, my arrow hovers over the reply button before I half-heartedly opt out? *Darling, your shawl is crooked.*

When I consider these *bros* and their reign on masculinity I wonder how it is they who've lodged themselves in my conscience when I'm out and about and spy their brethren in the street and I alter my gait to appear more masculine in order to sustain a fleeting glance. Where is that pretty little thing who could pull off those graceful bird-like dances clad in nothing but a shabby towel? The poor thing is smothered under bland, tasteless ideals imposed by one-dimensional takes on masculinity which have taken priority over spiritual strength and duty.

Inside, a voice tells me to retain some sort of integrity, to try, try again and resist the obscure pressure to succumb to generalized norms of gender and sexual identity as they have been modeled from both my Native upbringing and the remarkable control of white gay culture. Had I listened more closely I would have realized it was a voice telling me that these imposed definitions don't work for me. It isn't that my laptop guardian spirit has steered me wrong by providing me glimpses of a hypermasculine world I think I desire. I don't look for real-life sexual encounters online, but I'm turned on by teasing the possibility. I think this is just a way to solidify myself as a desirable item in an on-screen world where the feedback is almost always favorable because my cam is set to my good side, focused on my good parts. Yet more and more my online personality is leaking out into how I treat others in real life, and this is something that causes a certain amount of apprehension. I find I view men in the gym, in the club, and in the street as profiles, as chat windows personified. It's easy not to care about whatever truths they're hiding or embellishing because I know that all I might want is to tease the notion of (and sometimes partake in) sex. Forget the possibility of a great connection or conversation with someone. I want to be physically desired. And as much as the straight-actors annoy me, when I see someone who would probably refer to himself and others as *bro*, I hover and consider an approach as if my entire appeal depended on it.

I've also realized that I've forgotten manners and tact when a mission must be aborted because I'm so used to the ease of exiting a window or telling someone I'm going offline. I've got to find a balance somewhere. I've got to create an opportunity for the growth of something rooted in spirituality, sexuality, and pride, but also in humility and kindness. Where is the time

and place to challenge this complacency in upholding brainless and system-
atic ideals of sexual appeal, and encounter some sense of sexual satisfaction?
The battle is an internal one of the self against contempt. The first challenge
I need to confront is the detachment of my spiritual training wheels in the
acceptance of my sexual self. More directly: I am not a Two-Spirit. I respect
and admire the Two-Spirit movement, and will remain supportive, but I
don't think this model fits me simply because I'm Native American. I have
toiled over this question for years. Am I a Two-Spirit? That's not the same
question as "Am I gay?" I know I'm gay. I'm gay as hell. Yet I'm doubtful
of whether there is in me a man and woman who shift between duties or
situations. That would still define roles for each as if either one or the other
will surface in order to handle its respective affairs like gender roles of the
spirit. I cannot restrict myself that way.

Getting a hand job in the backseat of a car doesn't take away from my
spiritual self, yet there is no box in Native America for the slutty vision
seeker. If it's a shortage of insight or an absence of foresight that points me
down this path, such a lack is as good a reason as any to embark on the
quest. If this is a search for enlightenment, or more specifically, a vision,
then it is a search I'll gladly take on. Because, darling, contempt is such a
crooked shawl.

THE UNLIKELY BAREBACKER

Shepperton Jones

Getting fucked without a condom used to be out of the question. I worried about the major and minor sexually transmitted diseases with equal paranoia. I worried about what I could catch from blowjobs traded in the darkness in Buena Vista Park. And girl, there were lots of those. In spite of my paranoia, when I was 18, I worked for an "escort" agency in San Francisco. But see, I was an uptight hooker.

I had recently arrived from the rural South and I personified some of the stereotypes that go along with that. I was a very demure girl, but oh so slutty underneath. So much inner conflict, honey. My extreme social awkwardness somehow explains and defines why I became a hooker. To do the job, I had to be willing to put myself on display, which was difficult, but I could do it without the small talk, the explanations, and the facade of normalcy, and still get the validation that I needed. I didn't know how to meet men in any ordinary sense, but I knew that lots of men wanted to have sex with boys who looked underage, and from what I saw in the back pages of the *Bay Area Reporter*, I knew they were willing to pay for it.

I came across an advertisement for Ocean Escorts, which specialized in providing barely legal boys. I called the phone number in the ad and asked the guy who answered if they were hiring. He said I could come for an interview and we all know what *that* means. On the train ride to the interview I thought about all the possibly sad and frightening scenarios that might await me, but I also felt compelled to follow through with it. Becoming a hooker would give me access to the gritty, urban world that I had dreamed of for so long, even if it meant slurping on this wannabe pimp's extra-large penis, which I did. I mean, is there any other good reason to live in a gay ghetto besides getting paid for sex?

My hooker dreams were highly influenced by Paul Russell's mid-nineties novel *Boys of Life*. Tony, the teenaged protagonist, is plucked from rural Kentucky and taken to New York by the underground filmmaker Carlos Reichart, where they go on to make several Passoliniesque films together—shot entirely on location in Alphabet City, of course. Tony is a hooker on the side, seamlessly mixing the downtown avant-garde art scene with Times Square seediness. I wanted that mixture of grit and glamour, too. Instead I ended up with Steve as my fumbling, drooling pseudo pimp-daddy. He told clients I was "Czechoslovakian," which gave me and my clients something to laugh about. It's true that I'm tall, thin, and white, but I can't really pull off an Eastern-European accent.

Ocean Escorts was a sad little operation, but it was as avant-garde and edgy as I could get. During the day, I was a shy, ultra mainstream-looking gay boy who worked retail in the Castro, but at night I had sex with strange men in strange beds, and somehow this made me feel alive. But I was still uptight about everything. About all the drugs suddenly circulating around me, about working for a pimp, and especially about the risks of unsafe sex. Part of me wanted to lose control, do a line and spread my legs for whoever wanted some, but the fear was greater than the desire. And just to be sure to squelch any of those urges, I became the prissy, uptight, well-read hooker who knew she was better than all the rest.

Back then, I rarely let anything come close to my hole except for a finger, a nice tongue, or the occasional butt-plug. I was not like my escorting colleagues who would do anything for drugs. No, I was prim and proper, slightly sassy Ms. Louisiana I'm-too-good-for-all-of-you-and-you-know-it-so-don't-even-look-in-my-direction. I'm here for the *experience*, honey, and you're just the gritty wallpaper of my hooker experiment. One day soon I'm going to walk out of this sad little apartment on grey, grey, grey Ocean Avenue and get on with my highly successful life. So that means I'm not letting that freak do me for some bad drugs, or some good ones either because I don't even do drugs. Can't you see he's not worth it, I asked them silently. Can't you see that nobody is worth it? *Please*. I thought I was special. And I just didn't understand their risk-taking. I'm still not sure that I do. Theirs, or mine.

Because now, at thirty years old, my escorting days long over, I've become an aggressive bareback bottom. I know, girl! Online hook-up after online hook-up, all I want is a bareback top. The phrase "Safe Only" has become such a turn-off. I have locked my condom drawer and slapped the hand of any top who dares go near it. If he does manage to get a condom on, I pull it right off and toss it aside (more on this later). *Wow, you really want it raw don't you baby?* Raw, don't you love that? *Oh yeah, my boipussy is begging for your big daddy cock.* As difficult as it is to believe, I have recently uttered those exact words. Girl, how did it come to this? How did I go from uptight hooker to wannabe cum dump, giving it away for free? I'm not sure and I don't know how to stop.

It's true, I have been a self-destructive girl, lately, for all the usual reasons: because I'm not happy, I'm depressed, I'm alone. There was a boyfriend a few years ago who gave me hope for something else. I thought: maybe I won't always be alone, after all, stepping in dog shit and falling down in the dark in Buena Vista Park. Was his name Paul? I can't remember now, but it was definitely a serious relationship. So of course we had unprotected sex because we were monogamous. Or so I thought, right? Now I'm not so sure. Like the time when we hadn't seen each other in two days and I started kissing him and he said he had just jerked off. He said he didn't know why. I didn't really believe him, but I didn't want to question him either. And that time at the Vietnamese restaurant when I told him I had been a hooker, because he wanted to know about my past and I wanted to shock him, and then he totally flipped out and laid in bed face-down all evening, but it wasn't because he wanted me to fuck him. The prissy, uptight girl that he loved was gone forever. But what he neglected to tell me then was that he had been a hooker too, and that his photo had been posted on one of the escorting websites the whole time we were together. Can you believe it? So many lies, girl. I was saving myself for this? Our relationship ended soon after my disclosure at the Vietnamese restaurant, with a burst of unexpected tears and sadness. I told Paul it wasn't working out, and there I was stumbling in the dark all over again.

But it was exhilarating to be independent again. I felt more confident about meeting new people and I was ready to try new things. For, like, a millisecond. In my attempt to escape the perils of Buena Vista Park, I ended up on one of those horrible online hook-up sites where it seemed like everyone was barebacking. After looking at the profiles for about six consecutive hours, I decided I wanted to join the party, too. I'm not masculine, the seemingly ubiquitous requirement for online hook-ups, but I am flexible and I was more than willing to prove it. The first guy from an online hookup to bareback me was a young medical doctor. Must be safe, right? The next one was a bit older and slightly conservative. Totally safe, I'm sure. The one after that was my neighbor from a couple blocks down the hill and he wouldn't lie, right? But is that facial wasting or just the signs of aging? Who can tell? Probably safe. The list just started getting longer and longer, and then there was no going back. It was similar to the measured risk of being a hooker: I'm going to take risks from which I get momentary pleasure that blurs the pain and nothingness of daily life, but I'm going to find ways to make it all safe, at least in my mind.

After barebacking for a while, I began to realize that I was narrowing my sights to Asian tops only. I was telling this to a friend, trying to figure out what it meant and why this felt safe to me. And she said well, statistically Asians do have lower rates of STDs. I took those unverified facts and ran with them, right back to my computer. I didn't tell her that I was the one who often initiated the unsafe sex. But it's true; I instigate unsafe sex with college-educated, professional, middle-class men of Asian descent. If he's got a master's degree from Harvard, I figure he doesn't have AIDS. That's my shaky logic. But I don't know if I really feel safer about STDs with Asian guys or if I just feel safer with them in general. Most of the Asian guys I meet seem less masculinity-obsessed. But there I go stereotyping again. I guess I like the idea of getting fucked by guys who those white, masculinity-obsessed "straight-acting jocks" would never consider possible tops. But when I'm searching for Asian tops on Craigslist, I worry that I'm a racist. I feel like I'm playing into the stereotype that all Asian guys want to have sex with white guys. And wouldn't it be an extra special privilege to bareback my white ass, too? So, you must say yes when I ask you to fuck me raw. This is the moment you've spent you're whole gay Asian existence waiting for. Fuck me raw because we're both in this together, both marginalized in the mainstream gay world, but obviously better than the rest of those barebacking whores.

But I don't advertise myself as a bareback bottom to these guys I meet online because only truly dirty whores do that. I want to bareback safely. Is that too much to ask? Like with this guy Peter who meets all the qualifications for, in my mind, safe barebacking. He's Asian, of course, well-educated, socially-conscious, drives a Saab, etc., but of course he is so perfect that he doesn't want to fuck me without a condom. So, in the spirit of flexibility I let him do me with a condom. I knew it wouldn't work. I knew I wouldn't feel desired in the way that I needed to. I asked him to stop for a second and then I took the condom off his cock, somehow thinking that he would be ready to bareback me, once he knew how good it felt to be inside me, right? I tried to get him to put it in my hole without the barrier, but no, he wasn't like that. So we tried again with another condom and then, amazingly, I did the same thing again. I pulled the condom off and tossed it aside and with it went my self-worth. It was just ridiculous. I wanted to curl up in a ball and cry. I felt so low. I didn't know how it had come to this. I was risking the possibility of a new relationship just for one night of barebacking. But I never really thought it would work out anyway, right? I mean, I don't think my life is going to work out. And maybe that's the real problem.

Peter was paranoid about the possibility of catching some nasty disease from me. He talked about all the people I had fucked before him and how, by having sex with me, he was having sex with them, too. He was considering whether to continue having sex with me at all. Girl, if he only knew how many men I've had sex with—safe and unsafe, and every combination imaginable—and I'm still here. I tried to explain to him that I'm not *really* a dirty whore. But then I thought wait, I'm really not different from those guys 12 years ago who were taking risks for drugs or money. I'm just taking risks with no real goal except for that elusive moment of connectedness.

REHAB FOR THE UNREPENTANT

Francisco Ibáñez-Carrasco

While screwing me hard, a fuckbud of mine often processes his life: a combination of urges, debts, hockey scores, and suburban heartaches. He makes me feel like one of those dime-a-dozen talk show counselors. Pinned down by his 30-something, 6'2' frame and 200 pounds of 100% Alberta beef it's hard to breathe, let alone give sound advice. At 45, 5'6" and 150 lbs, I am lithe but greedy. Yet Fuckbud seems angry at times, as if all he wants is to exorcise his homophobia by fucking me harder.

Like accidental airplane companions, fuckbuds often pour their hearts out to near strangers, knowing that danger laughs under the wings. Fuckbuds demand advice as a fringe benefit, give it till it hurts. Give advice and take some too, the hard way. If bad shit can happen at any time—say a plane crash or an infection—one must spit out the demons first. Infected queers know plenty about advice; in the 1980s, we outlined "safer sex" commandments almost exclusively for gay men. Some of my advice I pull out of my ass, some comes from years of teaching (ah the arrogance!), some from burning my eyelashes with porn pixels, teen magazines, and social science research I have to read at work. So, here is some of my philosophy, fibrillated under the weight of a fuckbud.

The bigger they are, the easier they roll over. This premise of sex between men has not faltered me yet. It works in gay environments as well as with heteros and it surely worked in the particular case of this fuckbud (and in the case of my manly handyman at home). Be it a biker, a stern leather dad, a trucker, or any big guy who looks towering and intimidating, rest assured that beneath the facade lies a man screaming to get his hole worked over. Get on your knees to give a non-threatening fellatio; thumb his rosebud slowly and feel the reaction—the sphincter muscle doesn't lie—slide under and in between his legs and eat the ass you will soon fuck tenderly!

I carry the curse of the queen: I am more often giving than getting. The big and young and beautiful all want to be cared for; they are infinitely vulnerable. Every stud can become high and available at 2 a.m.; he forgets he fucks the "clean and healthy" only.

"Cruising," that archaic, perilous roaming of the highways and streets, has gone virtual; hooking up online is efficient and spins a remix of the "private acts with public consequences" 1980s bit into a "public act with private consequences." Specialized sites for floggers, scatologists, or queer skinheads are like Sesame Street—everyone knows everyone else's "character." The same bullshit, fear, shame, and silence we have inherited as the 10% neurotic queer minority gushes through the veins of the internet. One is likely to encounter someone opposite from his virtual identity, or, even worse, a guy determined to check off each of the fantasy menu items he has listed online: "Now, let's do the enema scene, stop! Now, let's do the feltching, stop! Now, let's roleplay Nazi soldiers in heat!"

Boring! Specialized sites are populated by lonely gay men in kinky costumes fighting anxiety, fear, physical limitations, the effects of aging—or they are unripe yet equally lonely, playing the field/screen as videogame. The internet is a viral contagion slowly deteriorating the flesh of our community; no one will really meet with others anymore, no one will really infect anyone but himself. Hence my advice "the bigger they are, the easier they roll over" is followed by *cruise the ones in the flesh, not the ghosts on the internet*. I choose the sullen and standoffish—small Canadian towns seem full of them—they are often eager to be loved and fucked, just like you and me.

If you insist on using the internet to hook up, and if it means something that his pixx are not cut-out medical body parts without face, or that they were not taken in one drugged sex night years ago, that his advertised 9" is indeed erectable of natural causes, or that the guy is able to write half a sentence to save his life, you have to spell it out, but *don't ask for what you yourself can't give*. People online are terribly literal—they are literally full of shit or they literally do what they say they do. You want to put him to the test, make him call right away, meet you at the corner, act on it now. Most often, he will not call, and you will not dare to either; voices are far more revealing than internet images. If you get past my swishy voice putting on the leather top dad shtick, you are mine, baby!

The new millennium is rapid revolution without spirit, a spin cycle gone electronic. If you are HIV-poz, favor the old ways of finding lovers or fuckbuds, and you will get to the "negotiation" and "disclosure" part of the show much faster. And trust me, the unrepentant HIV-positive fag who insists on having a full sexual life is still the one expected to facilitate all negotiation. Getting in a stranger's car, going to a bathhouse, or scooting up to someone in a bar is terrifying but it gives you an immediate reality-check. How I met the Alberta truck driver I will never tell, but his wife was nearby, I can tell you that. And Steppenwolf was playing in the background.

My fuckbuddy dabbles in hard drugs during "high holidays" (long weekends and statutory holidays). It is eerie to help him push the plunger and see the cloud go into his vein bevel-up. A shroud casts upon his placid lake-gray eyes. He taught me to get hard on it and revel in the peculiar power and trust he gives me. I learned to slow down my morals. My advice is: *don't quit the drugs, but try and reduce the speed.* From social science research, we have clues that there are more of us in the poly-drug intermittent use category than fully addicted and doing a chicken dance in public. The technology of drugs is only bound to improve; the business side often booming as loneliness and anxiety keep on growing. We know that gay men who have survived stigma and the AIDS crisis, a number of whom are living with HIV, are vulnerable to using drugs to self-medicate, to combat depression and—perish the thought—to have fun. The point here is not the pernicious use of one single drug but the highly efficient social lubrication that drugs render, allowing us to mix and match and become fabulous in a world that craves the spectacular. Special athletes run marathons, Oprah tells us that 40 is the new 30, everyone wants to invert nature, so what is so odd about HIV-positive men wanting to experience surges of adrenaline, to glorify our survival through chemical regimens, to climb higher mountains of ecstasy? Overall, the human condition is lonely and greedy; we will always find ways to bend nature over and fuck it.

Advice: *don't fight your nature, but reduce the speed.* Once in a while, my fuckbud quits cold turkey and then shit happens, he gets depressed and calls in the middle of the night long-distance, tells me he beat up his wife or a tranny on the road, he spent too much money on a hooker or at the casino, got lost for days on the eternal prairie roads to Saskatchewan behind the wheel of his huge delivery lorry. Then he gets lonely and is shooting up again. He has it "under control," he says. Yeah, much the way he manages his man-on-man sex, I guess. Meth connects you anywhere, quickly, clearly, but the roaming calls can be costly—personal system crashes are common. My advice: *get a religion, meditate, move somewhere else for a while, lose the number for your supplier.* Or get a fuckbud on the side to witness the margins of your life. Someone to take a snapshot of how you look or give you the rundown of what you have become once in a while, someone to make you human.

Easy to write, and hard to accomplish. Using and detoxing is human, slowing down is divine. In Canada we call it "harm reduction," although the current Tory federal government is getting rid of this progressive health approach. Harm reduction is not easy when one is beaten down by depression, debts, aging, unwanted weight gain, problems with employment, fucked-up family memories, or future uncertainty. Advice: *get help from those who don't want to change you*. I keep this fuckbud separate from the rest of my world—no promises, no regrets, love is a battlefield. I accept that we will always live separate lives. I accept that sexual diversity is still only a vision and that "think globally, act locally" might be the least harmful action. I accept the contradiction of witnessing a magnificent animal dissolve like accelerated pixels on a hazy screen, and doing nothing about it.

Living with HIV = Living with Drugs. Granted, highly active antiretroviral treatment (HAART) is a combination of prescription drugs; however, like any other chemical cure, it puts us in a crowd—along with seniors and youth, and desperate suburban wives—inclined toward self-medicating and taking risks harder than bungee jumping or excessive plastic surgery. We take pills to get it up, pills to bring it down; we mix and match our drugs like sophomores. In the same vein, living with illness is living with pain. In one lifetime, I have had Kaposi's, Herpes Zoster, and Hepatitis C with its companionship of chemotherapy, radiation, amphetamines, morphine, and Interferon. Using illicit drugs is an extension of therapy, cosmetology of the mind, the individualization of medicine, the consumer's right. Accessing alternative forms of pain with temporary piercings, tattoos, flogging, breath control and the like is an extension of what we must do well: manage pain. Western media glorifies shooting, punching, fucking, and speeding, right? Why then such big fuss about HIV-poz guys getting high and barebacking? Why then such horror at poz men stretching the limits of endurance while suspended in slings? Poz men, however, are still terribly misunderstood, most of all by other queers, cloaked as they come in their little fears.

"Who is really at an infection risk here? Whose fantasy are we milking?" I said once to my fuckbud. "The fact is that those of us on HAART are physically safer than any straight man on the downlow." Fuckbud lost his vigor on that occasion. One can't fuck something so scientific. Choosing to live in a duplicitous world to which I contribute willingly, I respect his choice not to participate in such controversy. That day, he pulled out without juicing up my ass, leaving me wanting my dose of so-called intimacy. Who in their right mind chooses to speak about this while getting fucked anyway?! Guys write "healthy and clean" in their fastidious internet profiles, resenting the fact that we, the polluted, give it and take it raw. Hypocrisy makes us risk-takers, ambivalent. The clean and healthy are often the ones who crave it raw. HIV-positives, the druggies, the sexual radicals are often erected as sexual terrorists marching armed dicks in hand, shooting into a place filled with innocent bystanders. We annihilate all illusion of what is right, pure and beautiful in gay spaces. Our reality is a garish, bloated, complicated piñata you head towards with your little stick.

I choose others' loathing, not pity. HIV-positive queers live with the scorn, contempt, resentment and sometimes envy of our peers. I'm not sure what the stats are in each country, but for me it feels like being the 10% HIV+ inside the Kinsey 10%; there is no wonder poz fags seek each other out, in riskier situations, testing our physical and psychological limits. In the illusory market of gay sex, sullied queers have fluctuating currency. We end up entangled with fuck buddies like mine, with no interest in migrating to the gay side, ever. It is not uncommon that we branch out to a meat market even when risks of violence and illness are high, when the legal system has started to prosecute us as sex criminals, and when the potential for finding a long-term partner, a family, or a reciprocal relationship may be nil. I am fortunate to have a companion with whom I create family, but the parameters of our relation are queer, not heteronormative.

Have you ever been fucked by a portentous but whiny Caribou? When my fuckbud boohoos about his current wife, how little pussy she gives him, about the cost of living and his growing kids, the local hockey team's dismal scores, or taxes, I get impatient. The ride is interminable (yes!) and monotonous (no!). Once, I called him a greedy slut, "getting all the action you want, in all fronts, you can live normal." Silence. He halted the jack-hammering for a moment, and then resumed it vigorously. "Say something, you fucking closeted fag," I screamed (it seemed like something Kate Jackson would have yelled in *Making Love* in 1982). "Have some HAART, will you?" I added this cryptic line for mere affect, knowing full well that it was probably incomprehensible. He lunged a fist at me, quick and hard. We both, in different kinds of pain, lay down into silence again. He didn't leave.

My advice: *seek men of your own soul age*; be aware that time still brings about experience and forgiveness and sweet cool revenge, that dreams do come true but not in the way you ever suspected. It really is about wisdom—the flattery and the abuse of a small infected urban queer daddy gets men off big time. Sigh! One more man looking to resolve his father figure issues on my back. That day, his come print was bigger than the carbon print left behind by his hauling truck. Unlike other times, we didn't march into the bathroom to wash off the remains of the deed with gestures of misplaced apprehension and religious hangover. We both laid there, side-by-side in awkward silence. Intimate for the first time.

HIV-positive men serve in public but in silence: facing this fact is facing the spirit of our loneliness. Our HAART-lipoatrophied faces indicate a silent apartheid of desire that remains solidly installed in queer sexual cultures. Although the virus in our blood might be undetectable, on the surface our wiry gargoyle bodies are the radicalized gaze of queer desire. No matter how much I work out, inject steroids, fight my body, my body is not seen as normal in the queer spaces where it should be. The unrepentant, HIV-poz or not, are like gargoyles—grotesque, campy, kitschy figures that project from the gutter of a building to cast away rainwater or raw fluids. We protect you even as we scare you.

For a while my fuckbud and I will continue to hide behind fear and silence, until we find ways of accepting ourselves. He: his closets, his drug use, his risks, his sexual contradictions, his emotional compartmentalization, his vulnerability to my infectious and illegal charms. Me: my internalized (self-)hatred and my unfathomable voracity. Some days it seems that we understand each other; we were born alone to live strangers amongst strangers. One day, Fuckbud started murmuring lines of a Robert Service poem he had learned on a trip to the Yukon about "a race of men that don't fit in, a race that can't stay still; so they break the hearts of kith and kin, and they roam the world at will." I almost lost my straddling, I mean, in my condescension I didn't even know he could read! The moment passed, he did not let me kiss him more once the drug high was over or we were pummeled by the boiling shower to erase all traces of sex; but I have the moment of recognition to treasure.

I am skeptical of all Judeo-Christian angst about disclosures and coming-outs but never cynical of love. Maybe I am superstitious, and love is superstition, standing in awe of each other without theory, technique or technology. Even in silence, my advice is: *don't mess with love*. It allows us to reinvent ourselves away from the daily grind—the family, the medical appointments, all the menial things that remind us 24/7 that we are nothing but a system of suppressed immunity. In fact, we model resilience. I get busy somewhere else; so does my fuckbud; so does my partner. Compassion fills the days with gentle reasons to carry on. We focus on what keeps us together. In ten years my partner and I have settled in serene pools of compassionate silence, into a sexless marriage. Ah! Such ghastly taboo for gays barely glued by curdling protein.

Two men sharing a life together needs to remain abnormal; what really binds us is not sex but love in the face of fear, risk, and danger. Existing

REHAB FOR THE UNREPENTANT

with this abnormality is what makes us a queer couple or fuckbuds—the tacit bargaining, the willingness to witness each other's lives and not know absolutely everything, not to pretend that the other person can meet my every need, assuage my sidereal loneliness, that is true, that is love. The true rehabilitation for the unrepentant in you, in me, is not the eradication of all risky behavior but the injection of love in whatever you do—ejaculate in a raw ass, kiss and drink from him all night, engage in the trafficking of illusions on the internet, wait for the inhalation, ingestion, or injection. This is not soft-porn romantic, this is hard-boiled love infecting everything we do, always awake and often persisting.

I'LL TELL YOU WHAT I WANT, WHAT I REALLY REALLY WANT: HOMOLOVE AND ACCOUNTABILITY

Harris Kornstein

I'm lying on my back in my best friend Jeff's room. He's sitting on my chest, legs resting on either side of my small but chubby torso. He pins my arms up above my head with one hand, leaving his other hand free for gentle slapping and rough poking (he's always been stronger than me). Then again, maybe I'm not resisting. Maybe I want my hands to stay put, in a pose that indulges both an attitude of damsel-in-distress and acquiescence. My fingers swim through the tan carpet, grabbing shag that's caught too much dirt over the years, making it rough and clumpy. It reminds me of my grandma's rug, only hers is older and clumpier; this one somehow doesn't fit in Jeffrey's otherwise white and sterile suburban home. Jeffrey puts his hand over my mouth and playfully tells me, "just breathe through your nose." Next, he grabs my wrist and uses it to slap me in the face, taunting, "why are you hitting yourself?" When I pretend I'm mad at him later, he tells me all I had to do was ask him to "please stop." Jeffrey's not a bully—he's my best friend. We're ten years old.

Jeffrey and I met at a local summer camp after kindergarten, where we performed together in *A Chorus Line*. Wearing gold top hats, we sang "One Singular Sensation" in a chorus while demonstrating our best high kicks, and at the end I got to stick my arm out dramatically and say "That's all folks!" (I don't think that Jeffrey ever got over his jealousy, though he'd eventually play the lead in high school musicals.) Later that year, we found each other on the same bus to first grade and instantly became best friends.

Our friendship flourished through our bar mitzvahs, when he wrote in a card that I was "like a brother" to him.

Another memory: this time, I'm sleeping over. It's the middle of the night, and it must be summer because I'm on the top bunk wearing only a teal oversized t-shirt and underpants. After we've heard the "lights out" warning and finished our giggling and gossip, I'm ready to sleep but Jeffrey starts up a game of stealing things from my bed: first the thin fuzzy blanket, then the sheet and pillows. I probably just laugh and whisper at him to stop. I'm worried that his parents will yell at us, so I eventually de-escalate the game by trying to fall asleep despite his antics. I don't remember how it happens, but eventually he pulls my shirt off, leaving me shivering, the air conditioning rapidly cooling my naked skin. I may or may not yet be embarrassed by my chunkiness, but I know that boys aren't supposed to look at or care too much about each others' bodies. And besides, I still have my underwear on—the thin, white cotton that covers my most private of parts. Our ruckus wakes up his parents, and his dad makes him sleep in his sister's room. I'm embarrassed. I don't know what his dad is thinking. And even though Jeff gets most of the punishment, I've clearly lost the game too.

* * * * *

I was never a very sexual kid, or teenager for that matter—I didn't even masturbate until I was nineteen and away at college. I never thought of my childhood play as being overtly sexual either, at least not until recently. Nothing ever got so far as hand jobs backstage, "cornholing" at bedtime, or even furtive kisses by the piano, as many of the gay novels and memoirs I've read would suggest. Instead, my time with Jeffrey as a kid usually centered around stuffed animals, video games, and elaborate scenes of make-believe based on magical powers. Yet I can't (and don't want to) ignore those hazy memories—my shirt coming off or him sitting on top of me—that were not necessarily an exception, but instead secret parts of the fantasies and worlds we imagined as kids at play. Perhaps Jeff had a stronger desire than me for rough play, since his two older sisters bored him with talk about horses, *Saved By The Bell*, and heartthrob Jonathan Taylor Thomas. And maybe I, as the oldest of three boys, liked the chance to feel vulnerable, to shriek submissively, to resist without meaning it (or without it meaning anything). But beyond the shady explanations of pop psychology and birth order theories, I wonder about the details of our motivations and desires that we didn't seem to understand then, and I'm not even sure we can now.

I don't recall ever talking about these moments with Jeff—or with anyone else, for that matter—what was there to say? Nothing came across as wrong, nothing seemed to cross boundaries, and nothing felt confusing. We simply played our games and enjoyed each other's company without a need to process, or a desire to ask for more. But there's a part of me that now worries that I've forgotten exactly what and how things happened, that wants to invent something more explicit, and that yearns to know exactly why and when we eventually stopped. Did we lose interest in each other's bodies (or were we never really interested to begin with)? Were we each afraid to make the next move? Did we feel any shame then, or is that something we learned as we got older? Most importantly, why do these moments feel so important now?

Jeffrey and I eventually became a trio with the inclusion of Brad, a short kid who liked to draw and shared our interest in things related to magic and other worlds. Looking back, we were from day one something of a ragamuffin posse of baby fags—a tap dancer (Jeffrey), an illustrator (Brad), and a figure skater (me)—who artfully dodged the expectations of grade school masculinity by choosing arts over sports and closeness over competition. Our friendship was solidified in riding the bus to Hebrew School once a week, where we were all in the same class (a treat that never happened in day school). We created an identity for our trio by combining parts of our last names, and kept journals and sketchbooks where we wrote down jokes copied from TV and practiced drawing cartoon characters. We would beg our parents to let us have sleepovers with all three of us; sometimes even two nights in a row. We spent hours inventing superheroes, creating trading cards and spell books, and acting out games we invented, borrowing characters and scenarios from our favorite modes of fiction. Each of us chose a preferred niche or persona in a given narrative: a magical power, a favorite video game fighter, or a character in *The Wizard of Oz*.

Brad and I interacted in ways that were different from my time spent with Jeffrey. While Jeff and I were both excited about theater and school, Bradley and I shared a similar sense of humor and an interest in drawing. My relationship with Brad was also less physical, likely because it seemed that Jeffrey tended to initiate things, usually only when we were one-on-one. But he did fool around with Brad too. I have a hazy memory of a conversation with Brad about how Jeffrey was "too rough," and maybe even an intervention we staged directly with him. As a group, our tension generally centered around petty, girly, friend drama—who classified whom as a best friend, who got invited to what, who took credit for an idea. In fifth grade, as pressure grew to act cool, and as we found ourselves spending more time with each other in school and play rehearsals, we had a series of small but dramatic fights. Once, Brad threw his prized *Lion King* sticker book at me on the playground—which broke, and he blamed me—while Jeffrey ran off and cried.

Eventually, we got over most of our drama and the three of us stayed close throughout middle school, working the Electric Slide on the Bar Mitzvah circuit. In eighth grade, we all fell in love with the Spice Girls, each claiming a favorite and creating our own pseudonyms (my favorite: Mel B; my name: "Smarty Spice"). We ripped pictures of Hanson from teenybopper magazines to trade with girls in our respective homerooms for an endless array of Spice Girls pin-ups. Our drawings turned from the magic of wizards and the musculature of superheroes to the curves of these women's bodies, and, most importantly, getting the details right on the tiny outfits and gigantic shoes that adorned them. We were occasionally accused of being gay for our interest in the Spice Girls—and, given our various commitments to such activities as the spring musical and figure skating, as well as swishy walks and high voices (of which I was the most guilty), this was not the only clue or ammunition—but we brushed it off by explaining that we were totally hot for these pop stars. I recall desperately trying to turn myself on by staring at my *Tiger Beat* pull-out poster of Scary and Ginger in bras and hotpants. After all, as a generous classmate once rebutted in our defense, "Hello, how can they be gay if they're obsessed with *women*!?"

It was around this time that I had the first overtly sexual experience that I can remember. I was home alone one day after school and came across a bodybuilding competition on ESPN. I stopped flipping channels, and instead ogled the parade of men in their tiny, shiny swimsuits as they struck slow, confident poses, and rearranged their bodies to highlight one bulge after another (similar, yet different from those of the Spice Girls). After a while, I realized that I was hard—very hard—harder than I'd ever been before. Surely I'd had erections pop up every now and then, but they seemed to come and go on their own, not related to anything or anyone in particular. I certainly knew what they were, and to some extent how they worked, and repeated jokes about them and rumors about who saw whom with what size boner. But this was the first moment that it actually made sense as something that happened to me *for a reason*. I felt scared and embarrassed, betrayed by my body and confused by its reactions. Was I attracted to these men's sculpted bodies, their legs and nipples indulgently displayed before me in ways that were generally reserved for women? Or was I turned on by their signification of strength and masculinity, by the violence and power I knew they could yield, like the X-Men and Street

Fighters? I wanted to know if there was hope for me, a short chubby boy who played with My Little Pony and wore ballet leotards as a kid, to somehow achieve this kind of masculinity, both in body and status.

As high school drew nearer, we started learning what it meant to be popular and found ourselves making new friendships that sometimes gelled, but often didn't. We bought new clothes at the approved stores in the mall, watched *Dawson's Creek*, and started caring about what kind of music we listened to (hello Third Eye Blind, goodbye Spice Girls). It was also the time for dates and friendships with girls, which meant sitting next to your girlfriend at lunch (this wasn't hard, since we generally ate at the "girls table" anyway), calling her on the phone, and stepping awkwardly together at school dances. Another friend of ours invited us to sleepovers where we'd try to make out the scrambled images on the porn channels, pretending to see things the others couldn't. But growing up and trying to be popular also meant keeping secrets from and inventing things about one another as we aspired to perform the related modes of popularity and straight masculinity. Brad and I started referring to Jeff as "Stacey" behind his back—an attempt to emasculate him—and Brad reported finding gay porn on Jeffrey's computer (to this day, I'm not sure if this was fact or fiction). That was the first instance, in any context, that the term "gay" surfaced within our once-tight circle.

There's a part of me that's shocked by how easily we learned to throw around words like "gay" and "fag," attempting to hurt and discredit the others without tarnishing or implicating ourselves. While this is clearly how teenage straight masculinity is performed (oh, how I avoided locker rooms), I'm not sure how we thought we could get away with it when we were each failing in almost every way. We weren't friends with the popular kids who called us all fags, and we didn't really want to be—yet still we started rumors and tried to build strategic alliances in the halls of middle school. Why did we turn against each other, and what were we afraid of when it came to our relationships? Homophobia, external and internalized, is an easy answer, but one that feels too superficial and dissatisfying. Writing it off as childish doesn't seem to be useful either. It may be silly and moot to expect my fourteen-year-old self to have acted more responsibly, but there's a part of me that can't help romanticizing this moment as a potential time for rebellion, that knows that "it could have all been different" if we had been able to draw strength from each other rather than trying to win the usual games that we were always already set up to lose.

After middle school graduation, Jeffrey and I literally didn't speak for an entire year—summer vacation provided a good break for us, as he went his way and I went mine. And though the start of a new school year—with many shared classes and friends—could have yielded a new opportunity for us to reconnect, we still couldn't find the right words, or even the strength to look each other in the eye. It was, in many ways, a particularly hard year for me, but it also created space to explore new interests, to become politicized, and to find more confidence in myself. Eventually Jeff and I made up, not by working through our issues but by ignoring them and agreeing to put the past behind us. As a result, I'm still left with questions of who said what, whose feelings were hurt, and why exactly we needed that year of silence. Did Brad and I reject Jeffrey because he was too much of a liability, or did he reject us because we'd ganged up on him? Or had we just spent too much time with each other, and needed some time to ourselves, like our parents used to tell us when it was time to go home?

As high school went on, Jeffrey, Brad, and I remained friendly, though I would always be closer to each of them individually than they were to each other. We each moved in slightly different directions and into new cliques as our interests became more nuanced. We also each dated girls at various points, though nothing was ever too serious or sexual. For the most part, we avoided sex talk, clearly disinterested in and embarrassed by girls' bodies and what we were supposed to do with them. In one of the few exceptions, Jeffrey confessed how much he liked his girlfriend of several months, but how he just wasn't sure how to make the first move. (Honey, please!)

In this way, I suppose we offered a sort of tacit support to each other—finding and creating spaces in which we didn't need to brag about sexual conquests or perform a normative masculinity. Instead, we allowed ourselves to indulge in unpopular interests, express ideas and politics, and be friends with each other and with women without having to be sexual. And yet, this support was clearly built on a foundation of fear and vulnerability, paradoxically enacted in silences, in choosing to disregard our own desires and suppress our suspicions and histories. Certainly this was a way of getting through adolescence, though it was strictly a mode of survival, not self-empowerment or social transformation. Perhaps we were not only afraid of being "found out," afraid of the repercussions of being gay in a conservative community; we were also afraid of our proximity to one another—that one outing would lead to another, that we knew we were more of a target collectively than we were individually. More importantly, however, I believe we feared the questions that we would have to answer to ourselves: what were our true feelings toward one another? What did those childhood games involve, and what else might we have suppressed or forgotten? What did we really fight about? How had we failed one another?

It wasn't until I got to college that I finally came out to Jeffrey and Brad, with the safety of a couple hundred miles between us. I don't recall these conversations in detail, but I do know that they both gave me support and told me it wasn't much of a surprise (oh really?). But, there was no talk about their own feelings or questions, and no talk about our pasts together. Jeffrey came out to me about a year and a half later, in the middle of an argument about a homophobic email he'd sent me. I'd been cheekily replacing my usual email closing of "love" with "homolove," and he wrote me back a rant about how I didn't need to reduce my identity to queerness. I was pissed, and argued with him about how that was a homophobic thing to say, especially coming from someone who identified as straight. He told me he felt like I was trying to imply something specific with the phrase "homolove," trying to draw him out of the closet. I hadn't been, but then I asked him. I apologized for my point-blank question, but felt worse about the circumstances of our argument than my need to know. We kept arguing about whether his comments were homophobic when coming from a gay man (yes!), and thus began our never-ending disagreements about liberation, gay politics, and the use of the term fag.

It was about another year and a half before Brad came out, at a point when I was beginning to have my doubts that it would happen. He told me during our walk home from my twenty-second birthday party, and I said it was the greatest present I could have wished for. We spent a couple hours tipsily talking about how good he felt to have finally said it, our childhoods, how alone we'd felt, and some of the drama we'd started with one another. It was a productive conversation, but also superficial at times: we looked back at moments that were "so gay," and talked about how "terrible" it was that we turned against each other, and how people in high school thought we were a couple. We talked a bit about Jeff and how it was "weird, but made sense" that we were all friends growing up. I asked him if he'd ever been attracted to me (no), and confessed that I was momentarily attracted to him in college (awkward). I asked him if we could talk about what he was attracted to in men and he said he didn't want to—he said he wasn't quite sure what turned him on. After graduation, Brad went to Scotland and I moved to California; he called me to tell me about the first time he made out with a boy. Neither Brad nor Jeffrey officially came out to the other (but word does get around, girl).

* * * * *

I'm interested in exploring my earliest relationships because they continue to hold so many possibilities. I'm fascinated by the fact that, though I've shared so much (explicitly and quietly) with Brad and Jeffrey, there are many things that even now we don't want or don't know how to say. Despite, or perhaps because of, our closely connected pasts, we still seem to make each other vulnerable, to fear each other more than others. Perhaps our shame is buried deeper than we think.

While I may wish that I'd shared youthful homo pleasure or power with Jeffrey and Brad, I also realize that in many ways I still lack a sense of knowledge and confidence in how to interact with other fags, especially when it comes to negotiating the sticky boundaries between friendship and sex. And I don't think I'm the only one. How many opportunities are missed because they don't fit our expectations? How often do we hold back for fear of what our honesty might yield? Only recently have I found myself able to talk to friends (and only certain ones) about things that feel private and embarrassing—what porn I like, how I masturbate, and what scares and excites me about making a move. In my mind, these conversations begin to make up for the chats with older brothers I never had—or for the locker room talk that, while often exaggerated or offensive, also has the potential to be instructional and co-mentoring. For me, it's a consciousness—equal parts sisterhood and solidarity—wherein I try to get deeper than "he's hot," to not be afraid to call a friend "honey," and to talk explicitly about my feelings and politics.

* * * * *

Though we continue to live in different cities, I still see Jeff and Brad at least a couple times each year, and we're in consistent (if not frequent) touch. As we continue to explore new identities and communities, we each have new stories to tell, and our fantasies have largely shifted from magic to men. Last summer, Jeffrey and I went camping, and as we slept on a cold campground surrounded only by trees and cows, it was one of the first times that we talked about our sex lives in any personal detail. We discussed our feelings on dry humping, realized that his negative reaction to the word "fag" was met by my disgust with certain euphemisms for cock ("sword?" how medieval, masculine, and vulgar!), and vented about how difficult we find it to negotiate sex and dating, given our respective fears and hang-ups. Brad also recently visited me, perfectly timed to make a pilgrimage to see the Spice Girls' reunion tour (quite literally a second chance at something we never thought we'd have). I was surprised by how excitedly he accepted my proposal to go dancing on the first night of his visit, given his reluctance a year earlier to even enter gay spaces. I was even more surprised to discover how bold he acted, and was excited (and jealous) to see him hooking up with a noticeably older guy when I returned from the bathroom. As we headed home much later that night, he told me about what happened, how gently they had held each other, and how he was much more interested in cuddling than coming.

In thinking about these conversations, I take delight in recognizing the aspects of each of our personalities, our logics, and our values that haven't changed since we were kids. But more importantly, I find pleasure in realizing that our closeness to each other is no longer something we have to fear.

IT GETS BETTER?

Matthew D. Blanchard

In early October 2007, I was discovered alone and on the brink of death, after what doctors now believe must have been ten to twelve days of comatose confinement. I had apparently fallen unconscious, laying face down in bed with the side of my head pressed slack-jawed against a dirty pillow. In a painfully contorted position, I allowed eminently dangerous bacteria to enter my mouth through the constant stream of saliva that dripped between my lips and cheek. Alone in my bed, just days after my twenty-eighth birthday, I was stricken with an overdose-induced, HIV/AIDS-related PCP pneumonia and necrotizing bacterial infection of the face.

The San Francisco Fire Department busted down my door in response to an anonymous call, to find me covered in my own vomit, urine, and defecation. My face was blackened by corrosive decomposition, and all but nine of my teeth had fallen out. I was rushed to the nearest emergency care unit. For eight weeks, I remained in a medically-induced coma. After some quick and effective lifesaving maneuvers (i.e., blood transfusions, dialysis, wound care, heavy doses of antibiotics), doctors stabilized my fading heart; brain activity restored.

A team of San Francisco's leading diagnosticians, doctors, and surgeons fought valiantly, yet failed to defeat the necrotizing bacteria which infected my face. Their only option, in order to ensure my survival, was to perform an emergency debridement surgery. In effect, the greater portion of my upper jaw, mouth and nose were amputated, leaving a gaping hole in the middle of my face.

Plastic surgeons replaced the missing portion of my upper mouth and jaw with skin and bone grafts from my lower left leg. An 8"x16" slab of flesh eight layers deep was ripped from my calf, sutured and sewn inside and over the opening in my face, but only after a six-inch section of my left fibula was sawed off and screwed flat to the remaining portion of my jaw, forever destroying its natural curvature.

Early on in the reconstruction process, my surgeons told me flat-out, "You will never look normal again." When I asked if I would ever be able to smile, they responded with a long, awkward silence, and then one of them said, "You *will* be able to express happiness." As if that was any consolation!

Since waking from sedation, I wear surgical masks to hide my monstrous face from the curious, insensitive scrutiny of the public: the bystander, the spectator, the voyeur. Tragically yet tenaciously, I am learning to accept my new face and its continuing transformations. It has been an unspeakably difficult experience living through disfigurement, but I maintain hope and grace, courage and pride, and a damned dutiful determination in life, that I may live once again in pure and unabashed beauty. Beauty eternal! Beauty internal!

Suffering through a childhood and adolescence of incessant ridicule & fag-baiting, I planned my escape from the double-locked and triple-chained closets of conservative Southeastern Virginia. My choice to remain in Virginia to attend university was a decision I regretted for a very long time. During my freshman and sophomore years of college, I remained stubbornly closeted, despite the constant haranguing and harassment, not by homophobic straight students, but by the queer kids on campus. Early on in my freshman year—within weeks of my arrival—my loosely veiled cyberspace identity was discovered by a very "out, proud and loud" queer classmate of mine. After recognizing some photos I had posted of myself in Gay.com chat rooms, he wrote to me, threatening to expose me to our entire community. Then, he did just that!

The aggressively dispassionate and unsympathetic queer kids on campus ridiculed me incessantly. Bred to condemn and constantly contradict all accusations against my good Catholic, conformist upbringing, I adamantly maintained that I was not in any way a "faggot." Homosexuality was a sin!

I begged the culprits guilty of gay-on-gay cyber-bullying and rumor-mongering to let me be free to live my life at its own normal pace. I did not want them to force me out of the closet sooner than I felt comfortable enough to break down its doors. I especially did not want people telling me who and what I was before I had decided for myself.

I continued to traipse around in cyberspace chat rooms hunting for acceptance, enlightenment, and fulfillment of my unbridled lust. Still, I remained closeted; and in an undeniably defensive maneuver, I began to comport myself publicly with a conscious "better than thou" air. I recoiled further into the enticing yet destructive sexual subculture of gay cyberspace. Welcomed into the open arms of a whole different brand of hateful, dispassionate, and unsympathetic gay youth and men, I fell into the habit of clandestine weekend trips to Washington, D.C. for extended sessions of "party 'n' play." I frolicked there in the unabashed bacchanalia of sex parties where drugs were lavished upon me and condoms were rarely in sight.

Yearning dearly for the opportunity to accept and explore my sexuality more fully and openly, I decided to spend my junior year abroad, studying in Paris, France. There, in the "City of Lights," I discovered bathhouses and boyhood romance; mature, adult love, and mutual adoration. I returned to Virginia ready to throw my unremittingly out and loud gay pride in the faces of all those ferocious dykes and fags on campus who had tormented me the prior year, but disaster was looming. My final semester of university study was tragically interrupted by some devastating news, news that I had come to expect. On February 13, 2002, I called in to an anonymous HIV testing center to obtain my results. Sure enough, I was diagnosed positive. In an attempt to act responsibly after the fact, I notified each of my sex partners of my seroconversion, including two gay students on campus. Word spread fast!

In order to brutally expose my whorish escapades and deviance to the world, anonymous groups of antigay, AIDS-phobic bashers and trashers began to commit crimes of pure, unrelenting hatred against me. The ostracization I had first experienced as a "holier than thou" homo-hater was carved into the cement stone of the cinderblock walls of my dormitory hallways, tacked to my door in scribbled sketches of guns, nooses, and scathing epithets; sliced and slashed into all four of my car tires, and tagged in soap on my car windshield: A.I.D.S. WHORE! A.I.D.S. VERMIN! QUEER SLUT! YOU KILLED MY BOYFRIEND!!

Needless to say, the hatred aimed at me by the kids on campus at the time of my diagnosis translated into my own vehement contempt and hatred of the greater LGBTQ culture and community. My unmitigated misery as victim to this venomous hatred in turn intensified my suppressed queer kid self-loathing. In a last-ditch effort to free myself from such disgrace, discrimination and persecution by my peers, but tortured by the truth in queer kid judgments of my sexual irresponsibility, I fled cross-country. Amongst the ultra-liberal, gay-friendly folk of Northern California, I hoped to find the love and acceptance that had eluded me most of my young life.

I arrived in San Francisco with two hundred dollars in my wallet and all my earthly possessions consolidated into three suitcases, a duffel bag, a portfolio, and a computer case. I did not know anyone, and I had nowhere to go. After spending three days and two nights sleeping on the vinyl cushions of the waiting room chairs at San Francisco International Airport, I desperately dug into my pockets to spend the last few ounces of cash I could spare on an hour or two of exorbitantly expensive internet access.

While researching HIV/AIDS homeless youth organizations in the Bay Area for resources and linkages to housing and medical care, I returned concurrently to the gay sexual subculture of cyberspace in search of a one-night destination. The investigation into resources and linkages required most of my cyber minutes, but finding a fuck buddy was quick and easy.

As I mattress-hopped from one anonymous hookup's house to another, my continuing internet research during daylight hours soon paid off. I found Bay Area Young Positives (BAY Positives) online at the ripe age of twenty-three, when my hormones were high and mighty and my manhood potent and preserved. BAY Positives was able to assist me in finding permanent housing, public health care, and world-class social welfare services. I became a member, a volunteer, and then eventually joined the staff of the agency. As a gay youth living with HIV/AIDS, my involvement in the organization was primarily social, but I also became the capricious prodigal son of BAY Positives. After a short period as a client of the agency, I presented to the executive staff a detailed review of the organization's operations. My hopes were to help renovate the structure and function of BAY Positives in order to improve member relations & morale: I wanted the agency to shift away from viewing queer youth as passive clients to a focus on empowering queer youth to become participatory members.

Once my evaluation reached the desk of the Board President, the majority of the staff began to coddle my ego with empty praise. Their *laissez-faire* attitude and inaction nevertheless persisted; my suggestions of program and policy enhancements were ignored as baseless criticisms by everyone in the organization, except for my one lone supporter: Curtis Moore. A queer Afro-Caribbean Canadian with a Master's in Public Health, Moore was well aware of both the pain of ostracism and the potentials of youth empowerment, and welcomed with pleasure and aplomb each of my critical remarks. He went to great lengths to guide me in the composition of a written proposal. He promised to me that even if change didn't occur immediately, it would eventually happen just as I had envisioned it.

BAY Positives has indeed, through the tough-knuckled knock-downs of financial adversity, succeeded in its once tentative and now resolute transition. Curtis Moore is now the Executive Director, and BAY Positives no longer operates as a provisory client-based agency, but rather as a participatory organization focused on the education, advocacy and empowerment of its "members" as youth leaders in HIV/AIDS prevention. As my one true advocate through years of turmoil and tragedy, Moore has helped to cultivate and nurture in me a profound sense of philanthropy, volunteerism and altruism. He has taught me to be tolerant, loving, and charitable in spite of the immensity of my own suffering. I am indeed proud to call Curtis a friend, colleague, caregiver, and the primary agent of my final health directives.

My road from homeless destitution to professional development and leadership in this Fog City, however, was certainly marred by successive scrapes and stumbles. Early on, as a lowly client of BAY Positives, I remember witnessing the demise of nearly a dozen of my drugged-out, sex-crazed peers and playmates. We were all to-die-for adorable at twenty-something; each of us boys (and grrrls!) had climbed mountains in our Sisyphean struggle out of "Southern cruelty" and queer kid condemnations, and into the loving arms of San Francisco's skid row SROs. We naively assumed that "It Gets Better," but it never did.

Some of us celebrated drag princess pastiche or twink boy sex-tape stardom; some of us wanted to save the world through political action, civil rights coalitions or artistic agitprop performance cooperatives. We had all escaped the torment and turmoil of "home," searching for freedom and romance among the infamous hills, valleys and serpentine streets of San Francisco. Little did we know that we would instead be welcomed into the arms of a chaotically corrupt, crystal-lined, tina-torn, AIDS-quilted gay mecca.

For homeless and runaway queer youth, schooled in street-corner sustenance and leaning against colorful-but-uncomfortable walls, acceptance into the straight-laced gay social scene is damned near impossible. Nevertheless, I do remember one twink twenty-something friend of mine who scaled those walls with fiendish fervor and ease.

"Mr. Infectious," a name I give him more for his serostatus than for his contagiously pleasant personality, just happened to suffer from sociopathic sex addiction coupled with preposterously compulsive prevarication. We met for the first time at the first and only BAY Positives Monday Night Support Group he attended. We were both cute and charismatic; I quickly fell in love with his gusto. He seemed to appreciate the meek virtue of my loyalties.

His golden ticket into the "straight as a cockatoo" community of charming and cultured, career-oriented gay men was not his garishly gorgeous gay boy physique or his beaming baby blue eyes, but his gargantuan cock, and the millions of tricks he could play with it. After the support group meeting, he admitted to me privately that he didn't like people knowing he was positive. He figured that if guys knew he had HIV, then they sure as hell wouldn't let him fuck them. After all, he would "*only* fuck bare!" Such was his mantra, his calling. Whether this was due to the discomfort of latex too tightly sheathing his giant cock or because he was in fact a sociopathic seeder who got off on infecting new and unknowing victims with disease, I never knew.

After the meeting, he confessed that he thought I was the one attractive guy in the support group. "The rest of them homos were dog ugly," he teased! We did end up fucking that night. He made me bleed puddles from my anus, so he promised we would never do it again. We were now blood brothers, best friends! "BFF's don't fuck," he mused.

For the next two-and-a-half years, we were pretty much two peas in a pod. We hit the pipe and sex-parties together, never fucking one-on-one but always watching and egging each other on. We both were natural exhibitionists and enjoyed watching one another fuck and fill the nice, tight ass of some unsuspecting bareback bottom boy. We'd often egg each other on with hot, sultry sex talk while he was fucking or I was getting fucked. Sometimes, we'd even tag-team side-by-side in a four-or-more way, belting out cheers of encouragement. "Take that big fat dick, you cock-crazed, cum-hungry cunt boy," he'd yell my way, while he was fucking some random hottie next to me. "Fuck the faggot like you mean it, you whore," I'd shout back. There usually was enjoyment all around. Even when that wasn't the case, only rarely would I go home feeling guilty.

When we weren't on the sex party circuit together, he would tell me about the three or four new guys he fucked and filled with cum in a gym sauna, in a parking lot, or in the adult section of a video store. I watched him as he fucked the brains out of countless clouded minds, never thinking to ask him if he got off on infecting guys without telling them. His salacious stories of hookup upon hookup eventually came to seem so outlandish that on a few choice occasions I surprised myself by grabbing him squarely on the shoulders, shaking and pleading at the same time, "You've got to stop lying to me! I am your friend. You can tell me the truth!" In the end, I don't know why I doubted him. The way his eyes glinted and how he salivated after each conquest was for me confirmation enough of the fact that he didn't give one flying fuck who he gave the bug—as long as they enjoyed his cock!

Eventually, we fell out of contact. Frankly, while he was still busy spreading seed, my life of unrelenting hedonism was hampered by feelings of self-disgust, as well as disgust and hatred of other such wanton, woe-begone whores and hustlers of this Fog City. I figured that, in light of my experience, and as an effort to prove to myself that I still had at least a shred of morality, I could be of service as a safer sex advocate. So, I cleaned up my act a bit and decided to work toward establishing myself professionally in the HIV/AIDS prevention and advocacy arena.

After about five months of no-shows and silence, my friend found his way into my office. He was shivering, convulsing almost, and bawling wet, slobbery tears all over himself. He was drunk and cried out in a mumbled mishmash of dotted phrases something about how he had seeded this cop he had been fucking on and off for a few weeks.

He was convinced that the cop knew that he had infected him on purpose, and that the guy was going to throw him in jail. "Godammit! I need some vodka… This is it! I've gotta go kill myself," he chuckled in a frightfully serious tone. Before I could console him and council against suicide, he ran out of my office building, slamming the door abruptly. That was the last I saw or heard of him.

After witnessing this tragic spectacle, my own life proceeded to escalate into numerous episodes of similarly tempestuous drama. When my friend and fuck buddy spoke of suicide and mirrored back to me the sad and sinful nature of my own deviance, the guilt mounted in me to such an unbearable degree that I in turn began to fall into a deep depression. We were one and the same, I thought. How sad!

I shan't forget the illicit, alluring beauty of my tight little tush and thighs, which tempted and fed far too many head-spun, tail-furious tweaker tops tucked away in the sex stalls and playpens of Berkeley's lone bathhouse or beneath the bent and broken branches of San Francisco's Buena Vista Park. Sorely self-indulgent substance abuse fueled my freakishly scandalous sexcapades and then, sadly, a six-month schizoid-delusional psychosis ensued. Prescribed psychotropics slaughtered my sex drive, and the social malaise that came with no longer having the sexual stamina to survive midnight marathon man-on-man action made me feel like I'd curtailed any chance for sustainable romantic relationships inside or outside of the "party 'n' play" scene. I was left alone, forgotten and denigrated, deteriorating toward death until the paramedics busted down my door.

The only difference between me and my "infectious" friend was that I never contemplated taking my own life. Suicide wasn't even a passing notion after "a killer crystal meth and HIV/AIDS combo" completely corroded what once were my soft, sultry and quite kissable lips! Perhaps, in full appreciation of remaining alive despite disease and disfigurement after so many near-miss forays toward death, I am convinced of my extraordinary good fortune and blessings. Or, maybe, all that's keeping me alive today is gut-wrenching gay boy guilt.

Sadly, I haven't had a single sexual encounter, or any true physical intimacy in my life, since months before my untimely illness and injury. Years have gone by, and not a single kiss has been laid on my misshapen leg-flap lips. That is to say, not a single kiss apart from the smother of wet, slobbery tongue lashings I gladly get from my god-awfully gorgeous companion pet: my super-duper, cutie pie puppy pooch, Tanner Baby! The only muscle with which I've been mouth-to-mouth since misfortune befell me is droopy, drooling, far too flaccid, fresh from nibbling his nether parts, Tanner-tongue.

I often dream of intimacy, but my dreams don't amount to much. I have thoughts of spooning with a beautiful young man I may once have known before growing so ugly in the face. I desire to be kissed, to be fucked, to be loved, yet when I turn my head around to get that kiss or to beg for that cock inside me, all I get from the anonymous queer kid behind me is a vacant stare and a somber shake of the head.

THE SOUL OF OUR WORK

George Ayala and Patrick "Pato" Hebert

We share a belief in the power and importance of creating cultural production as a form of community building—in this case as a dynamic response to the impact of HIV/AIDS on gay and bisexual men of color. For eight years we have attempted to prioritize and hold open a space for this approach within AIDS Project Los Angeles (APLA), one of the largest AIDS service organizations in the United States. One of our most popular and contested efforts was *Corpus*, a creative journal that utilized visual art, creative writing, and critical reflection to explore the socio-cultural context of HIV among men who have sex with men (MSM).

Seven issues of *Corpus* were produced from 2003–2008, with guest editors developing theme-based issues and calling for content from artists and cultural workers (including the editor of this anthology) all over the United States, and, over time, the world. *Corpus* was printed in editions of 5,000 and distributed for free to AIDS service organizations, schools, libraries, prisons, public health departments, researchers, hormone clinics, and bars and clubs throughout the United States and at two International AIDS Conferences. The AIDS industry in general, however, has moved in a very different direction over the last decade, emphasizing evidence-based, top-down interventions and increasingly bio-medical approaches to prevention.

GA: I don't want to sound too romantically nostalgic, but the early days of the epidemic seemed more energized. Gay men mobilized and responded with a series of creative, community-based prevention programs aimed at disseminating information, providing social support, and changing community norms. The community response from gay men was a nationally-coordinated, locally-driven, profoundly social and political process. Action and activism were swift, creative, unapologetic, and stewarded significant social and cultural change. Belief in the power of multi-ethnic and cross-gender organizing was palpable.

As the HIV/AIDS industry became more professionalized or bour-geois-ified, public health approaches to HIV prevention took center stage. The operating paradigm narrowed in its focus on behavior and individual responsibility, with little regard for the "we." The emphasis specifically asked (and still asks) queers to vigilantly question our own intentions, mo-tivations, and personal conduct, as well as those of our sexual partners. I can't help but think that this created a sort of second guessing and self-differentiation, adding to the complexity of negotiating HIV within our relationships.

Pato, I think the AIDS industry has contributed to a community ethos that has us believing that there are good gays and bad gays amongst us, by creating confusion, fear, shame, and questions about trust. Yes, the over-whelming impact of HIV on men who practice same-sex desire has finally moved into public awareness, and edged towards mainstream health policy. Interestingly, though, and perhaps not so coincidentally, this sudden aware-ness and acknowledgement of queer folk is happening at the very same mo-ment that the AIDS industry seems creatively bankrupt and beholden to sci-ence. Surviving progressive activists and thought leaders are abandoning the industry in droves, leaving it to paid HIV professionals, who in turn have either become overly reliant on essentializing ideas about our communities or engaged in an Atlantis-like search for the one-size-fits-all magic bullet.

In some places, HIV prevention has become reduced to a routine of HIV case finding and the delivery of pre-fabricated, hand-me-down inter-ventions. In an increasingly bio-medicalized AIDS industry, community discourse and vision about participatory processes that include open, criti-cal examinations of sex, race, community, risk, and resiliency are largely ig-nored and actively undermined. HIV prevention has lost meaning. And the potential of bottom-up, collectively derived solutions to the social problem of HIV/AIDS is squandered. Although science is important in our work against AIDS, science idolatry is not. Such unquestioning faith in science may be having the unintended effect of limiting the role that community can also play in modeling more participatory praxis.

As AIDS advocate and researcher Robin Miller and others have as-serted for several years now, the emphasis on evidence can limit innovation and efficacy by promulgating a narrow view of prevention and by creating the false impression that multiple, co-existing, and mutually informative approaches are not possible. This is why cultural production is so critically important. I must admit, when recently asked at a meeting to explain to colleagues what I meant by "cultural production," I was tongue-tied.

I have a sneaking suspicion that the net effect of top-down, evidence-based approaches is the dulling of intellect. After all, workers and consumers in the industry have been asked to stop thinking; we're told the scientists have done that for us. If I had my wits about me when asked, I might have explained that cultural production is our chance to reproduce ourselves as social, cultural citizens. It is a way of making things together—of making meaning, shared understanding, and solutions. It is a way of giving back, of becoming more socially integrated. Ultimately, I think of cultural production as the democratic expression of diverse views being brought to bear on the problem of AIDS, offering all stakeholders equal footing.

PH: Jaime Cortez, our colleague and the founding editor of *Corpus*, talks about two things that I think have been really important to the work we've all done together: first, Jaime describes the body as a repository for knowledge. I would also suggest that the body is a producer of knowledge in concert with other bodies. Jaime also talks about how our work in HIV prevention, cultural production, and in the organizing of queer men is about the negotiation of who gets to tell the story of HIV at this time. What does HIV mean, what has it meant, and what might it mean, in the future, to gay and bisexual men?

For me, Jaime's understanding of storytelling as central to the way we respond to the disease and to our needs is really valuable. Storytelling is very instructive; it's where cultural production might dovetail with research at its best, and even advocacy. Without losing critical perspective, I think research is a potential way for folks to wield voice and shape narrative, and advocacy at its best is the strategic positioning of narrative towards greater resources and opportunity. Together we have tried to understand cultural production as part of a suite of responses to the epidemic and the scale of the need.

But I realize that storytelling as a concept risks sounding a lot like sitting around the hearth, as though it's so far removed from what really matters. But that critique of storytelling misses its tremendous critical and generative potential. It also falsely assumes location and authority for certain kinds of knowledge production (academic research, governmental public health initiatives) and devalues others (community-based mobilization, interpersonal and social exchange). Yet I know in my heart, as an artist and also from the years of work we've done together, that it's precisely during the telling of stories that people lean forward in their seats, that people start listening, and that people begin to share. And it's in the story, however subjective or even fictional it might be, that we can make and grapple with meanings and truths that often elude empiricism.

If you say, "Hey, you wanna talk about HIV?" people may not want to get together or be forthcoming, but if you say, "Could you tell me your greatest trick story," or "Tell me about the pros and cons of trying to come out to your family, if you ever did," or whatever the invitation or prompt may be, all of a sudden people have another angle by which to come at the terms and the meaning of their lives. Then we can deepen and strengthen our sharing with one another, our connection with one another. When people are committed to an ongoing, reflexive process of critical storytelling together, it serves to undo shame and build community, all the while sharing and shaping knowledge. Such a process would necessarily engage queer men's fears of one another, our affection, and what we mean to one another, as well as to the broader world.

GA: Research is really about storytelling too, but it's also about the process of soliciting stories and synthesizing those stories through particular sets of lenses. And then retelling those stories through those lenses, and with very little critique about what happens to the story when you put it through that process. You can say the same thing about service providers, 'cause service providers tell a different kind of story, in a different way, about the people who are most impacted by HIV and AIDS—in this case gay men.

If you don't privilege the voices of the people who want to share the stories, or if you don't come to the storytelling process with the perspective that collecting stories is really how we come to know or how we come to make sense of HIV in the big picture, if you don't come from that perspective then storytelling can also be a way of distancing yourself from the people who want to share those stories. Providers do that all the time, 'cause we also have a tendency to want to cast the people we serve as clients, and by retelling stories with a different set of lenses and from a different perspective.

For example, I've heard gay and straight providers say, "Oh, he should have known better," after they've delivered an HIV-positive test result to someone. In that regard, I think people's attitudes about gay men come into play, right? Distancing becomes an accepted way of expressing dislike of gay men or expressing discomfort with homosexuality. As a provider, it's easier to deal with your discomfort about homosexuality by casting gay men as the clients and the clients that have something wrong with them. Within this logic, the provider therefore has to somehow fix the pathologized client. And some gay providers may be well-meaning, but can easily lose sight of the importance of reflexivity and criticality, the importance of being vigilant against a distancing judgment and a pathologizing fear.

PH: Right, and this is rather distinct from a model of empowerment or solidarity. There are certain conventional public health models that are really about control and isolation. When prevention is approached from such perspectives it really misses the possibility of socio-cultural mobilizations, which can cultivate, nurture, and build wellness—a wellness that is grounded and growing, not prescribed and controlled.

I also think about this other crucial aspect to storytelling, which is audience. Storytelling in oral traditions, in familial traditions, perhaps even in online chat rooms and social networking, is about synergy and experience. In the art of storytelling, storytellers understand that it's really about connecting with audience. A good story might well address fear, but its goal is not to encourage a dependency on fear.

In the AIDS sector, we must of course confront the challenges, despair, anger, and fear that arise from the catastrophe that is this disease. But our efforts cannot end there, lest we fail to share and develop the strategies that will see us through. Our storytelling and efforts must help us better understand one another, not fear or judge one another. Sometimes we may do this through allegory, sometimes through cataloging, sometimes through imaging, but always as a way to get at meaning, the making of meaning in the sharing of and the listening to the story.

Plus, because it's AIDS and because it's gay men, the storytelling must always make space for the sex, right? Yet in much formal HIV prevention discourse, there is, I think, this extreme distancing not only from gay men but especially gay sex. And, unfortunately, along with that, gay affection, gay intimacy, gay conflict, gay anything that would be a part of a sexual ecology. For me the danger is a distancing from the story, a distancing from the body, a distancing from the "we." Of course we can distance ourselves through sex as well, but at its best and most profound and most dynamic and scary and revelatory, it's about communion. There's a way that I think cultural production is that too, and allows us to talk about things that are difficult to talk about, or tell stories that we haven't told.

Jaime shared a beautiful story with me of a colleague who was a young writer who had been looking for himself in words. He was a bookish, gay Latino man, and had been trying to find himself in books, and so he read the coming out literature and he read the queer literature, and kept saying something you and I have heard and known for years, which is that you go into these bodies of literature, and until fairly recently and even still, there are huge gaps in them in terms of what kinds of lives and stories are represented, prioritized, privileged, etc. He talked about this sense of being able to piece together some understanding of himself as a proactive reader—reading as a form of making knowledge and meaning. Nonetheless, he also always felt absented and wanting until he came across the anthology that Jaime edited, *Virgins, Guerrillas and Locas*. He told Jaime that book made him "feel like men like me were possible, that this is how we make ourselves."

This shows how storytelling is not just the telling of something that has existed, but is the making of possibility. We make ourselves through storytelling. We reproduce the queer power of ourselves through our sex. When I evoke sex it's in a very fluid sense that's also about our intimacy, our sharing, our raunch, our connection. So I think about storytelling as a top priority, as crucial as any other strategy. In the same way that we would think that useful advocacy and the legal right to exist, or research that does give us a useful and accurate epi-profile—the same way that invisibility in those arenas is literally deadly, I would suggest that invisibility and absence in the storytelling arena are also really dangerous.

Which is why, for me, cultural production continues to be a priority. It's also crucial not to put it into a zero sum equation where it's either giving people antiretrovirals or publishing a collection of short stories, giving people groceries and helping with adherence to their treatment regimen or doing a night of original theatre by gay men about substance abuse. We have to step out of this reductive either/or narrative, and hold open this shared and contingent ecology, as difficult and expensive and unwieldy as that may be.

GA: I'm reminded of a conversation I had recently with a colleague—another gay man, who's doing international LGBT rights work. We were talking about the work that we were doing and I was talking to him about what it was like to be involved in global HIV/AIDS work. I told him that I felt privileged doing this work and that I felt strongly about the fact that to do this work well, you really had to love gay men, and then he said to me, "Oh, really? I don't—there's things about gay men that I really hate." And I left that conversation wondering, if that were true, could you really do this work well?

PH: I believe the subtitle to Jaime's book is "Gay Latinos Writing About Love."

GA: I totally forgot about that—it is the subtitle.

PH: I would say that it's difficult to do the work without love, but it's also okay, perhaps even necessary, to acknowledge the hate that arises within the work. I would be very scared and skeptical of a process that lacked love for gay men, but I would also be suspicious of the wholeness and honesty of a process that didn't acknowledge the pathologies that emerge, and therein lies the complicated rub for me. Can we talk about things that make us really uncomfortable, even if for some people that manifests as hate? Our love can be withered in the face of a culture that is persistently homophobic, does not have generalized healthcare for anyone, let alone gay men, and in a culture that has completely decimated its support of the arts, of storytelling outside of a profit narrative.

We have commoditized wellness and creativity, and so gay men are up against these much larger contexts that aren't particularly conducive to the strongest, healthiest, most holistic approaches. Access to basic healthcare, and a healthcare system that is not homophobic and that is responsive to the needs of gay men, would radically change the pressures and therefore the opportunities for those of us who work primarily within the HIV/AIDS sector of healthcare, whether in research, programming and cultural production, or advocacy.

Similarly with the arts: if we had sufficient and adequate funding for community-based arts programming—of all kinds, not just related to gay men and HIV—then it wouldn't seem so shocking and misappropriated to allocate some of those funds for gay men to tell their stories. So it's in this larger, structural context that we get forced into very painful conversations about prioritizing of funding, or what's most important, and it's always a reductive conversation because of limited resources.

But I do think you're on to something with love, and it begs another element for me, which is soul. Soul is a very difficult thing to talk about within the work because it carries with it a lot of loaded religious connotations. But I often think how soulful sex can be, how sex is a form of prayer, as sacrilegious as that sounds. And my thinking opens up further when I insert other words, which are dangerous to substitute because they come from different lineages, but what happens if I substitute for soul a word like justice, or a word like freedom, or imagination, or creativity, or communion—any of the many different ways I attempt to understand soul outside of a specific religious mandate?

So your comment about the colleague who wondered, "Do we really need love to do this work?" makes me then ask where is the soul of the work? Where is the creative soul of the work? This is an ongoing, generative question for me. There's no easy, definitive answer attached to it. Soul is not a fixed entity in terms of form, time, or space, so there's no definitive answer to questioning the soul of our work. Nor is outcome the goal. But the questioning of soul is one of the ways we strive to make our work more rigorous and meaningful. It's one of the ways we make and allow for meaning.

GA: Yeah, I think about it in terms of drive too. In some ways I guess you can do this work and hate some things about gay men, but then I wonder are we then just doing the work in a rote way, in a way that we were trained to do, or in a way that is somehow faithful to a set of professional ethics that we might have been handed down? If so, then what is the quality of the work at the end of the day? What compels us to come back and to do it again, and how does that wither our perceptions about who gay men are in the world and what their sex means?

I think about that a lot because I'm often shocked by some of the ridiculous ideas about what we should be doing in HIV/AIDS work with gay men, and by the total disregard for gay men's feelings and for how gay men have sex and how gay men inhabit their bodies and what sexuality might mean across cultures. For example, I'm always taken aback when I see gay public health officials get jazzed over promoting circumcision, or abstinence from anal sex, as promising prevention approaches for gay men. Really? Is that the best we can imagine for ourselves when it comes to HIV prevention? I keep coming back to the fact that these ideas can only come from people who really dislike gay men. I don't know how else to explain it to myself.

PH: Right. And I think the shared response could be invigorated and could be much more effective, in my opinion, if we could have a more frontal and honest and critical conversation about the hatred of queer men, including our fears of one another. Perhaps that starts, on one level, by critically engaging stigma and homophobia. These are the social and cultural viruses we must confront. I agree with you that without a more purposeful acknowledgement and dismantling of that, the work will always be inhibited, and limited.

GA: Impoverished.

PH: Though some elected and public health officials might disagree with me, I often understand HIV work in the United States and in many parts of the world as also being queer liberation work. I wonder about how untrue that is for many, many other people, in part because of a hatred of gay men, as you say, but also because HIV prevention and queer liberation are not synergistic, let alone synonymous for many, many people.

GA: Yeah, I certainly don't think that the HIV/AIDS sector is the only place to do that work. It should never be the only place to do that work. But without liberation work, without social justice work, HIV/AIDS work is really futile, in my mind. I'm quite humbled by stories that I hear, or examples that I see, of gay men, LGBT communities around the world who do this work, often under very, very difficult situations, where it's really unsafe to do this openly. Yet activists find creative ways to do it, often at great personal costs to themselves and to their families and to their social networks.

Because of this duress, it's much easier outside of the United States to link social justice with HIV work, because the realities in some ways are much harsher in some parts of Africa, parts of the Caribbean, parts of the Middle East and Central Asia, and Eastern Europe. In many of these places, homosexuality is illegal, and we're literally witnessing cleansing programs directed at homosexuals at the national level or regional level. And scapegoating is used as a political wedge, as a way to secure political power, because LGBT communities are easy targets. Torture and murder are happening on a regular basis, on a routine basis, so it's much easier outside the US to link the work that we do around HIV and AIDS work with gay men to a social justice agenda. That's really important for us to keep in mind here in the United States, because it's not a coincidence that HIV in the States is hitting hardest with black gay men and Latino gay men. That's not a coincidence in my mind. And yet we're very slow to call that a social justice issue or speak about human rights in the context of HIV work here in the United States. So as I do global work, it really offers me an opportunity to bring back those kinds of frameworks and those kind of lenses, 'cause I think they're useful in the context of the United States.

PH: This is why folks in this country, we must learn to strategically take our cues in concert with our global colleagues, right? It's interesting to me to substitute justice for soul, community for soul, wellness for soul, freedom for soul, because if those values are important—and it should be stated that they're not valued by everyone everywhere, but if they are—then it always takes us to the soul of what we mean to one another, whether it's in our sex, whether it's in the divvying out of national and global resources, whether it's in the prioritization of genuine wellness versus profit.

GA: I think that's really important. And the soul of the work to me is really about everybody's ability to take part and to leave the work feeling, "I have a say in this. I have a role." Otherwise HIV/AIDS work just becomes cold and removed and disconnected.

DIRT STORY

Lewis Wallace

I remember the field at Camp Trans, that volatile open space that is hot and uneasy each August, aching with energy, idealistic and rough. That fine dusty dirt and hard grass in West Michigan is where I first saw two trans boys fuck each other. It was dusk, I was sixteen and I just leaned against a tree and watched, feeling gutted because I couldn't imagine sharing in that feeling. Their bodies buried in patched clothing reminded me of injured birds, delicate and strong, small beaks angularly exploring each other. They pulled each other's hair, rolled in the dirt. Shadows turned to the glow of night, leaves and tree trunks lit thinly by the moon. Back in my tent I couldn't even masturbate, I just shivered and slept, heavy with the vague desire of becoming.

I met you a year or two later and we flirted on that same dirt, and then quickly tore each other up, broke our bodies open with one another, our muscles and bones chisels and axes against one another, holding each other like rocks in our hands. I was raw before I could blink twice, plummeting into my body. This was what I'd wanted.

First loves are messy but first lusts might just be worse. The memory sticks with me—of your rough grimy fingers under a sky full of stars; of a sky so distinct that it filled me with longing to look up; of a small boy with bony and broad shoulders, tying my wrists with a bandana or spilling whiskey down my back. You were that first spine and cheekbone I followed to their end, the first lips I fixated on. The first boy to take off his belt and beat me until I came close to my wit's end; and then we jumped into the cold creek together and bathed naked, skin hot and scarred.

That summer, you dropped out of college after your first year, just a few weeks after we'd met and next thing we knew we'd left your apartment in

New York for a ride to Tennessee and another one to New Orleans. In New Orleans it was really just the two of us for the first time—18 and 19, cut loose from sheltered lives, sleeping on the black tar roof of a punk house. You were always in your black Carhartts, and I was in my baseball cap and jeans, trying to steal your favorite t-shirts. I remember waking up delirious and warm on that roof and feeling you sink your nails into my back, flip me over and fuck me in the sweaty heat.

We still carry the feeling of fighting one another down by a damp bayou, but don't remember what we fought about. You hated the heat because it made you groggy and depressed, and New Orleans took us over like a cloud of black flies. I think we argued about the future, where we would go after this sweaty mess, the reality of when and how we would pry ourselves apart looming silently ahead. The future never served us well during those moments. We scammed bus passes and when the scam stopped working we hitchhiked West, passed through Texas unflinching and admiring the landscape. We kissed dangerously by the sides of highways and waited in the blue darkness to find another ride.

All the time we were pretending we came from some place other than the sterile pasts we shared—both white, both alienated from rich families, both guilty and sincere at once. We were angry at the system but each of us had a ticket out of sleeping under train bridges, each lived a credit card or a phone call away from a warm bed. We each vehemently blamed the other for our own shame, so set sometimes on ripping the past to shreds that we came close to doing the same to each other.

So many trans boys are raised in a way that leaves us bruised. I see the women I know struggle to be inhumanly tough and sensitive, to suck it up or let it go depending on the moment. It's a constant dance, with complicated steps. You and I carried all that weight even as we dashed quickly away from the pasts we had shared with girls we'd known. We had spent so long feeling like we didn't make sense, what we were expected to become never fitting with what our bodies' gravity drew us towards.

It wasn't easy for two such boys to try to hold each other up. Sex was harsh, awkward, perfect for that short time. We kept crashing into each other—you were injured and distrustful, I was ignorant and demanding. The last time you fucked me in a tent at Camp Trans I left it laughing with a black eye that lasted for days. It was one of those nights with no moonlight and I couldn't see your face. Even when everything was sour I kept clinging to you until you tore yourself away. I found new boys who wanted to swap cigarette burns and fist fights, and lie and watch the dawn creep through the window talking about what happens when we die.

I've fallen in love a couple times now with people whose bodies push through convention and into that broad atmosphere of possibility. The solace of the open space our small freedoms create only seems to exist within us or between us; we become so secretive. The outside world is a harsh place when your body does not exist according to any story you've been told, any dominant version of "reality." My trans lovers have held me whole, no matter which doorway I pick to walk through on a given day. It's only in retrospect that I see how brave we were to come so close to one another; for all those mistakes we did something right just by trying.

Sometimes now I think we could have poked our eyes out, swinging around the way we used to swing. I remember the way your tattered shirts would hang over your thin shoulders, the frightened face you showed me when you had surgery. Our bodies met long gazes in waiting rooms, the familiar silence of icy eyes trying to figure us out. I remember what it meant when I broke down, started picking at you with my sharp words after you'd waited all day for me to come home. I remember how little I felt for your fragile body in my bare bedroom, how hollow I felt taking you to the hospital, making pay phone calls from the lobby. It was too late by the time we were there in the hospital: the harshness of seeing myself in you, seeing your weakness and exposure, had already driven me away. I felt you wanting me to take care of you and I think that scared me more than I could admit.

I looked away when I knew I'd left you alone and I could never meet your eyes after that, even in the months after, as you healed and we silently touched each other in the bathroom, on the living room floor. Hurting you felt too much like hurting myself, and I let you take the fall, let you wait for me with betrayed eyes. Still it was the kind of perfect that shows up between the black flashes of a strobe light when two bodies seem just exactly right together, even if it's just the moment, the lighting or the drink you just downed. Sometimes two boys together is just the sweetest thing, even if it's a toxic risky sweet. I wanted that moment to stretch out easy and ripe before me.

Years later we walk together on a city sidewalk, kicking trash, bundled for winter, talking about people we still know in our strange separate worlds, becoming grown-ups. We've felt growing pains every year and we're just more used to them now, I think, knowing that confusion and ambiguity is not just about youth or newness but about a system that doesn't want us, that doesn't want us to be brave or fall in love or fuck in public or behind closed doors.

I have seen a man emerge in you out of the boy I thought I knew, and in me a sweeter, stronger faggot out of the spiky sharp creature I was. After tearing each other apart looking for ourselves it's almost funny now to see how little we resemble each other. Our baseball caps and young faces used to make us fags or dykes or freaks in other people's eyes. Now I hover outside of being a man or a woman and you've eased into passing; you're suddenly comfortable in sweaters and suits, your light hair cut short.

Touching you last winter, I could feel that the brilliant dropout I knew was gone, and I felt different to you too. I glowed with a new calm. Your scratchy face was like a stranger's face and we eyed each other's angles and curves hesitantly, at the edge of admiration but afraid to see what had changed. Our old fierceness together had created a tower of barbed wire and boy smells, delicious and divisive; the feeling is still tempting even if it's dusty and dangerous, even if it can't last. There was no innocence and no urgency to our muscles' push against each other this time, and we both cried for a minute and then cleaned up. We stayed up late talking in the dark between clean sheets and it was that easy, and that hard, to move on.

GENERATIONS

Mattilda Bernstein Sycamore

I met Truly Outrageous Chrissie Contagious just before the March on Washington in 1993, the biggest ever of its kind, a million white gays in white T-shirts applying for Community Spirit credit cards but at least that meant the freaks, we found each other, and fast. Chrissie and I met in Dupont Circle because she liked my hair and then later that night I saw her dancing naked in a tree and screaming girl!!! I didn't realize she was screaming at me until she came down with eyes bulging from Ecstasy and took my hands and said you know you know you know you know you KNOW we're sisters.

Chrissie loved to tell stories, so it made sense that other people loved to tell her stories too. Like when she stole some trick's car in Seattle and decided to drive cross-country, I can't remember if she was trying to get back to Florida where she was from or to some club in New York that didn't exist anymore, but anyway she ended up crashing into a cop car, spent time in jail in Wyoming, but then somehow she was back in Seattle where she became the manager of the poshest boutique hotel in town, this was weeks or years later but it all ended when she decided to throw a party and serve up all the liquor bottles earmarked for the mini-refrigerators. Or maybe that's when she stole the trick's car, you know how these stories work. With Chrissie there was usually someone kicking her out or locking her up but then she was back at the bar and all the other legendary messes would giggle knowingly or snicker, and keep on drinking and doing bumps because at least they hadn't ended up in jail in Wyoming.

We were both crazy queens who spent too much time in worlds of clubs and drugs; we both sold sex for a living and moved from place to place in search of something we would never find. We both turned tricks for way too long until it made us distant in ways we hadn't expected. We believed in runway and reading and rage and rapture, but I don't mean to suggest that we were similar. Even when we first met in D.C. at the very end of our teenage years, I was there to protest and she was there to party. I'd returned to the horrible place where I'd grown up, and she had so much fun that she moved there.

We were looking for different things, but we were always looking. I remember the first time Chrissie stopped doing drugs, I guess it was soon after I first stopped doing drugs, now that I think about it, but I didn't think about it then. Chrissie started going to the gym and drinking protein shakes to bulk up and she bought blue contact lenses to cover her deep brown eyes and she tried to imitate some kind of upscale preppy look that before I'd always thought she was making fun of—but the worst part was that she didn't want anyone to call her girl anymore.

I remember when Chrissie first came to San Francisco, maybe a year after the march and she was working big fake eyelashes and some store-designed club outfit and she took a look around at how people were reacting to her and said girl, I need to change out of this. And I said honey, don't ever let them make you change. I remember that moment because Chrissie told the story over and over, and I loved her for it. And also I loved her.

There was never anything balanced about our relationship—I knew she was completely unreliable, and so I never relied on her. She always trusted people who I thought were repulsive. Still I respected her because she could let everything go, over and over again, in hopes of finding what she wanted. She never did, but neither have I. One time, after drugs were gone from my life but before it felt that way, Chrissie came to my house with gray skin and black knuckles, fresh from the hospital and another abscess she called a spider bite, sipping Dust-Off from the straw that came with the can, girl I got cab vouchers. That's not a spider bite, I said, so she wiggled her tongue and asked if she could shoot up in the bathroom. Me first, I said, and we took a cab to a restaurant. Outside, she started shivering, and when I took her hand in my hand or really the mitten covering my hand, she said something about how her head hurt so much, she was sick of it all, she was angry that everyone was always letting her down—that's when we were really sisters.

The last time I talked to Chrissie, she had just listened to me on an NPR program where I was telling the world that the gay marriage agenda was draining resources from everything that mattered. Chrissie was so annoyed at the announcer for calling me she. We call each other she all the time, Chrissie said, but that's because we're camping—I couldn't believe that announcer, it was so disrespectful.

I never understood how Chrissie could live in worlds filled with freaks and fruits and perverts and whores for so long, but still she wanted to be normal. Sure, she could pull stunts that made everyone else look tame and prudish, but only on drugs.

A few years ago, Chrissie went back to Florida to get away from crystal, and I became someone she would call late at night when she'd been drinking for twelve hours the way she'd been drinking for twenty years almost, and even though she mostly stopped the rest of the drugs there was always a cocktail waiting. She'd demand updates on the most notoriously obnoxious people in San Francisco, and always acted surprised that I avoided them—sure, a few of them had once been my friends, but the rest I'd barely even spoken to. Then she'd go to the kitchen for more ice, get back in bed with her cocktail and start yelling at the TV, a play-by-play commentary on Hillary or Heath Ledger or the latest dildo infomercial. She loved Hillary and Heath and was somehow scandalized that dildos were for sale on TV, but sometimes she would surprise me with a drunken insight—Obama came on one night and Chrissie started screaming: What are you selling me, just tell me what you're selling me!

Maybe you've figured out that Chrissie's dead. Her heart stopped, that's what they said. Later they said it was because of huffing, but I'm sure that's not the whole story. I wonder what Chrissie would yell at the TV during the sudden flash of news stories about an epidemic of queer teen suicides, an epidemic we all know has been going on for generations. I'm wondering about those of us who do survive—for how long?

PRISONS AND CLOSETS

Jason Lydon

I walk in the front door. The yellow walls are covered with art. Pictures of pink and white flowers entangled in long green vines wind around thick legs, and silly cartoons peek from behind ears. I hand the tall, butch, blond-haired, tattooed man my image: a pink-and-black star, anarcho-communist style but with pink instead of red.

"Is this it?" he asks.

"Actually, I want it to say 'queer' across it in typewriter font, all lower-case."

As his face changes and his friendly tone disappears, I remember one of the reasons for this tattoo: closeting myself will never again be so easy. I hope that any time I try to pass, the new star on the inside of my arm will burn a little.

* * * * *

I sat on the cold concrete floor, surrounded by thirty other men with the same questionnaire. Everyone was going through it. One guy to my left was having his translated from English to Spanish. We were all in our bright orange uniforms; everyone else wore boots, but I still had only socks—two days before, I'd informed a guard that my shoes didn't fit, and he'd taken them away and offered no replacement. Everyone was zipping through the questions, seemingly without thought. I was stuck, but not because of any language barrier.

One of the questions read, "Have you ever used illegal drugs?"

I checked the No box without hesitation. It was a complete lie. The day before my trial, I'd stood outside in a circle with a number of my co-defendants, passing around an apple, which had been carved into a homemade pipe, for some excellent upstate New York marijuana.

Another question read, "Have you ever been diagnosed with mental illness?"

My pencil marked an X perfectly in the No box, but according to the psychiatrist I saw as a teen, I had a chronic panic disorder that I was prescribed 150mg of Zoloft to control.

The only question left unmarked read, "Have you ever engaged in any homosexual experiences?"

I read the question more than a dozen times, but I couldn't bring myself to answer it. I clearly had no problem lying on the other questions, why was this one so different?

* * * * *

Only a few months earlier—in Muscogee County, Georgia—I didn't even get the opportunity to fill out a questionnaire. Standing before the judge in my black shirt with a pink triangle at center, I outed myself to him, the people in the courtroom, and the US Marshals who dragged me off to the notorious Muscogee County Jail. After the first night sleeping on concrete with no pillow or blanket, I was cuffed, shackled, and ushered out of the tiny one-person cell. As the guard tugged me along by the elbow I asked if I was going to be held with any of my co-defendants.

"No kid, there's a special homo bin for people like you."

I nearly tripped over my shackles. He took me down the cold, spotless white corridors and into a steel elevator. He turned it on with a giant metal key that had its teeth hidden by a silver sheath. We stopped on the fifth floor of the shiny, high-tech, newly-renovated county jail and he hustled me over to the cellblock in the back corner. The door opened after the guard raised his right hand and gave a thumbs-up. I walked through and the door closed behind me with a thunderous bang. I slid my hands through the open slot and the guard removed my cuffs. Turning around I looked into the eyes of more queens and queers than I'd seen since before my trial began.

I was immediately greeted with hugs, hands smoothing my hair, and soap to take a shower. Skiboe opened the bunk in his cell for me and informed me that he'd have my back. I didn't know at the time that really he just wanted to fuck me. Miss Knockout told me she was the head queen on the block and if I wanted to know anything about the 23 other folks around me, she was the one to ask. We played spades and chess all day. We gave each other privacy in the group shower. I watched the girls braid each other's hair; they stood up to the nurses when they didn't bring someone's AIDS medication. My surprising new family cared about me and took me in. We talked about love, sex, AIDS, politics, *American Idol*, makeup, and gossiped about who was fucking whom. This was our survival.

The guards used our homo bin as the outlet for their ignorance. On Tuesdays, when we received clothing changes, we were forced to give our clothes up in the day room and didn't get any replacements until everyone was undressed, leaving Miss Michelle blushing and uncomfortably covering her genitals. While Clay Aiken sang his heart out on *American Idol*, the television would magically flicker on and off, outraging Santos. This segregated cell was supposedly created for our protection. I wonder if the preacher who raged on Sunday mornings in our block about the abomination of homosexuality got that memo.

* * * * *

"Have you ever engaged in any homosexual experiences?" How do I define that anyway? What about that one strip search?

The tall, angry, muscular, scowling guard took me into the back room. He was one of the new guys, so he was forced to do the dirty work. He shut the door behind us; no other guard had done that in the past. He seemed to sneer at the latex gloves on the table. He was supposed to cover his hands before touching me. He didn't.

"Remove all of your clothes, including socks and underwear," he growled.

He stared me down as I peeled my sweaty, smelly shirts, socks, pants, and underwear off my long-unwashed body. I had decided after the second strip search I suffered through that the only way to resist the anguish was to let go of myself completely. I would imagine my body somewhere else and allow my mind to quiet as much as possible. I stripped as quickly as I could. Standing with my head up and eyes halfway closed, I imagined myself kicking this man in the face the next time we crossed paths.

Then I got the standard, "Open your mouth, lift your tongue, cough, cough deeper, lift your nuts, turn around, bend over, spread your cheeks, squat, cough."

But then he kept going. "Turn around. Pull your foreskin back, push it back, pull it back again, push it back again, pull it back again, push it back again..."

He was almost smiling at me. My half-closed eyes began to water. Rather than imagining kicking his face in, I got lost in images of my 12-year-old self surviving a different sexual assault. Back in reality, the guard put his hand under my balls and lifted them himself. I rose up on my toes and made a tiny squeak that felt like a scream. He let go of me and stared. He threw a bar of soap at me and barked, "You fucking smell, take a shower."

He grabbed a new uniform, threw it at me, and said, "Put these on after."

He walked out the door and locked it behind him. I fell into the shower, unable to really cry. I hadn't even had a chance to name my sexuality and already a man couldn't keep his hands to himself.

I continued to stare at the question. The whole time, I knew which box I was going to check. My brain needed justification. My heart sought resolution for my betrayal of the last eight years of my out queer life as the bullies slammed my head against lockers, as I stood before the Board of Education decrying the silencing of queer students, as I kissed a boy for the first time. The room, filled with guys yelling, talking, and pissing in the open-trough toilet, felt almost silent as I put an X in the No box

In that holding cell where I sat, I was one of the only white people. I had received the shortest sentence. I had access to huge amounts of support outside prison, from my family and from hundreds of strangers who supported those of us who got locked up for doing civil disobedience against the School of Americas, a military training school for Latin American soldiers, based in Ft. Benning, Georgia. I had no major mental health issues. I checked that box to grab on to the only privilege I was missing. I was sure, with all those advantages lining up for me, that I would serve the last four months of my 6-month sentence at the prison camp, where I could go outside, have access to books, run the track, eat with other people, read in the prison library, avoid getting locked down in the hole. The betrayal and pain I felt checking that box would be worth it.

One by one, people were called out of the cramped holding cell. Each person was designated—hospital, Segregated Housing Unit, Camp, Level 2. My name was called, and I shuffled out to the intake table. The guard pushed my fingers into some ink and rubbed them on yet another fingerprint chart. I smiled Cheshire-cat-style for the picture.

He smirked at me, "What do you have to be so happy about?"

"The airplane y'all put us on didn't crash. Sounds like a good day to me." He wasn't amused. I handed him my form, likely damp from the sweat accumulated in my hands. As his eyes glanced over it and his pen marked SHU, I wished I had been braver.

* * * * *

My stay in the Special Housing Unit (lovingly called the hole) lasted fifteen days. I found ways to make the time pass in that cell, lit up twenty-four hours a day by a fluorescent light. Only a shitter, bunk, small table, and open shower surrounded me. I sat on my bunk, lay down on it, did hand-stand pushups (since there wasn't enough room for regular ones), jogged in place till my calves burned, desperately searching for anything to keep my mind and body distracted. Though I was often sure I would never make it out, one day the guards shackled me up again and released me to the prison camp where there were no walls, fences, or barbed wire, and prisoners had nightmares of accidentally walking off the prison grounds and getting an extra five years added on to their sentence.

I was in prison the summer the Supreme Court was overturning the fucked-up sodomy laws. Almost every day, for a couple of weeks, as we sat in the television room, some newscaster would interview this pro-homo or that anti-homo white guy about the case. One morning, after reporting to kitchen duty a couple of minutes late, the young, usually hung-over, arrogant guard pulled me aside.

"Lydon," he said, maybe a little slurred, "sometimes when inmates irritate me or I'm curious about them I google their names. Last night I got on my computer and dropped your name in. Do you know all the shit that comes up? There's quite a number of pages. Not all of it is about why you're in here. You're probably paying close attention to the big court case now, huh? You don't want to end up back in here."

He glared at me as he made it clear he knew my secret. I walked away from him and into the kitchen. He flicked on the cafeteria television and put on the news. Of course it was about the sodomy case. One of the other guys looked over. The guard called out, loud enough for everyone to hear.

"Lydon's not just a hippie terrorist. He thinks fags deserve rights too. That right Bin Lydon?"

"People should be able to fuck who they want to fuck. It's none of any of our business." We all returned to work. It wasn't enough for that guard to control my life; he needed to dig inside me.

Around the yard, there were whispers. Rumors passed from person to person, curious about the relationship between me and Darnell, another prisoner. He was a fag, clearly. I was a fag, clearer than I wished it to be. We hung out together. We ate together. We talked about politics together. I had a huge crush on him. He had a crush on me. We never fucked. For those six months I couldn't even put my hand on my own cock, never mind someone else's. As my release date came closer, he pulled away as my friend.

On the day I left he wouldn't even give me a last hug. He had to stay inside; I was going home to my friends, family, and freedom to fuck safely.

* * * * *

As the cute tattoo artist starts outlining the star on the inside of my arm, I think back to that X on the No box. Like closeted actors, teachers, parents, and politicians I was afraid to lose something. We betray those who need us. All those queer kids in search of role models and alternatives, all those fags, gay boys, trans folks, and bi guys in Muscogee County Jail. What does the lack of solidarity mean? Who suffers when we choose privilege over the experiences we treasure?

The tattoo gun keeps buzzing, dripping drops of blood down my arm, and I know that I have a permanent mark in the Yes box.

A ROCK AND A BIRD

Book Edouardo

I step off the ferry in Sausalito and look around for the supervisor. He waves to me from a car that I do not recognize. As I walk toward him, I notice that the vehicle has no license plates.

I slip into the front passenger seat. He tells me that he bought and paid for the new Lexus convertible on impulse. His mother gave him cash when he visited her in Philadelphia for her eighty-eighth birthday, and he used the money to buy the car.

The supervisor complains that he is now broke and has "no money." I think about how having "no money" means something completely different for him than it does for me. I compliment his purchase. He explains that he could have bought a hybrid if he had put his name on a waiting list, but he does not like to wait when he buys stuff because it takes away the good feelings.

The first time we met, the supervisor said that he liked my strong sense of spirituality and my special aura. I was sitting on the floor at a local animal rescue shelter playing with a feral kitten and a feather toy. I did not notice him until he knelt down beside me and introduced himself.

He told me that he was the supervisor of the volunteers at the animal shelter and at Ocean Animal Rescue, but that both jobs were unpaid. He asked me if I wanted to work with him at both shelters. When I said yes, he offered to give me rides.

The supervisor pulls out of the parking space. He tells me that I look too happy and asks me why. I say that I am glad to be away from San Francisco. I wonder how to convey my experience at the SRO where I live. The hotel is a world away from him but just across the bay.

More than ninety percent of the people who live in my building have coped with their circumstances by using drugs and/or alcohol. Approximately fifteen percent panhandle in various locations around the city. A few lie on the sidewalks too drunk to move, and sometimes I have to step over them in order to get into the building where I live.

Recently, one of my neighbors jumped off the roof of our six-story building. I do not know why. When I heard about it, I imagined that he, like me, could no longer stand living in the six-by-nine-foot room, with jail-like restrictions.

The building manager found two of my other neighbors dead after they overdosed together. My current next-door neighbor often threatens me. He follows me into our bathroom, or down the hallway, or to my room.

When I first moved into the building, I recognized him from the news because he was featured in a report about sex crimes. The reporter said that he was among the most dangerous sexual predators in the state. Late one night, I accidentally bumped into him in the private entryway we share. When I walked into the bathroom, I found a knife on the toilet seat.

I told the building manager that I was afraid for my safety. His hand waved my concern away, as he told me that I was intolerant and that I needed to accept the situation. My neighbor had nowhere else to go. As I got up to leave, the manager lowered his voice and cautioned me, because the authorities had just released the man from prison for kidnapping, rape, and murder.

To limit my interactions with my neighbor, I go to the bathroom in a five-gallon paint bucket, lined with a plastic trash bag and layered with cat litter. When the lid is on, the bucket is my only chair. I have not taken a shower at the SRO in more than a year.

"I like being at the Marin Headlands. To be near the beach and mountains," I say, and, after a moment, "Is your shirt vintage?"

"Yeah," the supervisor says with a laugh, while watching me from beneath the corner of his sunglasses. "Pink flamingos... I was wondering, what's your race?"

"I am Latino," I say. "I like your shirt."

"You don't look Latino."

I want to say, "What does a Latino look like?" Instead, I ask, "What race do you think I am?"

"You look white like me," he says. "Like me."

I smile again and look inside his light-blue eyes and at his streaked, platinum-blonde hair. A large, gold necklace hangs loosely around his neck and accentuates the flecks of sequins sprinkled lightly on each flamingo of his shirt. I try to formulate an explanation for why we are unalike but am speechless when I recount to myself all of our fundamental differences.

I wonder how he would feel about me if he knew that my birth certificate says female and that I am not simply a gay man. Would he become angry? Would he feel duped? Would he threaten me? Would he try to hurt me?

My answer to his question about my race lacked specificity, so it did not challenge his assumptions about race. Perhaps, if I could provide a more complex answer, he would understand me better. I could start by explaining how the government added the term Hispanic in the 1970 Census.

"Is something wrong?" the supervisor asks.

"Huh?"

"Your sigh. It was really loud like you have something important on your mind. Do you want to ask me something?"

"Oh, no. I was just thinking."

"What about? Probably about some hot date you had over the weekend."

"No, about race. One can be…."

"I think you're good looking," he says. "And really well hung."

Once, I watched a retrospective of gay pornography at the Roxie. The theater was built in 1909. It is the oldest in San Francisco.

One of the characters in the movie was looking for a "date." He said, "You're really well hung" to another character. This seemed to do the trick, because before long, the two went at it hammer and tongs.

The audience laughed when the character said the line. I wonder if the supervisor is trying to be ironic.

"Ah…ah how long have you been out?" I ask.

"I came out in my early twenties when I started working at TWA, but I wasn't out at work. When an opening came up for a supervisor's position, I applied for the job and got it."

"Were you there until you retired?" I ask, and he nods. "How did you stay so long?"

"After work everyday, me and a friend of mine would do lines of coke and then go discoing. Back then, dancing was great. Sylvester would sometimes come by and sing, and he always brought an entourage of the most fascinating people—Marty Blecman, Patrick Crowley, Harvey Milk, and a lot of other local celebrities. I was such a good dancer that my feet never touched the floor. You probably can't tell, but I wasn't always an old fart," he says laughing.

"I can see you being a good dancer."

"I felt like I was flying. But I'm probably boring you about the good old, gay days."

"I like gay history."

"We had a lot of fun and did some crazy things. When I decided to retire, TWA made me get tested for HIV. I was sure I would test positive. I was so nervous about having AIDS that I promised myself that if I tested negative, as a way to say thank you to the universe, I would give up drugs and alcohol and become a Buddhist. So, when I found out that I was negative, I kept my promise. You know, I could have bought a big house in Sausalito with the money I made, but instead, I spent it all snorting coke and partying."

"You made a lot of money?"

"Mmm...yes, A LOT of money," he says and switches on the CD player. "How about you? Ever do any partying?"

"Recently, two of my..."

"This is my favorite song."

The supervisor turns up the CD player. His head bobs up and down as he sings first to "Dancing Queen" and then to other ABBA songs. His voice echoes through the canyon.

We wind our way up the hills behind Sausalito. When we reach the top of the Headlands, I smile at the brown jutting cliffs and the blue-green ocean. We turn into a winding dirt driveway and park along the side of an embankment. From the trunk, the supervisor pulls out several plastic bags full of supplies. He hands me the heaviest ones to carry. He pats me on my back and calls me his "strong buck."

With my hands full, we make our way up the road. The cool ocean breeze blows dusty sand into our hair and faces. I look back toward the sea.

The closeness of the ocean makes me want to run to it, to dive off the highest cliff and into the cool water. I want to disappear from the human world. I want to swim away from the land and toward the sea lions and seals.

"You'll assist me," the supervisor says and winks. "I made sure that my schedule's open."

"Thank you," I say. "I like doing grunt work."

"Don't be silly," he says. "We'll give you something interesting to do like feeding the sea lions and seals."

A woman approaches us in a dirty blue jumpsuit. She has tied her grey straggly hair into a knot, but it has fallen akimbo. She tells the supervisor that Animal Care and Control has just brought a dead sea lion into the backroom. The supervisor tells me to set the bags down in the front office. After I do, I catch up with him in the laboratory.

The woman tells the supervisor as much of the history of the sea lion as she knows. She explains that she will call the pet supply company when she finishes the autopsy. They will pick up the body, take it to their plant, and turn it into dog food.

She closes the door behind her. We are alone. He whispers.

"She's one of the only people who gets paid for working here. Watch out for her. She's a real bitch."

"She seems really…"

"The runoff from the farms kills the sea lions and seals because they get too near the drains."

The supervisor sounds like a tour guide. Then his demeanor transforms. His shoulders round. His whole face sags into a frown. A single tear rolls down the crevasses of his right cheek.

"You…you okay?" I ask.

"You'd think I'd get use to this by now."

He waves at the dead sea lion. From his front pants pocket, he pulls out a white, linen monogrammed handkerchief.

He folds it in half and wipes his nose and face.

"It seems hard to get used to."

My feet shuffle from side to side. One of my hands jiggles the change in my front pants pocket. I rock back on my heels and then forward onto my toes, back and forth, and back and forth.

"Your special powers could really help send this poor creature off to a better place." The supervisor's voice scratches. He blows his nose. His hand clutches one of mine.

"Would you help me prepare the sea lion for his next life?"

I wonder what he means by my special powers, "You…you believe in reincarnation?"

"Yes, yes I do."

The supervisor drops my hand. He dabs his eyes with his handkerchief. The flamingo-pink monogram bumps along the ridges of his face.

"Reincarnated how?" I ask with a nervous smile.

"The sea lion's not really dead because his soul will be reborn into another animal," his voice shakes.

"What…what would you come back as?" I ask.

My hands comb my hair back. I look around the room. My eyes rest on one of the corners of the ceiling.

"I've always thought that being a bird would be the best."

The supervisor refolds his handkerchief and puts it away. He walks towards the dead animal. His voice becomes strong again.

"Imagine flying all over the world under your own power. Wouldn't that be wonderful?"

"Yes."

"You know just what to say to make me feel better," he says with his back to me. "I love you."

"I…I like to help."

"What about you?" he says turning around and looking at me. "What would you come back as?"

"…A…a rock."

"A rock? That doesn't make any sense."

"Yes. A rock, like a cliff against the sea or a ledge in a forest."

"You can't come back as a rock. Rocks aren't alive."

"You do not think they…?"

"Of course not. You should come back as something wonderful. Something like a beautiful bird, like a…a…"

"A flamingo?" I ask and point at his shirt.

"Yes," he says smiling. "Not a rock. But a beautiful pink flamingo. We could fly around the world together."

He turns around, walks to the animal's side, and meditates over it. I stand nearby, waiting. When he finishes, we start to work.

I clean out the trashcans. They smell really bad. Their crevasses have many dead fish parts lodged deep inside. The supervisor says that no one likes to clean them. I turn each trashcan on its side, climb in and then scrub it with a soaped-up wire brush. I like cleaning the trashcans because it is something I can do well, and nobody notices when I lose my balance and fall down.

I like it when I am alone. I do not have to worry about holding a conversation. I do not have to worry about saying the wrong thing.

During lunch, the supervisor and volunteers eat and sample wines from a local vineyard that one of them owns. They all seem to be the same race and are rigidly gay or straight. As they eat, I whisper the proverb to myself, "With the rich and mighty, always a little patience," but I cannot remember its origins.

At the end of the meal, the janitor cleans up. His right hand, cupping a sponge, skillfully sweeps over the table's surface. The leftovers fall into a trashcan that he has balanced on his left hip.

Nobody acknowledges him or his work. When the janitor notices me staring, he grimaces a smile. I mouth the words "thank you" and smile back. He nods up and down and then shuffles away.

The supervisor tells me that cleaning out trashcans degrades me. I explain that I like to clean them because it is helpful. He insists that I work with him instead.

The supervisor changes into a pair of stained and dirty blue coveralls. He tells me a long list of directions that I cannot follow or remember. I walk behind him with a ten-gallon bucket of dead fish parts so that we can feed the sea lions.

I try to look down when the animals stare even though my impulse tells me to stare back. The supervisor yells at me to pay attention. The animals feel threatened and can attack me when I make eye contact with them. He yells that I am not listening. I wish that I could clean out the trashcans with the wire brush.

The supervisor has taken my picture in front of one of the seal tanks. He acts as if I am a tourist on holiday. At the end of my shift, the photograph is ready for me to keep as a memento for completing my training.

One hour before the last ferry departs, the supervisor and I get back into his car. We wind down the hills and around the mountains back to Sausalito. We are both tired from working a full day. We smell like a rotting ocean.

Smudges of dead fish parts cover me from head to toe. My dark-brown curly hair sticks to my forehead. Sometimes my vision blurs because even my eyelashes have dead fish parts imbedded in them.

"How is your meditation going?" I ask when I realize that the supervisor has stopped talking and is staring at me, "Do you still go to World Buddhist Center?"

"My guide tells me that I need to meditate more," he says with a laugh. "She's my best friend. I pay for her advice but then don't follow it."

"How often are you supposed to meditate?"

"Every day. But the only time I can is when I'm with her."

"Oh."

"I just can't seem to get into it."

Once, I visited the supervisor at his cottage on a hillside in Sausalito. Trees, ferns, and long vines of ivy surrounded the entire house. We walked through his winding garden and up to his front door.

Inside the cottage, his meditation cushions sat on the ground in a corner. He lay upon them, his leathery body against a heaping pile of plush greens and pinks. Then he demonstrated for me how he meditated everyday.

Nearby was a gold framed photograph of him and the Dalai Lama, which he handed to me. I looked at the two seated at a banquet table without decorations. They leaned into one another and smiled broadly—the kind of smiles that I do not trust. According to the supervisor, a friend had bought the picture for him as a present, because it cost more than $1,500, and he did not have the cash.

My hand clasps the door handle, and I turn to say goodbye. The supervisor's arms stretch up into the air. As they come down, the right one rests on the back of the passenger seat's headrest just behind me. His sunglasses have slipped down his nose, and he winks at me.

"Some of my friends and I are chartering a plane and boat," he says. "We're going to Alaska to watch the whales migrate."

"That sounds like fun," I say. "Then I will wait to hear from you about coming back to Ocean Animal Rescue."

"I wasn't telling you because of the schedule," he says. "We have an extra seat, and I thought you might want to come."

"Mmm... no."

My head shakes. The passenger seat squeaks, as my butt scoots to its edge. My face turns towards the direction of the ferry.

"Your spirit is so special," he says. "I think you're reincarnated from a very old soul."

"Thank you," I say. "But no."

"We have so much in common," he says, as he leans nearer to me. "I'm an old soul too."

The horn from the ferryboat sounds. As I get out of the car, I smile and say goodbye. The lines on the supervisor's face have tightened. His lips purse into a narrow smile.

I close the door and wave, but he does not acknowledge me. Instead, he adjusts his sunglasses. As he stares towards the road, his face looks like a bug with sensors instead of eyes.

I return home on the ferry to the city where I was born. As I walk the few miles from Pier 39 to the SRO at Sixth and Howard, I think about sending the supervisor a card trying to explain that he has mistaken my autism spectrum disorder for spiritual powers. Perhaps I could mention my gender non-conformity too.

When I get to the SRO, my neighbor is waiting for me. He leans against the doorframe smoking a cigarette. The doorway leads to our rooms.

My neighbor is somewhere between thirty and sixty years old. I cannot separate his biological age from the environmental factors that have affected his body. He has a long jagged scar on his face that runs from the right side of his forehead through his eyebrow, down his eyelid and cheek, through his lips, down his chin, and ends with a healed jagged scar near his collarbone at the base of his neck. He stands with his hands clasped behind his back and his legs spread apart, which adds squareness to his already boxy frame.

"Faggot, pussy, it, it," he repeats the staccato phrase over-and-over in a baritone melody and then laughs.

He follows me inside our entryway. When we arrive at my door, he stands over me as tall as he can, his arms crossed in front of him. I fumble for my keys.

My neighbor says that he knows my secret—that I want him to rape and murder me because I am a freak. I look straight ahead and pretend not to hear. As my hand places the key in the lock, his aria continues. After I close the door, I move the barricade I have made out of stack of six boxes of books in front of the doorframe. I turn on the radio and can no longer hear him.

Maybe I have email, I think. My phone line screams as it connects to my computer. I wonder if the supervisor still wants me to go to Alaska.

More than anything, I want to get away from the SRO at least for a little while. Going with him would be unfair, though, since he does not see our differences—how or why we are unalike. His knowledge of who I really am would fundamentally change our relationship.

Perhaps he has more interest in me than just as someone he supervises. This would be a problem. I want to continue to volunteer at the animal shelter and Ocean Animal Rescue.

I open an email from him that begins "My Dear One." The supervisor says that had we met in the past, before he was a Buddhist, he would not have minded my disinterest. Now, his spirituality dictates clean and clear relationships.

Apparently, he finds my ethereal wisdom too attractive and too enticing, but he does not elaborate. He tells me that I can no longer volunteer because it would be unfair to him. The situation makes him uncomfortable, although he never says this directly.

As I get ready for bed, my neighbor makes a lot of noise. Our shared wall begins to shake. I hear and feel him ripping the pressboard cupboards from their hinges and kicking new holes in the walls as he has done previously.

The word "unfair" pops into my head. My chest hurts and my breath becomes shallow. I flush as if bees have stung me all over my body.

When I lie down, I purposefully breathe as deeply as I can from my diaphragm. I picture myself naked at the Headlands. I jump from the highest cliff into the ocean. My breathing calms down, as the seawater cools off my body.

I float out to sea. The sea lions and seals swim to meet me. They do not mind that I am looking at them. Just before I fall asleep, I think: tomorrow I will need to look for a new place to volunteer.

SLOW BOIL:
AIDS AND THE REMNANTS OF TIME
Eric A. Stanley

One arm around his back, tightly holding the weight of our histories, hoping they would not fall to the earth. Salty nape smooth with hairless skin cradled my face; the promise of flesh, the promise of his flesh, was that it would stitch my wounds tight. And that these wounds from past harm might divide into the strength of scarred skin able to withstand more than before. Slow pushes grew with force, pounding away the hurt of growing up different, the guilt of surviving when one ought not. As his come met our chest I fell deeper into him.

"AIDS KILLS FAGGS DEAD," the homophobic snap of 1980s apparel, taught me how to be a fag. I was born along with the virus or at least its discovery, in the late 1970s. Unlike the generations of faggots before me, I never knew a time without AIDS. And unlike the generation after me, I could never know the dangerous contemporary denial that argues AIDS is over. The discursive practices of the public and private culture I inhabited made me sure of at least two things. The first was that the semiotics of my small frame and fey body was indeed that of a faggot. I didn't need to go any further than the playground to be reminded of this reality. The second truth was that as a fag, I would die of AIDS. In this co-presence, AIDS and faggotry were forged as one, in the blood of those that were dead and dying and through the AIDS-phobic representations that brought both to my pre-teen eyes.

Dry eyes and a slow kiss only new lovers can give welcomed me. His shirtless chest quaked against mine. A sheetless mattress guarded one corner of the room and caught our bodies as we fell back into his pillow. The energy of seeing his face again bounced my organs out of place and aligned them all the same. Geography made our love grow slow, and compressed the time we shared. His body felt much warmer than usual, which was always warmer than mine. Earlier that day he'd said he was feeling sick, a bit of a cold or maybe a spring flu, so I brought him some organic orange juice and a can of chicken-free noodle soup. After we each gulped down a glass of the juice we fucked on his damp mattress. Ravaged from sex and a sick and sleepless night, the fibers of the bed felt cold against my skin. Even warmer than before, we laid together in silence teased by the hot Central Valley summer air falling in though an open window. The Streets played on a loop as I traced the outline of his hip with my mouth, tasting the effect of simmering blood. His fever grew and the medicine offered nothing. I filled a cold bath and forced his desperately burning body deep under water.

Dan Rather's voice echoed nightly through the dusk of my parents' den. News of the Sandinistas and the Los Angeles Olympic games was sliced with sensational stories of a new "gay cancer" emerging in large urban areas. As the reports mounted over those early years, the growing body count and images of thin flesh draping the bones of hospital-bound bodies filled the screen. Even in the confusion of my six-year-old eyes I knew they would never be leaving those beds. Captured in the frame, their dying bodies were to remain entombed in the scandal and sin that was gay sex. The reports told stories of God's wrath here on earth, of multiple partners and a disease so deadly a single kiss was more than enough contact to ensure death. Deadly saliva and communicable little boys whose houses and bodies could only be washed away in a baptism of flames, this caustically made me feel less alone. The manufactured hysteria and fear was also joined in my psyche by an identification with the ghosted men dying. I saw my ancestors in the faces of those abject corpses.

He said almost in passing that he was going to get tested. My skin stood still as it always does when a past or current lover gets tested. Every moment of contact is retraced in hopes of not finding gaps where the presence of the moment failed to give way to the dogma of latex. His voice read a little nervous but not unlike most fags when faced with the possibility that this might be their last negative result. I assured him with a kind of performative certainty that everything would be fine, as he assured me. He surrendered his blood to Planned Parenthood. The week went by and I attempted to inhabit a hypnotized forgetting of the travel of his blood now fractioned and held captive in an outsourced lab.

It is not that AIDS only kills fags. For sure, we know that the global pandemic kills millions throughout the world, most of whom are not fags.

However, within the US context, fags will always be imbued with the crushing reality that AIDS is our destiny. The rectum may in fact be a grave, but not because of the wish fulfillment of a suicidal death drive, but because AIDS offered the wish fulfillment of a homicidal culture that knows fags have always been, and must always be already dead.

525. "It came back positive," typed out in unmistakable keystrokes and sent to my instant messenger, burned me into ash. The cold anonymity of the virtual world was made into flesh. His phone had been turned off so he was unable to call. Alone in the scarcity of his room he sat with the news as my mind collapsed history and logic to undo what was being done. The fear was not at first from the possibility of him vanishing before his time. My muscles froze and my heart made it heavy to breathe for the fear that it was I who infected him. In a panic I rushed to the only clinic still open that night offering rapid results, the Berkeley Free Clinic. There I was met in the waiting room with the usual chaos and gloom that fills the lobbies for those who cannot afford anything else. The clinician lectured me for almost 15 minutes on the dangers of "finger sex" and how even a small cut on my hand could lead to AIDS. After an hour I was reassured that I was not the source of the viral multiplication.

The homophobic gaze of normative culture that first offered me the possibility to look on as my ancestors lay dying also turns inward. The mechanism of various forms of microscopic and photographic technologies, as well as the affective currents of grief, denial and shame opened my body for compulsory viewing. I, and all faggots, inherit this position as objects for medical surveillance. The emerging HIV/AIDS apparatus not only policed my body as a kid, but even worse, taught me how to undo desire in the name of fear. The crucial knowledge that comes from HIV/AIDS research is translated through the tongues of state violence into information that continues to remind me that gay sex is certain death.

620. The doctor said they could find no evidence of drug resistance. His viral load was low enough and his CD4 count high enough that they suggested blood work every three months and no medication, yet. The crumbling of time realigned our newly forming cosmology from that of clumsy lovers to a biological intimacy much ahead of our time. We went from random encounter to bounded lives in the force of a day. Awakening love and ethical obligation to build possible worlds where "community" and "family" might be given a name and a purpose that cause less pain than their previous incarnations compelled me, compelled us, to try to forge a bond that was much too full to hold either of us. He moved from his apartment in the Central Valley to a residential hotel paid for by a nonprofit

specializing in HIV+ people 25 and under. He shortly aged out of that situation and found himself in a long string of precarious living arrangements. The continuing instability of his life now seemed haunted by his serostatus, or maybe it was the other way around.

Ours is a time out of time. Faggots of my generation, who were born in the time of AIDS, have no claim to a history that was anything different or to a future that can be at all. If I am to think of kinship beyond the bounds of heteronormativity, in hopes of constructing an anti-narrative of history and generation, then where can I look? If the past is written in the negativity of death, then how can there be a present, let alone a future? The tragedy of AIDS is, among other things, the forced passage into dying before one's time. In the time after death a gap is made where history and bodies ought to be. There is no martyrdom in a faggot's death. Here in a time outside the logic of sacrifice there is only decomposition and bone.

450. The water ran red and I jumped back a bit. We rarely showered together; the heat of the spray irritated my sensitive skin or maybe the proximity of water and space was too much for a relationship riddled with growing suspicion and doubt. The razor traced the contours of his jaw, slicing away just enough flesh to liberate its contents. My fear of blood was also the fear of his blood. With an unthought utterance I asked him not to bleed on me. But what he heard, and maybe what I said without words, was "don't make me like you." He referenced this shower with a calibrated precision when, in the drama of a lover's fight, he wanted to expose my AIDS-phobia as a lack of commitment.

AIDS is, among other things, a time of death. Not because it is simply a "death sentence," but because even when one is living with AIDS one is haunted by the specter of death in a way much different than for those who are negative. What, then, might the necessarily polemic "living with AIDS" really mean, if AIDS itself is tethered to death? Or, in other words, what kind of faggot's life is not lived under the shadow of AIDS? For sure, the declaration that HIV+ folks are still living is politically and psychically necessary. However, denying the deadliness of AIDS might not be the best way of apprehending its power.

300. He was living the death that first taught me how to be a faggot. The images of people dying of AIDS that ironically gave me a terrorized hope that I was not alone now left me with a constellation of feeling too much. Our relationship and love wore on and I began to tell the seasons by bloodwork and dropping CD4 counts. With each result I feared the news would bring him closer to death. I did not know how I would cope, what my last words to him would be, or how his hand would ice over as

the blood stopped flowing. How could I hold the guilt of another? How could I leave the hospital room when I knew he never would? I imagined, as I still do, if time would pass without him here. Unable to live this collective legacy of genocide still in the making, eventually we broke. Beyond recuperation, I am left with these fragmented endings and displaced desires which bear the weight of our history which is yet to come.

EXCELSIOR

Jaime Cortez

Four in the morning is the soft place between days. The hour does not deliver the decisive cleavage of midnight, the raunchy last-call spillage of two
AM or the sweet exhaustion of three. Four in the morning is SFPD cruisers
gliding up Mission Street like mantas. It is tattered hunters spearing coke
cans in the wet of the gutters. Crack chickens hunching over and scratch-
ing at the sidewalk. Taqueria crewmen scrubbing down the stoves, stacking
up the chairs, silencing the jukebox cumbias, and retreating to apartments
warm with the heat of too many bodies. Four in the morning is the Excelsior District rumbling with the snores of immigrants from Manila, More-
lia, and Guangdong on streets named after the fabled capitals of Europe,
dreaming their California dreams in chopped-up English.

Four in the morning is me, hopped up on insomnia and layered crav-
ings, loneliness on horniness on restlessness on I don't know what, but it
has me seeking escape in the driver's seat. On some blocks not one soul
is visible so I entertain myself by authoring drive-by biographies of each
solitary pedestrian. A narrow-assed boy with his jeans drooping about his
thighs waddles up Mission. He is afraid to go home, I guess. Stepdad's a
prick. Mom's whipped. So he waddles up the street, hoodie up, headphones
on, vomiting DMX's strangled lyrics all over the sidewalk. The Chinese
lady with the stirrup pants and tragically sensible haircut is headed to a
Chinatown bakery, I imagine. I picture her filling hundreds of tiny tart
shells with golden custard for the Sunday dim sum rush.

The boy leans against the wall of Cinderella's Filipino Takeout. Hands
in the knockoff Niners jacket. Got some Mayan in him, I guess, but still
his black shock of hair is making its way back to mother Africa, frizzing
up in the fog. Adorable goatee trying to prove something. He tilts his head

upward in greeting as I cruise by. A dealer. He smiles a bit. Not a dealer. I vulture around the block for a second look, watching him from the corner of my eye. Paydirt. He raises a hand, draws a truncated arc in the air before sticking it back into his jacket pocket. That gesture is pure voodoo, it opens up a chemical valve that dumps something scintillating into my blood, and everything gets simple. My layered needs evaporate, leaving only the twin survivors, fear and desire.

He waved. What to do? What to do? This is crazy. I want this. But it's crazy. I want this. I park around the corner and walk towards him. He smiles, flashing white against his brown. Beauty.

"How you doing?" I ask.

"Good *papi*, good."

Dimples.

"So what are you doing driving around?"

"Restless," I say. "Looking for fun."

"Oh yeah? I like fun too. What kind of fun you like, big man?" I smile as the fuck or flight imperative gets my blood moving seriously now. I've got a hundred pounds on this guy, easy, but there's nothing more dangerous than a young guy trying to prove something. I'm on the edge of backing away from this thing we're sliding into, but he reels me back in.

"It's okay, papa," he encourages, "We're friends. You can say what kind of fun."

"Well, actually, I'm looking for sex."

"That's natural. Everybody needs sex," he says.

"True," I concur. I feel my heartbeat back around my kidneys. I become aware of my cock.

"So, big dog," he asks, "you live around here?" This is a perfect time to say I live in San Jose, that it's late, and I should be heading home.

"Yeah. Just up and around that corner." I point to demonstrate, and casually add the final bit. "Close enough we could walk there." He pauses. Shit. This whole thing is seesawing towards failure, and I smile.

"C'mon," I say, "I promise I'm not a killer or a freak."

"What's wrong with freaks?"

"Oh, you like freaks?" Now he's smiling too. We're close now. Very close.

"Okay, let's go," he says. We walk past Lisbon, Paris, Edinburgh.

"Where you from?" I ask.

"The Mission."

"No, I mean, are you originally from here?"

"No. El Salvador."

"Aah, a *Trucho*. How long you been here?'

"Six years. Almost seven."

"Your family in El Salvador or up here in San Francisco?"

"Some here. Some not."

He handles the interrogation well. I want to know how old he is, but I don't want to hear it. I wonder what he remembers of the civil war. Sounds. Goya tableaus in headlights. Maybe he was too young, and the war existed as a feeling he picked up from others. Black pillow of fear coming at his face. Suspicion that the day after tomorrow is about as far as one should plan.

We turn the corner, and as we near the house I run my "bedroom or garage?" calculus. The bedroom option would be sweet. I want to take him to bed. Have a proper fuck, maybe even kiss. He could be a virgin. Could be his first time. I could walk him through that door. I'm excited now, then I picture things going bad. Imagine a warm pistol hammocked in his hip hop pocket. I picture the robbery.

"Unplug that stereo." $140

"The watch." $15

"Gimme that painting." $1,200

"The Kangol. The real one too, not the fake one, fat boy." $30

"That laptop. Throw that Mac shit in the bag too." $1,750

Shit. This date is getting expensive. I opt for the garage scenario.

"I live in the green house." I tell him. " We can't go up or we'll wake up my cousins," I have almost convinced myself I really do have cousins upstairs. "We'd better just go to the garage," I say. As I fumble with the keys, he tenses up.

"Hey wait," he says.

"What's up?"

"I'm having a real hard time, you know what I'm saying? I was dishwashing. Fisherman's Wharf. But the restaurant cut a bunch of jobs. Mine."

"You want money?"

"Not a lot, man. Just a little money."

Fuck. We stare at each other for a moment. Nobody's happy about this. I have done some crazy, stupid things for sex, but in the predominantly pro-bono sexual economy of gay San Francisco, I have always maintained a strict policy of never paying for it.

"If you need money to play, I think you need to find someone else." I tell him. He sighs heavy and sad. The social service provider in me elbows his way past the slut and moves my lips.

"I'll tell you what," I say. "I got a few bucks back in my car. Enough for a burrito and a coke. You can have them. No sex, no nothing. You can have them." He looks stunned and soft. We walk back past Edinburgh, Paris, Lisbon. Nothing will be traded for cheap tonight, and we both relax.

"You like Shakira?" he asks.

"Not really. I liked a couple of the songs off that first album when she was real young."

"I don't like the prostitute look she has now," he says. "She wasn't like that before, but she'll do anything to be a number one USA star."

"Oh really?" I respond. At my car, I pop the glove compartment and fish out my wallet. I've got a five and two ones.

"Here's seven," I tell him.

"Thanks, *papi*. That's great."

"Here, take this too." I hand him a condom from the bottom of the compartment and shake his hand.

"Be careful out there," I warn.

"I will."

I turn and head up the street. I fancy myself a film noir angel, kind of fucked up, dumpy, tarnished, and sad, but generous and life-changing.

"Hey wait!" he says.

I turn. He walks towards me. My body tightens up.

"Hey listen, *papi*. I want to go with you. To the garage."

"You don't have to do that. Just take the money."

"No. I want to do this. For free."

"You sure?" He nods yes.

By the time we get to Paris, the gutter romance of it all engulfs me like a cloud of knockoff perfume. I want to hold his hand, kiss his cheek, fuck with him on the sidewalk, call him boo-boo or something sweet.

At the garage, I check again.

"You sure you want to play? You don't have to."

"It's all good. Let's go in."

Once inside, he is nervous in the dark. I take him by the shoulders and guide him to the wall. He shudders.

"Just lean back here," I whisper.

I drop to my knees and reach for his belt. My hands tremble. I fumble with the buckle and he unzips. I stick my nose in the opening, inhaling deeply. It smells good in there.

His dick is soft when I take it out. I study its rounded outline in the dark. He didn't have to share this. He wants to share this. My mouth goes wet. I run maddening calculations on this boy, this body, its history. I wonder how long he's been selling sex. I wonder what people paid for it in San Salvador. In San Francisco? I unthink this. I close my eyes and bury my face in the crotchy warmth. Funny how nuts all taste pretty much the same to me. At the end of a workday, a bike messenger's sac tastes pretty much like a waiter's or a telemarketer's or a trucker's. Dick, on the other hand, is amazingly complicated and variable and this boy's dick is a marvel of flavor. It glides into my mouth and it is perfect in bouquet with both sweet and salty undertones. He places his hand on my head. His fingers trace furrows through the stubble of my buzz cut. I slip my hand under his pants and grab a great girly handful of smooth rounded ass. He twists a bit, releasing himself from my grasp. I suck, deliriously contented. He sucks air and it catches on the way out.

He never goes completely soft and never fully hardens. I cup his nuts like newborns.

"Is this good for you?" I ask.

"Hm." His response is inconclusive. I probe some more.

"You want it harder, softer, anything?" He remains silent, looking to the left at the light coming through the pebbled glass portal on the garage door. I suck some more. I feel him backing out of his body. I want him back and vary the rhythm, licking his nuts, then his pelvic crest, then that warm crease where his leg meets his crotch.

"I want to see you come," I say.

He spreads his legs to keep his jeans up and begins rapid, high friction stroking. I encourage him softly. He strokes it, pulls at it, slaps blood into it, hoping to launch a full erection. It never manifests, and he continues stroking, switching his grip when his arm tires. My knees begin to throb on the cement. Finally, he goes tight. His mouth forms a great stretched "O" and I place my hand just under the crown of his dick. He shoots, one, two, three thin waves of come. In the darkness, it glows pale and warm against my palm. I shut my hand into a fist and rise. He zips himself up and gropes his way towards the door.

I locate the door latch for him and open it.

"Did it feel good?" I ask.

"It was okay," he mumbles as he exits.

"You need a ride, dude?" God, I just called someone "dude."

"No. Gotta go. See you."

"You want my number, in case you want to come by again later? Doesn't have to be for sex." He turns on his heel and steps up his pace, almost jogging by the time he disappears around the corner.

In the dark, I make out the derelict exercise bike my upstairs neighbor had purchased years ago and hardly used. I mount the machine and lean my head against the handlebar console. My knees throb. My loneliness is sudden, deep, and full, a cello sighing in the dark. The come is cooling in my palm, but my hand remains closed in a fist with a small pocket of air inside, as if I had captured a sprite on the wing and hadn't figured out what to do next.

MY FEAR, THE FORCES BENEATH

Willow Aerin Fagan

I could barely speak to the other gay boys at the LGBT community center youth group I attended in high school. Partially, this was due to adolescent awkwardness. I was afraid of getting rejected because I was too fat, because my nose was too big, because I was too nerdy, too mystical, too different. But there was also the barely unearthed scaffolding of internalized homophobia within me, a deep structure built up over years of fundamentalist Christian indoctrination in private schools, at church, at home. There was still guilt encrusting my queer desires, shame squishing my sexual fantasies. And whenever I tried to speak with another gay boy, the possibility of sex loomed so large it eclipsed any calm. I was utterly distracted by my yearning for and fear of sex, still frightened of rejection or punishment.

This fear of punishment was, in part, a lingering effect of the inherited Christian worldview I had recently abandoned. In its place, I enshrined a dark romanticism, rejecting both my fundamentalist upbringing and the fashion signifiers most popular among the homophobic boys at my school. Paradoxically, this identity also alienated me from the other gay boys; I had already rejected consumerist, disposable pop culture like their beloved Madonna, and their Abercrombie & Fitch clothes reminded me of the homophobic bullies who tormented me with taunts, who demanded, "You're a faggot, aren't you?"

Raised Christian or not, in the ongoing holy war that is "America," what queer man does not know the taste of condemnation? Whose queer desire is not somehow mixed with fear, in this land where faggots are murdered with intimate, suggestive violence, strangled by male hands or penetrated by knives? What person who has chosen, discovered, or been forced into the identity of "man," has not had his heart malformed in some way by the pressure to appear invulnerable, the demand to develop a seamless, silent skin that covers any potential vulnerability or opening, the expectation that "being a man" means enacting violence?

* * * * *

In high school, I attributed my inability to connect with the other gay boys to some failure on my part, some defect which I was terrified I could not change. I tried to externalize the self-hatred I felt to cultivate a bitterness I wielded as both sword and shield, but this only made my stomach hurt. I also tried to turn my self-hatred into a sharp instrument with which to cut my body into a thinner shape, a shape which I believed someone else could love. No one ever said to me that I could only be loved if I lost weight. But in my suburban, Christian fundamentalist world the only images of physical intimacy between men that I could find were in porn magazines bought for me by my older friend Sarah, or pictures downloaded furtively from the Internet while my parents were sleeping or out at a card club with their friends from church. All the men in these untouchable worlds were muscular and thin. I saw no one like myself—pudgy, shy, bespectacled. These manufactured fantasies of sex seemed seamless to me, a charmed circle of desire that I could not enter without shedding pounds of my own flesh.

I absorbed these glossy illusions and felt angry disapproval when I would see people whose bodies were too large to fit into them. *Why couldn't they control themselves?* I would think. I avoided looking at my own body, especially when I was naked. I wore as much clothing as I could at all times, wearing a T-shirt when I would go swimming in the local pool with the sharp tang of chlorine in the air, the wet shirt clinging to my chest like an artificial skin. I focused my attention on my arms, which were thin, and my hands, which I thought were beautifully shaped, simultaneously elegant and capable. I only looked at my face in the mirror from certain angles. There was something I was afraid to see, something relating to my body, a secret that my fat concealed and contained.

The first layer of the secret was this: while I was scared that no one would want to touch me because of my body, I was much more scared that someone would want to touch me, that someone would desire me. Seen in this light, my fat appears to be a protective barrier, a necessary insulation.

Why am I so afraid of being touched by men? This question echoes throughout the years of my life, deep into the hidden place where I locked memory away, where my father forced his penis down my throat on my fifth birthday, when he told me, "I'm doing this because you want it, faggot." And so I am afraid not only of other men, faggots, who might want to touch me in the places my father did; I am afraid of my own queer desire.

My father told me once that he could barely remember anything before he was twelve. When I asked him, "What was it like to grow up on a farm? To have eight brothers and sisters?" he replied, "There's not much to say. We worked all the time." He did not say, "My brother molested me." He did not say, "My father beat me and raped me."

* * * * *

Despite my fear, I could not hold the secret of my queerness, of my desire, within the confines of my skin, behind the gates of my teeth. I hinted and hinted to my mother, saying things like, "Did you know Ellen DeGeneres is a lesbian?" apropos of nothing, until finally she asked me, point blank. I couldn't bear to lie. We had a theological argument about whether gay sex was sinful. "But just because you want it, doesn't mean it's okay," she said. "What about pedophiles, or people who want to have sex with animals?"

In the years since I remembered that my father sexually abused me, I have realized that some of what turned me on—porn in which there's dirty talk, in which one man says to another, "You like that, huh, faggot?"—did so because it resonated with the violence my father inflicted. This uncovering brought about fearful questions. If some of my desire was rooted in or shaped by the abuse, how could I know which parts weren't? Was all of it tainted? Was I only attracted to men because I had been abused? Would I have to give up being queer in order to heal?

These anxieties echoed the homophobic narrative that queer desires are unnatural and twisted, that their origin is rooted in dysfunctional families or sexual abuse, that queerness is a mental illness that can be healed. This narrative appeared in the *Focus on the Family* magazines my parents subscribed to, and in documentaries at the private Lutheran high school where they sent me. Although both my parents were fundamentalists, my father was the true source of the zeal infecting my childhood world. He had been "born again" as part of the chaos of a psychological breakdown which involved the perception that a camera watched him from the television and which culminated in a real-life episode during which he locked my aunt in the garage after she stood between him and my mother, who was scared and trying to leave. But after my father was hospitalized and then declared stable, my mother squashed her doubts and joined him in a faith in which Truth was as black-and-white and clearly delineated as the printed letters in the big, leather-encased Bible that sat on the back of the toilet. This rigid doctrine propped my father up and, not incidentally, ascribed him the authority and final say as "man of the house." Despite this, he acted strangely childlike; he would spontaneously sing songs of his own creation and frequently make silly noises. But rather than appearing joyful, he seemed blank, as if an essential part of him was simply not there.

He did not question or explore this emptiness. He was filled with certainty; he knew what God wanted. God wanted him to teach his son what was right and wrong. Even when I was a child, my father could sense the deviance in me and was terrified or enraged by it.

* * * * *

Each year in high school, I grew more and more depressed, and more and more enamored of my depression. At first, in my dark romanticism, I believed in honoring sadness as a necessary counterbalance to a culture of relentless, superficial happiness, of endless plastic yellow smiley faces and upbeat television jingles cheering us on as we consumed the world to extinction. But as time went on I began to think of madness as beautiful in and of itself, and then death as beautiful, and then suicide as beautiful.

They put me on anti-depressants, of course, damming up my pain with chemicals while I lived with the man who had raped me, while I brushed my teeth in the room in which he had forced his penis down my throat. I did not yet remember this, could not allow the trauma to surface and still manage to survive in that place, but I knew that the happiness I felt was false, that the pills were not a solution. So I stopped taking them.

In my suicide note, I wrote in big, shaky, capital letters, "I'M A FAGGOT, DAD." I took a few pills, drank some of the wine cooler I had stolen from the refrigerator, and stopped. I was terrified. I didn't want to die. I called 911 myself, and somehow the operator knew that I was gay. She said something like, "Lots of people are gay, honey, it's okay," and stayed on the line with me while the paramedics came.

I thought I was home alone, but when the paramedics arrived they encountered my father upstairs. He was scared and confused, unable to understand why I hadn't asked him for help. He was in the same house but he had no idea that I was in so much pain. He could not see, refused to look at the wound he had inflicted, the wound which mirrored his own, which he also refused to see.

* * * * *

I have no rational or demonstrable way of proving that my father is attracted to men, and yet I know it to be true. I know because of the way he molested me, because of the way he began his abuse: we stood peeing into the same toilet. I looked at his penis with childhood curiosity. He said, "You like looking at it so much, you better come over here and touch it, faggot." I knew because of the way he stroked my hair seductively but with the threat of a hit or worse unmistakable beneath; because of the way he kept saying, "Yeah, you like it, you dirty faggot," in an attempt to force away the desire he saw as sinful and shameful, unspeakable, into me, into my body, a tiny vessel to carry his burden in silence.

A faggot, in my father's eyes, meant more than a man who wanted to have sex with other men. It meant a man who showed vulnerability, softness, a man who cried, a man who moved with grace, a man who did not live in the stable, traditional structure of masculinity, but was fluid, unpredictable, dangerous. A man open to the hungers and thirsts of his heart, and to the possibility of love, connection, those wild intimacies which expose one to so much potential joy, so much potential hurt.

* * * * *

Many of my father's ideas about masculinity remain current, despite some shifts in the social landscape. The core ideal of masculinity is still the rigid, invulnerable man, always in control. This image has been taken up by gay culture, polished, worshiped in the form of glossy magazine images and hard, gleaming bodies. There is a perverse circle: the masculinity we lust after, which we seek as rescuer and lover, is the very same masculinity which appears in those who attempt to destroy us, in body and mind, soul and heart.

There were many entrenched social forces supporting and enabling my father's sexual violence, pushing him away from healing his own trauma and towards inflicting new wounds on me. There was the hard wall built between "masculine" and "feminine," a border one could not cross without paying the toll of exile; the masculine prohibition on exhibiting vulnerability, or any emotion other than anger; the religious teaching of the divine right of fathers to set down unquestionable laws within their small, familial fiefdoms; the cutting up of communities and kinship networks into private, separate nuclear families; and on and on.

The shame, silence, and fear which choked my father's heart, turning his desire into violence, echo throughout society in a thousand ways, a thousand assaults on queerness and queer people. And yet so many queer men are rushing to embrace these forces, these images of masculinity, in their quest for normalcy, for the shining prize of recognition by a sexist society as "real men." A deep fear arises within me at the sight of this; this is not a fear rooted in illusion but a clear-eyed fear. There is so much danger, so much harm, down this path.

The roots of my fear lead to a terrible place, a scene in which I am wounded beyond words. When I return to this place, I discover again and again that the ideals of masculinity are upside down; making myself rigid and closed to the flood of emotions only locks me up with the pain; refusing to be vulnerable only isolates me from those who care, who would share the burden of my pain; there is no way to demand dominance without repeating the monstrous role of my father in some capacity. The trick, I have found, is not to reject all that has been labeled "masculine," but to remain flexible, fluid, able to cross borders when needed. It is from these experiences that I say: There is another way, there are other ways for queer men, gay men, men who desire men, to walk and talk, to sing and cry, to breathe and open, to open and open and open.

CELL BLOCK 6

Mishael Burrows

"I don't want that new cop to be our gunner," Officer Matthews says to me. We're sitting in our office outside of the housing unit. Officer Matthews is my partner three times a week in Cell Block 6.

Including myself, there are three correctional officers in the building. We're supposed to be supervising 128 maximum security inmates.

The new cop in question is Officer Bradley, who operates our doors up in the block's control tower with the department-issued rifle slung on his back.

"What are you saying that for?" I ask. "Bradley's been working up there for two weeks and he's doing fine."

"New cops don't even belong up on the gun," Matthews scoffs. He says this as if he's a fifteen-year veteran, when he only has a year in himself.

"Don't start with that shit," I say.

It's supposed to be fall in central California, but it's hotter than hell in Cell Block 6 because the A/C is out. The inmates are irritable and I'm thinking that now would not be a good time for Matthews and Bradley to have what our sergeant likes to call *a personal conflict in the workplace*.

"You know why I don't want him up there, Burrows." Matthews has his boots propped up on the desk. He's digging around in the McDonald's bag he brought in.

I have an idea, but I want Matthews to say it himself. "Because he's just out of the academy and only 23 years old?" I ask.

Matthews rolls his eyes. He and I are also in our twenties. "You know *why*."

"Why?" I press.

"He's a fuckin' faggot is why!" Matthews snaps.

He's mad that I made him say it out loud. He knows he sounds like all the other redneck and/or ghetto-fabulous guards we work with. Matthews likes to think he's better than our co-workers because he has a bachelor's degree.

He's not.

I sit there looking at Matthews, also aware that I'm dependent on him to help me stay safe at work that day. We also don't need *a personal conflict in the workplace.*

"What does that have to do with it?" I ask. "He went through the same process we did to get hired. So far he seems like a good officer."

"A gay cop is going to complicate things for us in here," Matthews says. "We're going to have to watch him all of the time."

"That's stupid," I say. "You might as well say you don't want to work with me either because I'm a chick."

"It's not the same," Matthews says. "The inmates already know he's gay. They're going to be on him like flies on shit."

"So?" I challenge. "The inmates know I'm straight. After you check them a couple of times they leave you alone. Bradley knows how to do that."

"You don't get it," Matthews says. "Just watch."

We have an inmate called Keno who is our designated porter. He's supposed to clean our office and the tiers in Cell Block 6. He's the largest white inmate in the building. Prison policy states that we have to give Keno the opportunity to come out and work during our shift. He spends most of his time at work passing notes and drugs on the tiers and giving orders to the other white inmates. Prison policy also states that we're supposed to give him written reprimands for this, but Keno is doing life without parole. A written reprimand doesn't even make a blip on his radar.

Matthews leaves me alone with Keno so he can sneak a cigarette and a cellphone call out on the yard. Prison policy prohibits the use of tobacco and cellphones by guards. It is lenient, however, about leaving female and/or homosexual staff alone with inmates.

"What's up with that new cop?" Keno asks casually, leaning on his mop.

Keno's face is scarred from fights and rampant drug use. One of the nurses brings him steroids at medication pass; he's tripled in size recently and doesn't engage in compulsive calisthenics. Keno knows that I'm aware of what the nurse is giving him. He tries to be my "friend," if there is such a thing in prison.

"Bradley's not that new," I say apathetically.

"But he's also not that old," Keno smirks.

When I don't say anything. Keno asks, "Why did they put a fish cop up on the gun? Is he Matthews's *girl*friend?"

"Don't start with your shit, Keno," I warn. He chuckles and walks back towards the housing unit, dragging the mop behind him and leaving a trail of slime.

A few days later, Matthews and I are in our office when we hear Officer Bradley yelling at an inmate. The housing unit's shower is in full view from the control tower. The inmate had started to non-discreetly masturbate and from the sound of it, Bradley was not impressed.

There are rules about masturbation within the prison population. Inmates do not masturbate in front of one another unless they have a sexual relationship. To do so is considered "disrespect." Inmates also test new staff by exposing themselves. If the staff member doesn't say anything to the offending inmate, the other inmates believe that the staff member is either aroused or afraid. Silence invites more sexual solicitation.

Matthews and I respond to the shower area.

"That motherfucker was in there whacking it!" Bradley yells at us through a gun port. I can hear the cell block stirring. Inmates are at their cell doors listening.

"What the fuck is your problem?" Matthews asks the inmate in the shower.

"Nothing," the inmate mutters.

"Were you disrespecting my officer?" I demand.

"He's a bitch!" the inmate protests.

"You're the bitch!" I say. "And right now you're a bitch engaging in sexual misconduct."

"That sounds like disrespect to me," Matthews says.

Matthews and I leave the inmate in the shower. We tear up his cell. I confiscate the inmate's homemade tattoo gun and tattoo ink. We handcuff the masturbator before we escort him out of the shower and place him back in the disheveled cell. He rants and raves that we have no right to search his stuff, saying that he never gives us problems. He kicks his cell door for the rest of the shift and demands to see our sergeant. He tells us he's going to sue us for cruel and unusual punishment. He threatens our lives.

I tell Bradley to ignore the inmate and let us know if he exposes himself again.

"I told you we were going to have problems," Matthews says.

"Shut up, Matthews," I snap. I'm pissed off that his hypothesis is coming true.

"I told you, Burrows," he laughs.

"Matthews, you'd be in the shower spankin' it to Bradley too if you were caged up in this shithole," I retort. "He smells better than your girlfriend does."

Matthews keeps laughing at me. He's smug and I want to stick him with the homemade tattoo needle.

The steroid nurse goes on vacation and a new male nurse works in her place. The nurse is flamboyant and carries the pills in a Victoria's Secret bag during medication pass. Keno asks the nurse if he knows what Victoria's secret is and Matthews won't stop laughing. I want to shank them both.

The nurse is pissed. He threatens to file a sexual harassment complaint against Matthews. This would name me as a witness to Matthews's behavior. I try to tell the nurse that maybe it would be better if he brought the medication in a different bag. He asks me if I am prejudiced. I tell him no, but he is making my job difficult.

It occurs to me that night, when I am home and away from the prison, that I am probably the only person in Cell Block 6 who doesn't spend most of the day worrying about whether two men at any place and time are engaged in sexual activity, or if they're going to be accused of it. I can't comprehend what the big damned deal is. Everybody eats. Everybody shits. Everybody fucks.

Keno refuses to come out and work the next day. He's hungover from drinking moonshine. I have to ask the AM shift's porter to do Keno's job. The other inmates call this porter Kicker. He's 19 years old and from Louisiana. He tells me he was arrested for armed robbery his second week in California. He explains that he'd been up for three weeks on crystal meth and used a toy gun to hold up a liquor store. He shows me a picture of his daughter.

Matthews and Kicker spend a lot of time talking about New Orleans whenever Kicker comes out to work. While they are talking I listen for Bradley to yell about inmates masturbating in the shower. The third or fourth time Kicker works for Keno, I hear Bradley yell.

The second masturbating inmate has a contraband Gameboy that I bust against the concrete. This inmate doesn't kick his cell door or make idle threats, he just informs me that I am "a stupid dyke".

When we're sitting in our office later on, Matthews is smug about the incident and I tell him that he's Cell Block 6's biggest faggot. He tells me that he is going to tell Bradley about what I just said and I told him that Bradley probably knows a faggot when he sees one too.

Matthew tries to get me back by calling in sick the next day so that I'll work with a partner that doesn't know the cell block. Bradley works in his place. As far as I can tell, Bradley doesn't do anything effeminate when he's in the housing unit. The inmates still laugh amongst themselves when he passes by. I watch the inmates gawk at Bradley as he escorts a female nurse for her steroid passing. Some of them look away when they realize I'm watching them watch Bradley. They put *Maxim* centerfolds up on their cell walls with the tape Keno steals from our office. And they make a point of showing the posters to Matthews when he comes back to work.

Another inmate exposes himself to Bradley during shower time. Matthews isn't smug anymore. He tells Bradley to switch places with me. I go up in the control tower and strap on the rifle while Matthews and Bradley haul the third masturbator to his cell. They stay in there with the inmate for a long time. It's the last time an inmate jacks off in front of Bradley.

Cell Block 6 is relatively quiet for a few weeks. Then Keno's cellmate transfers to another prison and Keno moves Kicker in. This makes me uneasy because Keno has sudden violent outbursts. He tends to beat the shit out of cellmates who change the television channel without asking. Kicker is no match for Keno. He hasn't done time long enough to extort a nurse into bringing him steroids. But the two seem to get along and Matthews tells me that I'm the only officer in the building that's worried about Kicker.

An inmate in Cell Block 5 tells on the Victoria's Secret nurse for having an inappropriate relationship with another inmate. Keno tells me that the inmate who snitched "was just mad that Victoria wouldn't give him some." The sergeant decides to call a staff meeting about the incident. Matthews refuses to go, and substitutes for Bradley in the tower.

Bradley and I sit together at the meeting. Some administrator from the prison's medical department tells us, the officers, and medical staff about how we must always work together. The sergeant and lieutenant lecture us extensively on why it is important to maintain professional relationships with not only the inmates, but one another. Then they remind us that turning a blind eye to staff misconduct is staff misconduct in and of itself, and that we are not true professionals if we don't tell on one another. Steroid nurse gives me and Bradley a haughty look from across the room.

An officer who works graveyard shift in Cell Block 6 tells Matthews and me that he caught Kicker giving Keno a blow job between the multiple overnight counts. Keno laughed when the officer saw them, but Kicker hasn't come out for work in three days. Matthews and the graveyard officer go on and on and *on* about why it is hilarious that Keno makes Kicker give him head. After about ten minutes of listening to them I decide that I've had enough.

Bradley's up in the control tower and I call him on the phone. I tell him to call Kicker out for an appointment at the infirmary. I direct him to send Kicker out to the walk-alone yard with me and to keep an eye on us while we talk.

I expect Kicker to come out of that cell with a black eye but he doesn't. He looks at me wearily.

"Look," I said. "I heard about what happened last night. I know you're not a rat but if I don't talk to you about it then I could get into trouble for allowing it to go on."

"I don't know what you're talking about," Kicker tells me.

"That's fine," I say. "But if you want help, then you have to help me out here. I don't really give a fuck about what's going on in there. If he's forcing you to do that shit then you need to speak up."

"I'm not a punk, Burrows," Kicker says angrily.

"I can't do anything about what people call you," I say. "I can get you moved out of there if you tell me you're not cool with this situation."

"You don't understand," Kicker tells me. "I got nobody, Burrows. I'm in here by myself. My family's in Louisiana."

Kicker looks away from me. His eyes are focusing on something else. Finally he says, "I'm not gay."

"It really doesn't matter to me," I tell him. "But if you don't like it when he makes you suck him off when an officer is coming around, you'd better say something right now."

Kicker looks at me for a long time. Then he says, "I'm not gay just because he does *that* to me."

"I know that. What I'm trying to find out here is if you *want* him to do *that* to you."

"No I don't," Kicker says indignantly. "Wouldn't that make me gay?"

"I don't know," I say. Because I don't. "Do you want me to move you away from Keno or not?"

"No. It would make this worse."

"Okay. But I don't want you to snivel to the sergeant later on down the line that I let this happen to you," I tell him.

Kicker grins at me. "I'd only do that to Matthews."

RICH MAN'S WAR, POOR (GAY) MAN'S FIGHT

Larry Goldsmith

A poor, young gay man from the rural South joins the US Army under pressure from his father, and because it's the only way left to pay for a college education. He is sent to Iraq, where he is tormented by fellow soldiers who entertain themselves watching "war porn" videos of drone and helicopter attacks on civilians. He is accused of leaking documents to Wikileaks and placed in solitary confinement where he has been held for more than a year awaiting a military trial. The President of the United States, a former Constitutional law professor apparently suffering amnesia about the presumption of innocence, declares publicly that this soldier "broke the law." The United Nations Special Rapporteur on Torture, Amnesty International, and the American Civil Liberties Union express grave concern about the conditions of his imprisonment, and the spokesman for the US State Department is forced to resign after calling it "ridiculous and counterproductive and stupid." A letter signed by 295 noted legal scholars charges that his imprisonment violates the Eighth Amendment prohibition of cruel and unusual punishment and the Fifth Amendment guarantee against punishment without trial, and that procedures used on Bradley Manning "calculated to disrupt profoundly the senses or the personality" amount to torture.

The National Gay and Lesbian Task Force, the Lambda Legal Defense and Education Fund, and the Human Rights Campaign, having invested millions lobbying for "gays in the military," have no comment. Of course not. Bradley Manning is not that butch patriotic homosexual—so central to the gays-in-the-military campaign—who Defends Democracy and

Fights Terrorism with a virility indistinguishable from that of his straight buddies. He is not that pillar of social and economic stability, only incidentally homosexual, who returns home from the front to a respectable profession and a faithful spouse and children.

No, Bradley Manning is a poor, physically slight computer geek with an Oklahoma accent. He is—let us use the word, and not in a negative way—a sissy. Having grown up in a dysfunctional family in a small town in the South, he is that lonely, maladjusted outsider many gay people have been, or are, or recognize, whether we wish to admit it or not. He broke the law, the President says. And he did so—the liberal press implies, trying terribly hard to temper severity with compassion—because he wasn't man enough to deal with the pressure. He did so because he's a sissy and he couldn't put up with the manly rough-and-tumble that is so important to unit cohesion, like that time three of his buddies assaulted him, and instead of taking it like a good soldier, he peed in his pants. And then of course he was so embarrassed he threw a hissy fit and sent Wikileaks our nation's most closely guarded secrets, like some petulant teenage girl who gets her revenge by spreading gossip. This is, of course, the classic argument about gays and national security—they'll get beat up or blackmailed and reveal our secrets. And NGLTF, Lambda, and HRC, with their impeccably professional media and lobbying campaign, based on the best branding and polls and focus groups that money can buy, have effectively demolished that insidious stereotype.

They have demolished it by abandoning Bradley Manning.

Why was Bradley Manning in the US Army in the first place? Why does anyone join the US Army nowadays? Perhaps a few join out of a sincere if misguided belief that tells them they are truly going to defend freedom and democracy. But if that were commonly the case, one would expect to see a certain number of the more affluent classes, those who never stop preaching the need to defend democracy and freedom by military means, eager to enlist. There would be at least a few Bush and Cheney children fighting on the bloody ground of Iraq and Afghanistan.

Dick Cheney famously explained that he declined to fight in Vietnam—and invoked the privilege of the student deferment five times to avoid being drafted—because he "had better things to do." The draft is now a thing of the past, and the vast majority of those in the US military are there precisely because they do not have better things to do. That is to say, there are few other opportunities available. The official national unemployment rate, now at 9.1 percent, masks a rate more than twice that figure for young people generally and more than three times that rate among young black men. Decent jobs are difficult to get, of course, without a college education. The US manages, in the midst of an international economic crisis, to spend half a billion dollars every day on the wars in Iraq, Afghanistan, and Libya, but the federal and state governments have drastically cut funding for education, and public as well as private universities have reacted to funding cuts with astronomical increases in tuition and fees. Publicly-funded financial assistance to poor students is a thing of the past—except as part of a military recruitment package.

Bradley Manning wanted an education. He also wanted to get away from his family and out of his small town. Military recruiters do not spend much time in middle-class neighborhoods. They seek out those like Bradley Manning: poor, isolated teenagers dazzled by the slick brochures, the cool technology, the lofty rhetoric of duty and honor, and the generous promises—or those who see right through the hype but know they have no other option. The military does not discriminate solely on the basis of sexual preference. In its recruitment it has always observed the time-honored and deeply discriminatory precept of "Rich man's war, poor man's fight."

This is the club that NGLTF, Lambda, and HRC would have gay people join. Let us leave aside for the moment the question of whether the club is a defender of freedom and democracy or an imperialist killing machine. It is in either case an institution that sends the Bradley Mannings of the world, and not the Dick Cheneys, to be killed or maimed—killing or maiming the Bradley Mannings, and not the Dick Cheneys, on the other side. Whatever collective psychosexual hangups or perverse ideological interests have in the past prevented it from openly accepting homosexuals (or women, or African-Americans in integrated units), it is an institution whose fundamental design is to send poor people to die defending the interests of the affluent.

We did not need Bradley Manning to tell us that the military is an institution in defense of a class society. But his case does uniquely reveal a seldom-acknowledged disjuncture between modern LGBT politics, based as it is on the individualizing concepts of "gay identity" and "equal rights," and the way in which political power continues to be exercised through social relationships of class. It was a complex combination of factors—a lack of economic and educational opportunities, and the absence of a community and culture where he could be himself as a gay man—that led Bradley Manning to where he is now. These factors cannot be separated into the neat, discrete categories of single-issue politics. Organizations like NGLTF, Lambda Legal, and HRC would like to pretend that Bradley Manning's case is not a "gay issue," or worse, remain silent because they know that

it is indeed a gay issue, one that threatened to undermine their careful-
ly-crafted plea for admittance to the military. Addressing it as a gay issue
would mean looking critically not only at the specific discriminatory policy
of the military, but also at the very purpose of the military. It would mean
taking a good close look at the patriotic rhetoric of "equal rights" to serve
in an "all-volunteer" military, whose purpose is to defend "freedom" and
"democracy," where LGBT people can be just as "virile" in carrying out organized killing as their heterosexual counterparts. It would mean considering how such rhetoric hides unpleasant truths about economic domination
in our world; understanding how such domination relies on structures of
power embedded in social relations of class, race, and gender; and recognizing that these structures cannot be addressed individually, but must be
attacked simultaneously. Organizations like NGLTF, Lambda Legal, and
HRC, which define "LGBT rights" as a single issue divorced from such
considerations, abandon the Bradley Mannings of the world not just to
psychological torture by Presidential edict, but at the entrances to universities barred to those without money, at the military recruiting stations that
have replaced the financial aid offices, and at the bases where soldiers, when
not engaged in killing the declared enemy, learn to entertain themselves by
bullying each other and watching war porn.

NOT TILL THE EARTH FALLS INTO THE SUN

Horehound Stillpoint

Nipple Night at the Powerhouse called out to me from halfway across the city tonight. But—damn—when I reach out to push my way past the leather curtain in the bar's doorway, I realize I need a moment. From some deep crevice of my consciousness, a ridiculous hope bubbles up to the surface as I remember the astonishing first evening I spent here, so many years ago. Then, from some bottomless pit in my core, fears arise that it will be as devastating as what happened later that same night. Crap. For once, I would like to walk in without having to fight with the leather or do a dance with the curtain, the way I imagine other guys do, no muss no fuss.

I'm older now, I tell myself. Tougher, and meaner. There's no way my experience tonight will come close to the ecstasy of the first time; nor can it be as soul-crushing. I'm not looking for adventure; I don't enter with a heart full of hope. It's just another Wednesday night, second Wednesday of the month, Nipple Night, and at this relatively early hour, I'll be lucky if there are five guys inside who are not wearing shirts.

Just an hour or two of cruising, of getting my hands on flesh, on leather, down a nice pair of jeans, or all over a guy in a jockstrap, whatever's available, I want it all and I'll take what I can get. Fighting fire with fire: that's the plan.

It was an awful night at The Breezy Ocean Diner. We started empty, then suddenly filled up with customers who were needy as hell, rich as fuck, and desperate to have that one perfect meal which would make their lives momentarily all right. But the chili wasn't hot enough, the steak came out overcooked, the banana brioche bread pudding was not up to par, and all these grown-up brats tipped like the stock market had crashed for a third day in a row. Which, of course, it had. Reality: I just wanted a break.

I was at the computer terminal when I saw my least favorite co-worker (gorgeous guy, but we don't get along) come in on his night off and give a little smooch on the cheek to the young woman working next to me. The moment he took off to go join his team for a soccer match, I turned to Teri and said: "I don't know why you're so friendly with that homophobic asshole."

Teri looked up at me. She thinks I'm this wise, sensitive, compassionate, poetry-spouting, long-term-meditating, yoga-working, gracefully-aging, still-sorta-hot, rock 'n' roll queer, because, you know…this is how I *present*. She respects me, she likes me, she lets me in, she thinks we are better friends than I think we are.

"What did he do?" Teri cornered me. "You have to tell me why you said…. You know we're dating? Of course you know, everyone knows."

I knew Teri and her girlfriend had broken up six months ago. I knew she had recently discovered her latent bisexuality, because she had asked me for pointers on giving blowjobs. I had definitely seen her getting all frisky with Oscar; I simply, stupidly, hadn't gotten around to adding two plus two.

"You know how it is when you love somebody," she moaned, "you don't always see them the way other people do."

"Oh my God, this hurts my heart," she said right before returning to her tables, under a cloud of doom and despair.

One brief comment, made in the heat of an irritating shift, provided me with two brand new motivations for wanting to blow my brains out at work. I had crushed, temporarily at least, a sweet young woman's love affair, and had possibly turned a handsome young man into a full-on enemy.

A century ago, it seemed, I used to look up at the night sky and wonder what in God's name was going on up there, and what in thunder was going on down here. As a boy, I really wanted to save the world. I thought Earth needed me. Or at least it needed something…drastic and astonishing. More than anything, I wanted to be a saint, to do something wonderful that would turn everything upside down and make everybody love me.

Damn, damn, damn.

The crescent moon glowed, gorgeous and mysterious, in the deeply misted San Francisco night, as I rode my bike away from the Diner. It didn't illuminate the night so much as it watched me pedal, in isolation. I had back-pedalled as fast as I humanly could with Teri. Tried to smooth things over. She still looked like a deer in headlights when I left. So, I rolled right past my apartment building, felt the lovely possibilities of my art-fag studio slip slide into the distance. Nipple Night, I'm coming.

And for one eighteenth of a second, after locking my bike up outside the bar, as I enter the Powerhouse, it's 1977, and I'm riding the waves of the LSD I dropped hours ago. My lover Michael has left me alone for the weekend while he visits some friend in LA. This is my first weekend alone in five years. I have already hopped over to the Haight and scored some acid in a gay bar, while these two acid-head fairies tell me about the good old days (pre-1967) when cops frequented this bar to demand blowjobs from guys on the back patio. Back when things were *really* fun. I have already bought Iggy Pop's *Idiot* album and played it three times—after the acid had kicked in—and decided it was the greatest piece of art since that other *Idiot*, the novel by Dostoyevsky. I've already gone to see *The Late Show* with Art Carney and Lily Tomlin and laughed so hard and gotten so scared I forgot to breathe.

So it was probably after midnight when I entered The Brig (its name before some less imaginative owner changed it to the Powerhouse), and I was pretty far gone. Since the Ramones had been a huge influence on me starting in 1976, I was wearing ripped jeans, a t-shirt way too tight, and an extremely stiff, no frills black leather jacket. The neat hair pegged me as absolutely middle class and the trimmed beard screamed ex-hippie, but everything else was pristine NYC wannabe punk.

Fuck me if the sound system of The Brig wasn't playing the Sex Pistols' "Submission," my favorite track on *Never Mind the Bollocks*. I could hardly believe it. Every fucking bar in town bumped 'n' grinded with high gay disco. Straight clubs played disco. Gay saloons played disco. The Castro throbbed with that one, single, beat epitomized by "I Feel Love." I had not once been able to enjoy a beer in a bar since the Bee Gees did the music for that fucking movie with John Travolta in that stupid white suit.

"Submission" ended and Patti Smith started intoning: "Jesus died for somebody's sins, but not mine…" I looked around and saw a mass of leather and Levi's. Bare chests and muscles. Huge baskets. Guys cruising so hard you could practically see the lust in the air; you smelled it for sure.

I made my way over to the bar and found just enough voice to mumble which beer I wanted. After paying, I stumbled up the five-step stairway into the upper deck where there were fewer guys and more speakers.

Patti and her band smoked their engines into the stratosphere. The guys up on this deck prowled without moving, without talking or smiling. No nodding of heads, no toe-tapping, either. I leaned against a wall, right beside a hardcore leatherman, of course, and could not keep myself from blurting out a few overly excited words about the fantastic music. The leatherman wasted no energy on me: he turned and walked to the other side of the room with enough body language to guarantee I got the message. *I was not being cool.* All right, whatever, I never could talk for shit on acid.

But the choice song selections just kept flooring me. The Stranglers, The Damned, the Ramones, John Cale, the Buzzcocks, Blondie, Iggy fucking Pop. I was hearing "Search and Destroy" somewhere outside my own apartment. Truly unbelievable. I started bopping around, no longer trying to fit in, no longer wanting to get laid even. I was already as happy as a human being could be.

I headed back to the bar, where there was now a line. It was almost my turn when one of the bartenders said to another, "I told you we'd get guys like that in here if we played this music," and he nodded unmistakably at me.

Shit.

Fuck.

Hellfire.

Can I just die please? Can I fall into a hole in the floor?

I mean, I knew I wasn't exactly on the same page as the rest of these guys, but I thought I was close enough. My leather jacket and jeans may not have been the absolute correct style for the perfect South of Market Fag Look, but shit, I wasn't in a dinner jacket and hush puppies either.

Fuck. I ordered my beer and moved back up to the deck where at least no one would mess with my head.

Out of nowhere, this skinny, redheaded, bearded, hippie-looking guy, in beads and a blue jean jacket, zeroed in on me like a heat-seeking missile.

"You know what your problem is," he started in, launching without so much as a hello. "You like all this angry music 'cause it does all your work for ya. Right?"

These days, I would answer "You're absolutely right. Thanks for pointing that out." Then, I'd grab my dick and pretend to see a friend on the other side of the galaxy. But back then, I was really still a boy. A boy hearing the Ramones in a gay bar for the first time. A boy who got effectively pre-verbal on acid.

"Fucking punk rock. Most pathetic shit in the world. And punk rockers are the most feeble excuses for human beings I ever saw. I could say anything to you and you wouldn't say or do a thing. Right? The only time you make a fist is to wave it in the air at your stupid shows in some miserable garage somewhere."

He jabbed me in the chest with his finger. I moved away, but the fucker moved with me.

"One two three four, poor me, boo hoo, the world's fucked up and so am I and there's nothing anybody can do, so let's not even try to learn how to play our instruments, 'cause what does it all matter anyway. Right?"

We did this little dance where I spun, walked a few steps, backed up, and kept moving while the post-hippie asshole somehow managed to keep himself in front of me so he could continue to stab my solar plexus with his knobby finger.

"I could probably stand here and poke you all night long, and you still wouldn't muster the balls to defend yourself, would you? You don't know how to stand up for yourself, you don't know how to fight, and if you did try to fight, you'd only end up losing. Right?"

Another poke. I went down the steps, hoping he wouldn't follow, hoping this would be enough of a victory for him, but he was on me like leather on a dick.

"'Cause you're a loser, same as the rest of your *punk rocker* friends."

Poke. Poke. Poke.

White noise buzzed in my head, drowning out the glorious rock 'n' roll. Next thing I knew, I was on the sidewalk. The creep chased me out of The Brig, and I let him do it. My one chance for Saturday night freedom had come to a thoroughly dishonorable end. My soul felt spanked, my spirit vanquished.

Thirty years later, I'm prepared to subject myself to the generic, not-quite-disco, not-hardly-rock 'n' roll, definitely shrill wallpaper music that will seep thick as oil into my ears once I enter. It's okay: I'm not here for the music, nor am I here to have fun.

I've got my strategy. I will pony up to the bar, order my brew of choice, pay up, tip heavy so I don't have to hear any flack from the bartender, saunter up those familiar steps, cruise the deck for ten seconds, and make my way into the smoking area which used to be the backroom sex space. I will stand around. I won't even bother to smirk. I know what works for me and how to throw my energy around. I'll pull my shirt over my head, and stuff the tail end into my back pocket. I might pull my dick out and start casually stroking. I'll probably nod at a guy or two, doesn't matter.

I know I'm supposed to be invisible, at my age. What's more, I'm supposed to be past all this, I'm supposed to have given up, utterly and completely, by now. Nobody wants fifty-five-year-old tits and ass, or cock and balls, if you believe the press. But even the laws of physics and attraction can be bent, if you know how to work the angles.

Guys aren't just looking for youth and beauty; confidence will do in a pinch. We're looking for somebody, anybody, who isn't squirming and crawling out of his skin. That's all I have to project: *cool, here, grounded, not dying, not afraid, no problem.*

In reality, I practically kill myself trying to stay healthy and sexy.

Besides getting seven hours of sleep a night, drinking a gallon of water every day, exercising regularly, meditating daily, doing yoga, not letting my body gain extra weight, eating vast amounts of fiber, starting my day with green tea and ending it with probiotics, not forgetting the beet/carrot juice in the middle, not smoking, not doing drugs, not drinking alcohol, not indulging in too much sugar or fat, not allowing myself to stay in a job I hate, not commuting to my job in traffic that causes off-the-chart stress levels, in fact, not driving at all, but making sure that I live in a city where the air is clean and the ocean is next door. I also shave my head, so no one can see the hairline, nor how much gray is in the mix. Plus, okay, my mother and father aged pretty well too. But it's work, maintaining, keeping with the program, drinking the juice of a lemon every day, slathering my body with aloe vera, staying committed decade after decade, so that, ten minutes after entering the Powerhouse, I can have one guy hanging off my left nipple, another on the right, some guy sucking my dick, and another appreciating the action with his eyes. Maybe somebody kissing me too. I need a scene I can get lost in. Maybe I'll get lucky; maybe someone will eat out my ass in front of everybody.

But the leather curtain is not cooperating, and I can't help but think about what an evil shit I was at work, which makes me feel about twelve years old, and that brings up all my old family stuff, and then the ex-lover stuff punches me in the gut, just as the fucking leather curtain smacks me in the face. Fucking hell. Everybody is going to see that I could not get past the curtain with grace, let alone with some butch version of *savoir faire.*

I don't know who I am anymore. I want to stop feeling sorry. Sometimes, I wish I were a future-human with immaculate control. Or at least like my coworker at the Diner who said, in the middle of his own terrible shift, "I'm not having another emotion tonight." If wishes were horses, we'd all ride off into the sunset.

Right when I think I've made it past the curtain, the goddamn leather slaps the side of my ass with enough weight that my legs have to stiffen to keep me from getting knocked aside. It's alive tonight, I swear, it has weight, it's testing me, making judgments, trying to ruin me.

Screw it. All I have to do is not react. Don't feel humiliated, don't feel at all, don't think about your life, don't think about Michael or Eric or Ned, don't think about your father, don't think about all the wonderful men you played with for fifteen minutes and walked away from with a laugh, don't think about the ones who said "I love you" and then stopped calling, erase everything but the here and now.

You can forgive yourself for everything, tomorrow. And everyone else can forgive you the day after. I would like to be all wisdom and light, I'd like to take my apologies to the next level, but for now, that's where I'm taking my ass.

Stick with the program. Settle down. Walk. Pretend you're sexy. It'll be okay, even if nothing is the way it should be.

Bar's over there. Be a man. Don't think about anything.

Deep down, I know when I will be able to trust myself completely and love myself unconditionally, and trust and love everyone else as well: When the earth falls into the sun, that's when.

DANCING WITH WHITE BOYS

James Villanueva

A beer bottle shatters against the floor, *crash*, another rowdy Saturday night in Texas. A flicked Pall Mall hits the back of a waitress's blown-out hair. The cigarette flies in the air as the waitress tousles left-over ashes from her hair. Then, before the teased-up hair threatens to cause a scene—enter the queer.

Straight men who know me act like I need to be saved. Straight women who know me act like I have nothing better to do than gossip and talk about boys.

"I should kick his ass," a stranger points to me between chugs of his Lone Star Longneck. "Eat my ass, you cocksucker," he yells in my direction.

The angry man's pool cue hits a table, warning me not to mess with him. Everyone else is angry; I laugh and persevere. All I can do is giggle, use my best Audrey Hepburn impression to assuage my angriest friend, "Peyton, darling, you're being a bore." He doesn't listen to my request. He wants to be another heroic straight man, rescuing the queer. The other guy continues to holler just because I am here, in his territory. Peyton puffs out his chest towards the man, and I sit quietly as they claim their territory. The angry man pretends to own the bar, Peyton pretends to own me. Nobody hears a sissy, but will kick ass to protect one, I think.

So I talk football because that is the language these guys speak. We talk about the Red Raiders; I am no longer just a queer. "I can talk football, even with a dick in my mouth." They laugh. I am OK.

This is the Wild West—not the old one, the new one. Sure, there are still cowboys going "yee-haw!" at night, but they no longer holler for celebration, it is now a warning because, as they say, "those queers are takin' over." I look around for more like myself. But I am the only one and there is a lot of takin' over to do. I take another sip of my beer.

All around me, boots continue shuffling through the door. I search for the guys that stare a little too long, turn away a little too quick. There's one and then there's another. Two women make out by the pool table, I guess they lost their game and now must suffer the consequences of kissing one another. I wonder, for a moment, had the men lost would they be making out too? "I've never done this," one of the girls claims, but continues anyway. The room goes into whooping and hollering; I search again for the cowboys who stare too long. They sit quiet, and their ten-gallon hats create shadows over their eyes. I go ahead and cheer on the girls.

The straight girl who owns me for the night talks louder about her orgasms. When I start talking about mine, she goes to the bar. I turn to the next girl, they seem to crowd around me. We giggle and talk about boys because, maybe it's true, I have nothing else to say. I become the property of another big-toothed girl wearing a tight sweater. She has a lot to say. Does she ask me about my life? Do I tell her that I am a teacher? She turns away to bat her eyes at a cowboy who looks down at his beer made sweaty by the hot air greeting the cold can.

Somewhere in the night, everyone in the bar becomes friends. Entire lifetimes are revealed. The hours are slipping away and the two-steppin' starts. Men twirl women around the dance floor and everyone seems to lose their inhibitions. Alone, one of the men with shadows over his eyes looks my way. I know what he is thinking and we meet in the back of the bar. I become what he wants for the moment—a spicy Latino—like the wetbacks that plow his father's fields. *Aye papi.* It is dark and the neon light in the shape of Texas is only half-lit. The pink glare shows his face; he is my age. I want to know about his life. I want to know what he does for a living. Does he come here often? When did he know he was queer? Does he know he's queer? Doesn't matter though because two mouths filled with saliva smelling of beer come together as half of the Texas sign frames us. The feeling becomes too much; everything spins and my eyes are shut too tight. I run to the bathroom. When I come out, he is gone.

Last call. Women and men leave, shuffling out the door arm-in-arm, already forgetting names. The ones that walk out alone head into the darkness too. We are back to being strangers.

Driving on the plains is easy because you just go forward, flying fast into the night, nothing to block the way; the lights become little lasers as they swirl past my window. I am still immersed in thoughts of the noise made by pool cues, that cowboy with beer breath, and the neon Texas sign that saw it all.

I pull into the next parking lot and everyone stares. I am judged, not by my car, but by whether I've been done already. I have. But they do not know that.

Inside the bar, older men who have given up on being gentlemen stare down as their boyfriends—twenty years their junior—dance together shirtless. Love should exist, love does exist—somewhere else.

"A gin and tonic." It's what I order because this is just that kind of establishment. I say what's on my mind—everybody pretends to listen. My words flow into the disco lights and the zombie stares of blond boys with Adonis bodies. They all believe that no other night will compare to this night. I was once one of them. It was here that all my dreams came true and went crashing down with the moon. It was here that I learned, "Hey, it's all right to be gay." But, then again, it was this same building where I learned that it wasn't. I was too young and it was too soon, but the men didn't care. There was Jason, Jeremy, Chris and then Josh, each one claiming their piece of my body. A body no longer rightfully mine but theirs. I gave up that right long ago in the search for love, yep, there's that word again, if only there were a different term? And, maybe there is—somewhere else.

My thoughts become lost in the loud music in a bar reeking of Pall Malls. So much for escape.

Friends, I've had many. It was the nineties and everyone was embracing and accepting. I didn't get beat up like the older queers. I didn't have to run away in fear. I was the bright future of a forgiving world. Isn't this why the older queers resent my generation? Always reminding us with each whisper, each snare, that we couldn't be who we were if it wasn't for them. They sip their beers and point out the poor young ones they own.

A boy with blue eyes stares. I smoke my cigarette because this is what has happened before. Another white boy just trying to get his Latino fix— I stare back because, well, because that's just what we do. No words are needed; I want to tell him that I'm a teacher, I want to talk to him about my short stories, but he just bats his eyes and takes me away because tonight he's ready for something spicy, something exotic—he gets what he wants because he is a white boy and around here they get their way. A whole civilization wiped away by another orgasm in the bar's bathroom. I think of my cowboy, his eyes haunting me still: this boy could easily be him.

We are done within minutes. Still no words.

My friends, that's right, I told you I've had plenty. They are here too, somewhere, but I am too drunk to care because they've been here their entire lives and aren't going anywhere. Even when they speak of leaving— "I'm going to Dallas"—they've said that since they were teenagers. Because that is where queer boys in West Texas go. Instead, I went away to college in New Mexico, got back and these queer boys were still saying the same thing. "I'm going to Dallas. They have better bars there."

I stand by the bar now, my zipper down but I don't know it, doesn't matter anyway. Someone dancing on the bar swings his leg high and knocks me, *smack*—right in the back of my head. My cocktail splashes onto my shirt. For some reason or other it is my fault because my head shouldn't have been so close. The man is angry and his hands are racing toward my throat. He throws punches, or maybe it's me, doesn't matter though. The bouncer drags us both out of the bar by our collars.

I am out in the parking lot, forcing myself to vomit. Can't drive home drunk, you know. So I think of a place where I can sober up. I don't have to think too hard because it is the same place always, I am there within minutes.

The dark room still smells like Pall Malls, or maybe it's me, by this point in the night I can't really tell. I'm barely holding myself up at the back of the wall; cigarette smoke drifts beneath the only light in the back of the building. I can hear music on the other side of the wall and I know that a stripper is making a living.

I passed by this building every day on my way to school when I was a kid. It's so far out of town, away from all the churches. The neon lights say one word, "Adult," and I think, "So this is what it's supposed to be like?"

Even though it is dark and all you hear is the dull music from the ruckus next door, men open and shut doors. They make their way into small rooms with small television screens playing porn. Between the walls there are holes that are waist-high, you know why.

Some of the men I recognize from the first bar. They still wear their cowboy hats and their boots shuffle against the floor. No one talks. There is no talking in the back room. A sign bleeds against the wall: "NO WOMEN ALLOWED." A few wedding rings sparkle in the darkness, no one will tell. Here, no one is queer, because we are all at the end of a desperate night, wanting the same thing—sobriety.

Unfamiliar sounds are heard—they are sounds that are almost pleasant, the sounds of two people making love, slow panting, soft heaving and gentle kisses. Not like the usual sounds of bodies hitting walls and deep quickening grunts while boots shuffle against concrete floors. We all ignore these unusual sounds.

The walls envelop me; they take me whole and wrap me in their giant concrete arms. Now I am a part of something. No one stares or makes a move. We all stand, motionless and limp, against the welcoming concrete, paralyzed and unafraid. At least for moments.

A hand reaches out and grabs my crotch. It is a cowboy with shadow-covered eyes. I shake myself sober and leave.

So this is what has become of the Wild, Wild West.

The cowboy follows me out the door; I want to run, but I'm too exhausted, my legs feel rubbery. The cowboy is angry at my rejection. I stumble to my car. My body sinks back into the driver's seat as the engine breaks the dark silence of the parking lot. The cowboy throws a beer bottle and it flies towards my car and smashes into the door as I drive away and the stars fly towards my window.

SOMETHING RESEMBLING POWER

Kristen Stoeckeler

In October 2006, I was visiting Austin, Texas, for the International Drag King-Community Extravaganza 8 (IDKE), an annual conference held in the United States and Canada. It was my first IDKE, and my first year of drag-king performance; I was a student newly obsessed with examining feminism, queer politics, and identity politics. To my delight, I found a conference well-structured to critically address issues and intersections of identity: there were discussions by and for both trans men and femme performers, a caucus for people of color, a panel on race and racism, and an interactive discussion on cultural appropriation. I had worked extensively in traditional theater until then, but I had no idea that places like this existed in the world of performance and I was exhilarated to stumble upon such a community.

I had recently escaped a serious relationship that felt seriously too straight, and had formally come out to my family as queer. My relationship to my body, gender, and sex was taking on radically new forms. Through gender transgression in my personal life and emerging performance work, I came to express a resistance to the feminine hetero-woman life I had been expected to lead. So, on the last evening of the drag conference, and my last night in town, I found myself at the performance showcase after-party dressed in men's clothes, not particularly interested in passing, though very aware of my slacks and tie, my bound chest, the way I carried myself and engaged with others, and of how I wished my masculinity to be perceived.

I had heard that this particular bar was generally known to be a gay men's bar, which was made evident by the oil-and-water effect of the crowd that Saturday night: it was not hard to pick out the dragsters from the regulars. Flooding the dance floor, 20 to 30-something-year-old genderqueers wearing suspenders, large mustaches, bright lipstick, sequins, suits and glitter danced it out to Madonna and Beyoncé, while the mainly masculine-presenting gay male regulars were partying throughout the bar but noticeably absent from the flair of the dance floor.

I stepped up to the bar, waiting to order a drink. Looking around, I smiled to the 40-something-year-old white man to my left. He returned the smile and with a gesture toward the dance floor said, "Quite a party." I nodded and smiled, telling him that it was a party for the drag-king conference that weekend. "Drag kings?" he asked. "Oh, you mean girls who dress up as boys." Feeling relatively comfortable, I responded with manly coy, "Who says I'm not a boy?" And then, without pause, he informed me: "I'm not into that." At which point he turned away, ending the conversation.

My heart raced. Not into that? Not into what?! My skin flushed from head to toe and I suddenly felt that I had given too much away. And in spite of myself, I felt embarrassed. That night I tried to shake that interaction off me and have a good time. I got drunk and let the incident go. Come morning, though, the experience rolled obsessively through my mind. To this day I can only conclude that a) by situating myself in proximity to him, Dude thought I was talking a little too intimately about my gender and b) Dude thought I was implying that I'd be a suitable fuck—and who knows, maybe I was—but also, by extension, that I was hitting on him. Regardless, he seemed supremely uncomfortable and a little offended by the idea that he could be identified with these queer-tranny-faggot sorts of people by virtue of sexual proximity to a person like that—specifically, I think, to a person with a body like that. Dude was into sleeping with guys, but not a guy like me. So, if this person was responding as much to my body as to my words, I have to give pause and wonder, what was so unfathomable and repulsive to this man about fucking, or even flirting with, a faggot with a cunt?

This is (surprise!) a bathroom story. Let's switch the set to later in the same year, winter in Minnesota. In order to combat my hibernation impulse and my college's attempt at psychic domination, I was frequenting my favorite local gay bar maybe once or twice a week. The bathrooms were small, separated into "women's" and "men's"—long lines were not unusual for the women's restroom, but everyone knew the stall in the men's room was usually empty. Trans women used the women's restroom frequently if not comfortably, and it was common for many people who needed to sit while peeing to use both. This is how I knew the state of things to be for many months. My friends and I spent countless winter nights happily dancing and peeing the night away with comfort and ease, and it seemed like it had always and would always work this way.

This common-practice subversion of the bar's normative bathroom set-up, however, would not last. Towards the end of one particularly crowded and drunken night, I noticed that a friend in my social group had disappeared from the bar. We called him and learned, to our utter dismay, that he had gone home after being physically assaulted while in line for the men's bathroom by a guy who aggressively told him to get out of line and use the women's restroom. I caught wind of other such occurrences, and before long the men's restroom was fronted by a security guard, discriminating flashlight and all, searching faces, scanning bodies, and checking I.D.s. M's were invited to use the restroom, and those with anything different were refused entry into the men's room on threat of vigilante violence and forcible expulsion. An indication of impending doom: my favorite gay bar had gone police state over night.

The story closes with some petitions, a bit of guerilla street theater in protest, and, hanging on the door of the bathroom in lieu of the bouncer outside, a lone and threatening 8 1/2" by 11" sign reading in big block letters: MEN ONLY. A gay male acquaintance of mine who was bartending there at the time unwittingly boasted to me that the reason the bar pulled the bouncer from the men's room was not because of political pressure, but because they couldn't afford to pay another bouncer. At some point, weeks or maybe months later, the sign came down and, blessed-be, a counterpart never appeared in the ladies' restroom. But I never used the men's room again and neither did my transgender friends. And even though I love that bar because on some nights you can find dykes, fags, queers, and black, white and brown folks from all different walks of life hanging out in a way that doesn't happen in any other bar in the Twin Cities, I find it's hard for my friends and I to go there now knowing how unsafe it can be for transgender folks.

Again I found myself wondering, why are these men so threatened by our bodies? What was so necessary about reserving the space for men, and exclusively for men with penises? The whole instance raises a distinction for me: the type of masculinity that vigorously and violently clings to bodies for substance—to cocks and flat chests, particular height range and fat distribution—requires the expulsion of femininity, and those bodies thus associated, in the name of integrity, as if what it means to be a man, or male identity itself, would crumble without such boundaries. This story of territorialism, replete with the trimmings of body fascism, speaks quite literally of the gender police. The effect is not only the expulsion of trannies, queers, and women, but also the degradation and invalidation of the gendered identities of all the exiles. Oh, Mr. Gay Bar, defender of gays the world over, model of post-feminism! But really, where is the line between transphobia and misogyny? Between misogyny and a fear of faggotry? Or female-bodied faggotry? Or trans faggotry?

However I might like to say this sort of misogynistic gender invalidation is exclusive to mainstream gay male spaces, the trope of "gender authenticity"—or natural, inherent, and true gender—is also used to question, judge, and ultimately control bodies in queer spaces. In my experience, a drag king who identifies as femme or dresses girlie on the street every day is rarely granted the masculine authenticity of a drag king who identifies as butch or trans. This often translates into less respect for femme-y drag kings by other king performers who end up taking the "authentically" masculine performers the most seriously. How ironic for what is supposed to be a culture of performance! This hierarchy in king-dominated drag communities has incited the formation of groups such as the Femme Mafia Milwaukee and the Femme Affinity Group (FAG) in Portland, both social activist femme empowerment groups born partially out of the marginalizing experiences of femme-identified drag performers of an array of bodies and genders. Perhaps these groups' most significant function is to assert femme identities as legitimately queer gender expressions. Within king-dominated drag scenes, this means working to spread a politic and promote a culture that doesn't automatically privilege non-effeminate masculinities. To draw a few parallels, femme performers are shut out of masculine privilege in queer drag king communities much the same as trans male folk are shut out of gay male spaces, much the same as gay men are ostracized by dominant straight culture. In all cases, people are either accepted or rejected based on their ability to approximate various components of dominant masculinities and/or manliness.

In queer space, where we are supposedly free to determine our gendered identities, how do our abilities to approximate dominant cultural standards of masculinity validate or invalidate our embodied experiences? Am I less of a man in performance communities because I also pass as high femme on stage? Is my masculinity flawed because I'm little and limp-wristed? Are these the things that determine my ability to pass within a masculine embodiment? Recently, I performed a drag piece in which I tapdanced in a spandex unitard bee costume. Although I was wearing my favorite handlebar mustache and an immodestly large packer under my unitard, a gay male friend later referred to that performance and character as the "Bee Girl." It was a minor annoyance at the time since I generally identify as a girl myself. But taken in the context of my other experiences working in drag communities, the instance brings up this gender dissonance between performer and audience. I certainly wasn't performing as a girl character, and besides, we were at a drag show and I had a huge 'stache. Sure, I had antennae and was wearing spandex, but what about my package?! Regardless of how well I presented as a man, the "feminine" characteristics of the performance—the spandex, the tapdancing, my thighs—overrode my presentation of faggotry because I have a cunt. Even beyond passing within normative masculinity and maleness, there seem to be limitations for female-bodied individuals inhabiting faggotry in gay and queer spaces.

In the spirit of change, I present another anecdote: The Day Boilesque Changed My Life. The year was 2007. It was fall again and I found myself back at IDKE, this time in Vancouver, among kings and queens and everything in between, all back together to talk queer politics and radical performance. On the last evening of the conference, my friends and I attended the IDKE Showcase, the most formally produced show of the weekend, featuring performers from all across the United States and Canada, and from Germany. Held in a large, old auditorium, the crowd that night easily filled the space with their enthusiastic response to the talent. Everything from modern dance to puppetry to acrobatics graced the stage, finding common ground specifically in intentional representations of gender.

Towards the end of the show, a king came onstage alone—which was odd because most of the numbers were group pieces—and started your basic drag-king lip-sync to a cover of the Rolling Stones' "Sympathy for the Devil." Drag king Flare was giving a sensual delivery, wearing a formal suit and hat, complete with a red ruffled shirt, red vest and matching bow-tie; I was sitting back for what I expected to be a standard, old-hat performance. "Please allow me to introduce myself. I'm a man of wealth and taste."

Flare was gesturing and swaggering about when, to my surprise and delight, he started to strip. At first just teasing off his bowtie, he swung it around his head like a dirty red lasso and flung it across the stage. His hands slid down to his crotch as he rolled his hips round and round. Next came the suit coat, his back to the audience, inched down one shoulder then the other and dropped nonchalantly on the floor next to him; then the vest, swung aggressively above his head as the crowd screamed and whistled. Facing the audience, Flare loosened the tails of his ruffled shirt, slowly undoing every button. Poised half-shirted, he turned around, rolling the shirt off each shoulder to reveal his bare, broad back. He returned to face the audience, holding the shirt up to cover his chest, and sauntered forward, taunting us, before he withdrew the shirt to reveal a full chest, a red sparkly tassled pastie covering each nipple. "Pleased to meet you. Hope you guessed my name!" he smiled, and folded the shirt deliberately before tossing it to the stage floor. Then, throwing his shoulders back and taking a grounded stance, Flare started shaking his chest in the roughest shimmy you've ever seen, towards the left, then the right, then straight on, arching his back and swinging those suckers balls-to-the-wall. Sequencing through a variety of bouncing motions that propelled him into a twirly frenzy, he spun around into a climax by ripping off his pants in a flourish. Tall black boots atop thigh-high red and black striped stockings flanked his thick legs, and he wore a small black thong. Flare took a moment to address the audience, "Just as every cop is a criminal and all the sinners saints," and then he removed his hat and rotated it between his hands until it came to rest over his junk. He raised an eyebrow and eyed the audience, "As heads is tails, just call me Lucifer."

"Oh, no, he isn't!" I squealed, and shrieked as he gently swayed to and fro, and slid his thong down his thighs, taking a moment to hold his hat over his crotch, pressed between belly and thigh, to step out of the thong entirely before swinging it around his head and tossing it to the ground. I think, at that moment, I wasn't breathing. In one deft maneuver, Flare flipped his hat back up to his head and spun around, revealing a long devil tail draped loosely over his ass-crack. In that moment, everyone in the house straight-up lost it, shouting and screaming their lungs out. Looking over his shoulder for a moment, Flare started wiggling his white ass little by little until it was gyrating and jiggling with the wile of an experienced stripper. Flare raised his arms in one final grand gesture, took a last stroke of his devil's tail and with a dismissive wave of his hand, and gracious nonchalance, made his anticlimactic saunter of an exitus.

I thought I was gonna pee my pants because within those five minutes I had been utterly ripped out of my mind and the things I thought I knew about bodies, about tits and cunts and fat and all. About masculinity and femininity. And I felt for the first time an integrated reception of male tits and cunts and of the boys I love so much. Returning home to Minneapolis the next day, I kept thinking about that performance, rolling it over in my mind, and giddily recounting the experience to everyone who asked about my weekend in Vancouver. It was a demonstration of the kind of relationship I want to have with my own body, when I am a boy, when I am a girl. And somehow that performance helped reshape some of my ideas about myself, recasting fear into something resembling power.

ACKNOWLEDGEMENTS

For tangibles and intangibles, special thanks to Eric Stanley, Andy Slaght, Kevin Coleman, Gina Carducci, Jessica Hoffmann, Jessica Lawless, Socket Klatzker, Ralowe T. Ampu, Queer Cultural Center, *Corpus*, Sarah Schulman, Jason Sellards, Jim Van Buskirk, Jory Mickelson, Yasmin Nair, Michael Bronski, Ananda La Vita, Ryan Conrad, Hilary Goldberg, Killer Nepon, Joshua Gamson, Kirk Read, blake nemec, Stephen Kent Jusick, Feminist Press, Dana Garza, Carolyn Cooley, Wheels Darling, Von Edwards, Jess Clark, Justin Ray, and Karen Sundheim.

A few of these pieces appeared in earlier forms in *Make/shift* (my essay), *If We Have to Take Tomorrow* (Khary Polk's essay), and on *Common Dreams* (Larry Goldsmith's essay).

Thanks to everyone at AK for believing in this project, and for taking it all the way…

CONTRIBUTORS

Ali Abbas is a New York-based writer and freelance journalist. Abbas received his B.A. in philosophy from DePaul University and is currently pursuing his graduate degree in Interdisciplinary Humanities and Social Thought at New York University. His activism and written work revolves around the new Middle East that is emerging in the face of globalization. Whether reporting for a major news network or blogging for a niche audience, Abbas is insistent on colliding the events that shape the world with critical analysis of power and resistance.

Dr. George Ayala currently serves as the Executive Officer of the Global Forum on MSM and HIV (MSMGF). The MSMGF works worldwide against HIV for the health and human rights of men who have sex with men. Dr. Ayala has worked in the nonprofit HIV/AIDS sector, managing prevention, education, capacity building, and community-based research programs for twenty years. A clinical psychologist by training, Dr. Ayala is a former research psychologist at RTI International. His research has mainly focused on understanding the mechanisms through which social discrimination impacts health among ethnic minority men who have sex with men.

Chris Bartlett is a gay men's health community organizer from Philadelphia. He directed the SafeGuards Gay Men's Health Project for ten years, and has acted as lead consultant to the LGBT Community Assessment in Philadelphia. He co-facilitates the Gay Men's Health Leadership Academy, a national meeting of leaders in the field of gay men's health and wellness. Most recently, he has received support from the Arcus Foundation to develop a strategic plan for LGBT leadership development. He's a regular tweeter at http://www.twitter.com/harveymilk, and is a proud member of the Philadelphia Radical Faerie Circle. He'd like to acknowledge the reviewers who provided generous comments: Michael Hurley, Tony Valenzuela, Angel

Serra, Bill Jesdale, Fred Swanson, Michael Scarce, Peter Lien, Matty Hart, Eric Bunting, Malcolm Che Gossett, and Nick Deroose.

Matthew D. Blanchard, "QHereKidSF," born and bred a White Trash Euromutt Slut American, escaped the closets of Conservative Virginia only to be embraced by a "GAY MECCA" of wanton, woebegone whores and hustlers. The life this queer kid has led since arriving in the Bay Area in 2002—a life predominated by "party n' play"—contrasts concretely with his former life as thespian erudite. However, with drug dependency, disease and disfigurement have come the recovery, reconstruction and resilience of his last-ditch, last-chance life. Today, Matthew is grateful for God's boundless faith in his purely imperfect, human desire for beautification & self-betterment.

Mishael Burrows is a former correctional officer living in Central California with a menagerie of birds. Her primary interests include civil liberties, seafood, and tattoos. She actively supports PFLAG, RAINN, AUFSCS, and NARAL.

Nick Clarkson is a graduate student in Gender Studies in Indiana, studying trans theory and gay masculinities.

CAConrad is the son of white trash asphyxiation who grew up selling flowers along the highway for his mother and helping her shoplift. He is the author of *Deviant Propulsion* (Soft Skull Press), *Advanced Elvis Course* (Soft Skull Press), *The Book of Frank* (Wave Books), a collaboration with Frank Sherlock titled *The City Real & Imagined* (Factory School Press), and other books that you can find at CAConrad.blogspot.com

Jaime Cortez is a San Francisco Bay Area writer, artist, and cultural worker. His stories have been published in over a dozen anthologies. He is currently working on a humorous, semi-autobiographical short story collection.

Debanuj DasGupta is a Doctoral student in the Department of Women's, Gender, and Sexuality Studies at Ohio State University, and a gender, sexuality, and human rights consultant. In 1994, Debanuj founded the first HIV/AIDS prevention program for men who have sex with men and gay-identified men in Kolkata, India. Since his relocation to the US, Debanuj has worked as a policy analyst and community organizer, primarily within immigrant and LGBT communities of color. He is the past Co-Coordinator of the People of Color Organizing Institute for the National Gay Lesbian Taskforce, and has served on advisory boards of the National Network for Immigrant and Refugee Rights, and the South Asian Health Initiative at the Center for Immigrant Health at NYU. Debanuj was awarded the prestigious New Voices Fellowship by the Academy for Educational Development in 2006, and holds a dual MA in Geography and Urban Planning from the University of Akron. He is a resident blogger with www.gaywisdom.org.

Gina de Vries is a queer femme writer, rabble-rouser, pervert, and Paisan. Her writing has appeared in dozens of places, including *Baby, Remember My Name, Dirty Girls, TransForming Community, That's Revolting!, Bound to Struggle, The Revolution Starts at Home, Femmethology, make/shift* magazine, and *Curve* magazine. Gina curates shows for long-running queer performance series San Francisco in Exile, teaches a writing workshop for sex workers at San Francisco's Center for Sex & Culture (where she also serves on the Advisory Board), and tours wherever willing pupils and audiences will have her. She can be cruised online at ginadevries.com.

Booh Edouardo received a BFA and MFA from California Institute of the Arts (CalArts). His artwork has been featured at many private and public venues. He currently studies as a MA candidate at San Francisco State University and volunteers as a tutor with Project Read at City College of San Francisco. The anthology *Kicked Out* (Homofactus Press), edited by Sassafras Lowrey, features more of his writing. He would like to thank Mattilda Bernstein Sycamore, Dominika Bednarska, Sarita Cannon PhD, and Catherine Ragazzi for their readings and suggestions.

Willow Aerin Fagan is a queer writer, activist and Reclaiming Witch living in Ann Arbor, Michigan. His writings have appeared in *Critical Moment, The Q*News,* and *Fantasy Magazine.* He blogs at phoenixantree.wordpress.com and would love to hear from you at willow.fagan@gmail.com. He is writing his way home.

Michael J. Faris is a queer feminist leftist faggot currently living in Pennsylvania. He grew up in the conservative farm fields of Iowa, taught middle school reading and language arts for a few years, and has been the slammistress for various poetry slams. Michael earned his Master's in English (emphasizing in rhetoric and writing) at Oregon State University, and is currently working on his PhD in English (emphasizing in rhetoric and composition) at Pennsylvania State University. He's an active blogger, coffee addict, drag queen, and writing teacher. He often identifies as an indignant, pretentious, bitter queen.

Thomas Glave was born in the Bronx and grew up there and in Kingston, Jamaica. He is a founding member of the Jamaica Forum for Lesbians, All-Sexuals, and Gays (J-FLAG), and presently teaches at the State University of New York at Binghamton. He is author of *Whose Song? and Other Stories*; the essay collection *Words to Our Now: Imagination and Dissent* (Lambda Literary Award winner, 2005); the fiction collection *The Torturer's Wife* (Lambda Literary Award finalist, 2008); and editor of *Our Caribbean: A Gathering of Lesbian and Gay Writing from the Antilles* (Lambda Literary Award winner, 2008). Glave has received an O. Henry Prize for fiction and a fellowship from the National Endowment for the Arts. In 2008–09, he was Martin Luther King, Jr. Visiting Professor in the Program in Writing and Humanistic Studies at MIT.

Larry Goldsmith is a historian and a former reporter for *Gay Community News* (Boston, Massachusetts), and has been active in anti-war, labor, and LGBT organizations since the late 1970s. He lives in Mexico City, and teaches at the Universidad Nacional Autónoma de México and El Colegio de México.

Patrick "Pato" Hebert is an artist, educator and cultural worker based in Los Angeles. He currently serves as the Senior Education Associate at the Global Forum on MSM & HIV (MSMGF) and teaches in the Photography and Imaging Department at Art Center College of Design. Hebert was the recipient of the 2008 Excellence in Photographic Teaching Award from Center of Santa Fe, and his work has been supported by the Rockefeller Foundation, the Creative Work Fund, the Durfee Foundation and the California Arts Council. In 2010 he received a Mid-Career Visual Artists Fellowship from the California Community Foundation. Recent shows include the 2008 California Biennial and solo exhibitions at Haverford College and the University of Maine at Augusta. He is currently developing a commission for 18th Street Arts Complex and working on two commissions at local elementary schools as part of LACMA's On-Site program. In the fall of 2010 he will serve as Artist/Activist in Residence at Swarthmore College and at the California Institute of Integral Studies in San Francisco.

Francisco Ibáñez-Carrasco, born in Santiago de Chile, migrated to Vancouver, B.C. in 1985, where he acquired his HIV in 1986, his Canadian citizenship in 1991, and a long drawn appetite for writing. His first novel, *Flesh Wounds and Purple Flowers: The Cha-Cha Years*, was published by Arsenal Pulp in 2001 and nominated for the Regional Commonwealth Prize in 2002. His erotica is collected in *Killing Me Softly/Morir Amando* (Suspect Thoughts 2004) and his non-fiction appears regularly in the US queer literary circuit. He is an advisor in the creative writing individualized BA program at Goddard College, Vermont; in British Columbia he is the community-based researcher for all AIDS service organizations.

Shepperton Jones is a high school dropout from a small town in Louisiana. He now studies Library and Information Science at San Jose State University because it's all about information, right? He blogs at http://sanfranciscoish.wordpress.com/.

Harris Kornstein is a sissy queer originally from the suburbs of Albany, NY, but now located in the beautiful Bay Area. Though he appreciates the stability of working 9-to-5, his true excitement lies in organizing with queer youth, strategizing for racial and economic justice, and building a Jewish anti-Zionist movement. His alter ego, Lil Miss Hot Mess, has been spotted around town in figure skates, in wigs and shoes of all sizes, and in Hillary Clinton drag. Harris sometimes identifies as an artist, designer, and writer—but often feels like a major wannabe.

Jason Lydon is the pastor at the Community Church of Boston. Along with ministering to his congregation Jason can be found trying to abolish the prison industrial complex, riding bikes, tearing up the dance floor, joining up for the revolution, or eating delicious vegan treats. Jason strives to centralize the experience of queer and trans people behind bars as we all struggle together to end the systems of white supremacy, heteropatriarchy, and capitalism.

Tommi Avicolli Mecca is a radical, southern Italian, working-class, atheist writer and performer, author of *Between Little Rock and a Hard Place* as well as co-editor of *Hey Paesan: Writings by Lesbians and Gay Men of Italian Descent* and *Avanti Popolo: Sailing Beyond Columbus*. He is the editor of *Smash the Church, Smash the State*, a collection of writings on the early years of gay liberation, published in 2009 by City Lights, in honor of the 40th anniversary of Stonewall. His website is www.avicollimecca.com.

Philip Patston is a creative and social entrepreneur and commentator, with fifteen years' experience as an award-winning, professional comedian. His work—an eclectic mix of entrepreneurial leadership, consulting, and speaking—sees him travel regularly and has taken him to Australia, the US, Canada, the UK and Belgium. Over the past 15 years he has combined working with people, entertaining, and running a consulting business to create innovative ways to manage diversity, creativity, and change. Philip is a patron of Rainbow Youth, New Zealand's largest queer youth organization. Born in England, he has lived in Auckland, New Zealand since 1972.

As a writer, scholar, and DJ, **Khary Polk** works as a cultural agent in New York University's Program in American Studies. He has written for *Women's Studies Quarterly*, The Studio Museum of Harlem, *If We Have to Take Tomorrow, Corpus, The Journal of Negro History*, and *Think Again*. Khary has also worked extensively with The Institute for Gay Men's Health at New York City's Gay Men's Health Crisis and helped conceive its 2007 crystal meth awareness campaign, *Hurricane Tina*. He is currently finishing a dissertation on race, sexuality and diaspora in the US military abroad. He lives in Brooklyn.

D. Travers Scott authored two novels, the internationally acclaimed *Execution, Texas: 1987* and the Lambda Literary Award winner, *One of These Things is Not Like the Other*, plus the story collection *Love Hard: Stories 1989-2009*. After earning a PhD from the University of Southern California, he currently teaches technology, gender, and sexuality as Assistant Professor of Communication Studies at Clemson University. He and his husband live in Greenville, South Carolina.

Eric A. Stanley is a high school dropout turned doctoral candidate in the History of Consciousness program at UCSC. Along with Chris Vargas, Eric directed *Homotopia* and *Criminal Queers,* a sequence of films that have been screened worldwide. Eric is also the co-editor of the anthology *Captive Genders: Trans Embodiment and the Prison Industrial Complex* (AK Press, 2011).

Horehound Stillpoint is a San Francisco writer whose spoken word has been heard from New York to New Orleans, Vancouver to West Hollywood. His work has been collected in anthologies, journals, zines, and websites.

Kristen Stoeckeler is a Twin Cities-based drag and burlesque performance artist driven to produce work that addresses the politics of gender, whiteness, and queerness, as a tool of radical community-building. She performs regularly as Dickie Van Dyke with the cabaret revue Dykes Do Drag, as well as in the Sirly Girly Show. Kristen is also interested in anticapitalist politics, D.I.Y. homemaking, and fostering radically cooperative space. Spending much of her time disguised as a barista, you can otherwise find Kristen hanging out with the Femme Mafia Twin Cities, or enjoying such radical pleasures in life as playing dress-up and petting kittens.

ML Sugie is a queer brown drag queen faggot currently living in Oregon. He was born in Tokyo and moved quite a bit as a child, so his "hometown" is nowhere. After earning a Bachelor's degree from Oregon State University in Chemical Engineering, he stayed and is earning a Master's degree in Applied Ethics. During his time at OSU he's also emceed a few drag shows, won the 2003 OSU Queen of the Beaver drag competition, written a column for the OSU Daily Barometer, and generally tried to ask good questions about hard subjects. He's a fire sign, after all.

Former competitive gymnast, nationally ranked cheerleader and one time third-grade hula hoop champion, **James Villanueva** now carries a new label—writer. A graduate of Eastern New Mexico University, James writes feature stories for *The Slatonite*, a small town newspaper serving Slaton, TX, is a blogger for *The Lubbock Avalanche Journal* and is the current Editor-in-Chief for Southwest LGBT Press. His freelance work has appeared in *Gay Lifestyle Monthly Magazine*, *Latino Lubbock Magazine*, and *Campus Pride*. His coming out story was featured in the May 2004 issue of *Texas Monthly Magazine*. He lives and writes from a small house in Slaton, TX with his dog, Stella, at his feet.

Lewis Wallace is a young, white transgender activist, student and writer proudly located in the Midwest. His essays, poems and articles appear in magazines, 'zines and anthologies under the name Sailor Raven. He is fiercely dedicated to the projects of community-building and creative resistance.

Ezra RedEagle Whitman grew up on the Nez Perce Indian Reservation in north central Idaho. Ezra has written and performed for Native American children's theatre, received awards for original dramatic monologues, and appears in several anthologies. Ezra will be starting an MFA program in creative writing at Pacific Lutheran University. When not dancing in the street like a little girl or feeding a whey protein habit, Ezra pays his bills through nursing.

ABOUT THE EDITOR

Mattilda Bernstein Sycamore is a delicate faggot and a charming queen. She is the author of two novels, *So Many Ways to Sleep Badly* and *Pulling Taffy*, and the editor of four nonfiction anthologies, including *Nobody Passes: Rejecting the Rules of Gender and Conformity* and an expanded second edition of *That's Revolting!: Queer Strategies for Resisting Assimilation*. Her writing appears regularly in a variety of publications, including the *San Francisco Bay Guardian*, *Time Out New York*, *Utne Reader*, *Bitch*, and *Bookslut*, and she's the reviews editor and writes a column for the feminist magazine *Make/shift*. Sycamore made the short 16mm film *All That Sheltering Emptiness* with Gina Carducci, and the pair are currently working on a second film. Sycamore is thinking of making Lostmissing, her public postering project, into a book called *I Almost Hate You*. She recently finished her first memoir, *The End of San Francisco*, which will soon bring tears to your eyes—look out for it! Mattilda loves feedback and propositions, so please do write to her via mattildabernsteinsycamore.com.

AK Press is small, in terms of staff and resources, but we also manage to be one of the world's most productive anarchist publishing houses. We publish close to twenty books every year, and distribute thousands of other titles published by like-minded independent presses and projects from around the globe. We're entirely worker-run and democratically managed. We operate without a corporate structure—no boss, no managers, no bullshit.

The Friends of AK program is a way you can directly contribute to the continued existence of AK Press, and ensure that we're able to keep publishing books like this one! Friends pay $25 a month directly into our publishing account ($30 for Canada, $35 for international), and receive a copy of every book AK Press publishes for the duration of their membership! Friends also receive a discount on anything they order from our website or buy at a table: 50% on AK titles, and 20% on everything else. We have a Friends of AK ebook program as well: $15 a month gets you an electronic copy of every book we publish for the duration of your membership. You can even sponsor a very discounted membership for someone in prison.

Email FRIENDSOFAK@AKPRESS.ORG for more info, or visit the Friends of AK Press website: HTTPS://WWW.AKPRESS.ORG/FRIENDS.HTML.

There are always great book projects in the works—so sign up now to become a Friend of AK Press, and let the presses roll!